# Contents at a Glance

# Using

## MICROSOFT®
# Office 97

**que**®

Jill T. Freeze

# Using Microsoft® Office 97

Library of Congress Catalog No.: 97-68683

ISBN: 0-7897-1442-6

99 98 97     6 5 4 3 2 1

Interpretation of the printing code: the rightmost double-digit number is the year of the book's printing; the rightmost single-digit number, the number of the book's printing. For example, a printing code of 97-1 shows that the first printing of the book occurred in 1997.

All terms mentioned in this book that are known to be trademarks or service marks have been appropriately capitalized. Que cannot attest to the accuracy of this information. Use of a term in this book should not be regarded as affecting the validity of any trademark or service mark.

Screen reproductions in this book were created using Collage Plus from Inner Media, Inc., Hollis, NH.

# Table of Contents

## III | Working Together to Achieve Even Greater Results

# Credits

**PRESIDENT**
Roland Elgey

**SENIOR VICE PRESIDENT/PUBLISHING**
Don Fowley

**PUBLISHER**
Joseph B. Wikert

**PUBLISHING DIRECTOR**
Karen Reinisch

**PUBLISHING MANAGER**
Jim Minatel

**MANAGER OF PUBLISHING OPERATIONS**
Linda H. Buehler

**GENERAL MANAGER**
Joe Muldoon

**DIRECTOR OF EDITORIAL SERVICES**
Carla Hall

**MANAGING EDITOR**
Thomas F. Hayes

**DIRECTOR OF ACQUISITIONS**
Cheryl D. Willoughby

**ACQUISITIONS EDITOR**
Lisa Swayne

**PRODUCT DIRECTOR**
John Gosney

**PRODUCTION EDITOR**
Lori A. Lyons

**EDITORS**
Tom Stevens
Bill McManus

**PRODUCT MARKETING MANAGER**
Kourtnaye Sturgeon

**ASSISTANT PRODUCT MARKETING MANAGER**
Gretchen Schlesinger

**TECHNICAL EDITOR**
Dave Shinn

**ACQUISITIONS COORDINATOR**
Virginia Stoller

**SOFTWARE RELATIONS COORDINATOR**
Susan D. Gallagher

**EDITORIAL ASSISTANT**
Jeff Chandler

**BOOK DESIGNER**
Ruth Harvey

**COVER DESIGNER**
Sandra Schroeder

**PRODUCTION TEAM**
Heather Howell
Christy M. Lemasters
Tony McDonald
Paul Wilson

**INDEXER**
Ginny Bess

Composed in *Century Old Style* and *ITC Franklin Gothic* by Que Corporation.

*To Wayne, for your undying confidence (not to mention patience!) in me. Without your love and support, my dreams never would have come true. I hope you realize just how much I love you!*

# About the Authors

**Jill T. Freeze** is a freelance management consultant who has worked with such organizations as the Kennedy Center for the Performing Arts, the National Endowment for the Arts, the Smithsonian Institution, and the White House. She has also helped organize several startup companies such as Calamity Jeans and Just Plane Crazy. Her formal education includes a bachelor's degree from the University of Massachusetts at Amherst and a master's degree from George Washington University. Jill has been using Microsoft Office products since 1991 for everything from calendars to nursery school newsletters. Jill and her husband Wayne have written six books on a variety of computer topics ranging from ActiveX to Visual Basic to WebTV.

# Acknowledgments

A special thanks to my new friends at Que: Lisa, Jim, Karen, and John, for giving me the opportunity to sink my teeth into this project. I hope I've earned my stripes! And to all the production and indexing people who turned those boring, marked up pages into a "real" book. Lori Lyons, you deserve a vacation for all your work on this one.

To Wayne for contributing his years of experience and wisdom to the Access and macro chapters.

Love and hugs to Christopher and Samantha who gave up their summer fun so Mommy and Daddy could write. Look on the bright side, guys—this will help us get into the "big house" sooner!

To Dad and Goose for encouraging us to make the big leap to full-time writers—thanks so much for the support!

To "Papaw" and "Gramma 'Rie" for brightening up the kids' days while we worked. It helped to know they were having fun.

Finally, to my friends Veronica and Tracy who kept me sane during a frantic work schedule. You guys are the greatest!

# We'd Like to Hear from You!

Que Corporation has a long-standing reputation for high-quality books and products. To ensure your continued satisfaction, we also understand the importance of customer service and support.

## Tech Support

If you need assistance with the information in this book or with a CD/disk accompanying the book, please access Macmillan Computer Publishing's online Knowledge Base at **http://www.superlibrary.com/general/support**. If you do not find the answer to your questions on our Web site, you may contact Macmillan Technical Support by phone at **317/581-3833** or via e-mail at **support@mcp.com**.

Also be sure to visit Que's Web resource center for all the latest information, enhancements, errata, downloads, and more. It's located at **http://www.quecorp.com/**.

## Orders, Catalogs, and Customer Service

To order other Que or Macmillan Computer Publishing books, catalogs, or products, please contact our Customer Service Department at **800/428-5331** or fax us at **800/882-8583** (International Fax: 317/228-4400). Or visit our online bookstore at **http://www.mcp.com/**.

## Comments and Suggestions

We want you to let us know what you like or dislike most about this book or other QUE products. Your comments will help us to continue publishing the best books available on computer topics in today's market.

John Gosney
Product Director
Que Corporation
201 West 103rd Street, 4B
Indianapolis, Indiana 46290  USA
Fax: 317/581-4663
E-mail: **jgosney@que.mcp.com**

*Please be sure to include the book's title and author as well as your name and phone or fax number.*

We will carefully review your comments and share them with the author. Please note that due to the high volume of mail we receive, we may not be able to reply to every message.

Thank you for choosing Que!

# Introduction

We've all said it a thousand times—if only we had more hours in a day in which to get things done. When facing mounds of work and seemingly evaporating amounts of time, it's only natural that we seek more efficient ways to get our work done. Office 97 with its tightened integration and new Web functionality gives users the tools they need to accomplish tasks quickly and professionally on the job and at home.

And if you have your doubts about Office 97's worth, consider this little statistic: In its first quarter of sales, Office 97 sold an average of one license per second! Before you launch Excel to figure out how many new users that comes to, I'll save you the trouble. It's eight million, and growing by the day.

*Using Microsoft Office 97* sets out to give you the most succinct step-by-step directions in as little space possible. For you, this translates to saved time and money because you have a shorter, less expensive book that cuts to the chase to give you what you absolutely need to know.

What's more, we've made the steps generally specific so that you can tailor them to meet your individual needs. No more wasted space on functions you won't use in a million years!

And if something doesn't work quite right, we'll tell you up front. There's nothing worse than beating your head against a wall during a tight deadline only to find out that a piece of Outlook that doesn't work as you expected it to really requires Microsoft Exchange Server to do its thing.

And finally, we realize that many of you inherited Office 97 Small Business Edition with a recent computer purchase, so we've done our best to give you a sampling of what these applications—Microsoft Publisher, Automap Streets Plus, and Microsoft Small Business Financial Manager—can do when combined with the rest of the Office suite. ▓

# Who Should Use This Book?

Because of its succinct steps, portability, and affordability, *Using Microsoft Office 97* is the perfect book for you if:

- ▓ You've worked extensively with one of the Office applications and want to build on what you already know to learn other applications in the Office suite.
- ▓ You're new to computers and want to learn how to do neat things with Office quickly without wading through a bunch of technobabble.
- ▓ You own a previous version of Office and want to get up to speed on Office 97's new features.
- ▓ You need professional-looking results quickly.
- ▓ You want to learn how to pull the elements of Office 97 together to achieve even greater functionality.
- ▓ You need to learn how to collaborate on projects using Office 97.
- ▓ You want to sidestep purchasing more expensive Web authoring tools by using what you already have to establish a Web presence.

So no matter who you are—a student wanting to go the extra mile on a term paper or a corporate executive needing to get in better contact with your staff—*Using Microsoft Office 97* is the book for you.

Although this book assumes that you are at least somewhat familiar with Windows 95 or Windows NT, you need not know anything about the applications in order to get the most out of this book.

*Using Microsoft Office 97* covers Microsoft Office 97 Professional Edition, Microsoft Office 97 Standard Edition, and introduces you to the applications in Microsoft Office 97 Small Business Edition.

If you have Microsoft Office 95, you'll notice some differences in menu options and screen appearance. Furthermore, you will obviously not be able to use new Office 97 features like Outlook and Web capabilities.

Screen shots for this book were generated in Windows 95, so their appearance may vary slightly depending on whether you're using Windows 95 or Windows NT, your installation of Windows, your installation of Office, and your system configuration.

# How This Book Is Organized

*Using Microsoft Office 97* is divided into three parts:

- Part I: Common Features and Functions in Office 97
- Part II: Getting the Most from Each Application
- Part III: Working Together to Achieve Even Greater Results

Part I presents the common elements and features found in Office 97 so that you can build on what you know/learn instead of learning each application from the ground up. Chapter 1 looks at Office 97's new features while Chapter 2 explores common ground in the Office 97 applications. Chapter 3 covers correcting mistakes, printing, and getting help a variety of ways in Office 97. Chapter 4 takes a look at opening and saving files, and then Chapter 5 goes on to look at finding and managing your files. Finally, Chapter 6 shows you how to work with wizards and templates in general.

Part II breaks information down by application: Word (Chapters 7-10), Excel (Chapters 11-14), PowerPoint (Chapters 15 and 16), Publisher (Chapter 17), Access (Chapters 18 and 19), and Outlook (Chapters 20-22). Each chapter focuses on some of the most important and widely used features available in this latest release. In addition to these essentials, you'll find advanced topics designed to improve the quality of your work and save you time on the job.

Part III shows how to get your applications and your colleagues to work together to accomplish even greater things. Chapter 23 examines issues related to sharing data between documents and applications. Chapter 24 presents the tools and functions needed to collaborate effectively with your workgroup on reports, spreadsheets, and so on. Chapter 25 builds on everything else in the book to help you establish a Web presence or post your documents to your company's intranet. Finally, Chapter 26 introduces you to macro design using Visual Basic for Applications (VBA), the new standard macro programming language.

# Conventions Used in This Book

You can use both the keyboard and the mouse to execute Office 97 commands. A typical command sequence in this book might look like this:

Choose Edit, Copy, or press Ctrl+C.

This book also assumes your mouse is set up for right-handed use. Thus the left button is used for clicking an object, while the right button is used to access shortcut menus.

Other elements found in this book include the following:

**N O T E** Information found in Note boxes may help you avoid a potential problem, or they may simply communicate other relevant information you should consider while executing the current steps. ▪

**T I P** This box is often used to suggest easier alternatives to accomplishing a task or step.

**CAUTION**

These boxes will warn you of procedures that could potentially result in data loss.

Cross-references like the following direct you to related information in other parts of the book.

▶ **See** "Suite-Wide Enhancements," **p. 8**

# Common Features and Functions in Office 97

# CHAPTER 1

# What's New in Office 97?

**O**ffice 97 represents much more than a simple version release. Its changes and enhancements were so marked, in fact, that over 8 million users jumped on the Office 97 bandwagon in its first three months of existence. And that number has grown each day as Office ships with new computers, and more people discover what the suite has to offer.

It's almost unfortunate that this powerful suite carries the name "Office." Sure it has everything most offices, large or small, will ever need, but it also lends itself well to use at home. Whether you're preparing a newsletter for your son's nursery school, calculating the mortgage on your dream home, or designing a Web page for your favorite nonprofit organization, Office 97 is up to the task.

If you own or run a small business, Microsoft has customized its Office suite to meet the needs of most small businesses. Referred to as Microsoft Office 97: Small Business Edition, the suite contains Word, Excel, Publisher, Small Business Financial Manager, and Automap Streets Plus.

Office 97 bundles together a group of applications designed to enhance your productivity and has loaded each application with a variety of new features. They have even added an application, Outlook 97, to help organize your schedule, tasks, and contact information. ■

### Common user interface
Standardized menus, toolbars, and dialog boxes make learning the entire suite much easier.

### Customizable toolbars
Gain quick access from one Office 97 application to another via multiple, customizable toolbars.

### Simplified data exchange among Office 97 applications
Use object linking and embedding with hyperlinks to exchange and link data from one application to another.

### Powerful applets shared by multiple Office 97 applications
With WordArt, The Clipart Gallery, and AutoShape, among others, you can tap into a variety of useful applets from within most any Office 97 application.

### Sharing documents with a workgroup
Use Office 97's features to collaborate with a workgroup on large projects.

### Publishing Office documents to the Web
With Office 97's new Web capabilities, it is now possible to save ordinary documents as HTML and publish them to the Web.

### A uniform task automation language
Use Visual Basic for Applications to automate tasks from within Word, Excel, Access, or Outlook.

# Suite-Wide Enhancements

A number of changes have been made to the Office suite as a whole. The most noteworthy of these are described in the sections that follow.

## Changed Menu and Toolbar Appearance

Users of earlier versions of Office may notice that the buttons on the toolbars no longer have a 3-D feel to them. In Office 97, the buttons (including selections on the menu bar) appear flat until you point to a specific icon or menu name. Only then will the chosen item take on a raised 3-D appearance. This feature was added to clarify which button was about to be pressed. After a second or two, the familiar ScreenTip box appears, which gives users the name of the button in question.

The menus have changed in Office 97 as well. When you bring up a pull-down menu, you'll notice that selections represented on the toolbars now display their corresponding icons on the menu as well (see Figure 1.1).

**FIG. 1.1**
The pull-down menus in Office 97 give users an additional opportunity to learn icons found on the various toolbars.

New Document icon
Open Document icon
Save icon
Print Preview icon
Print icon

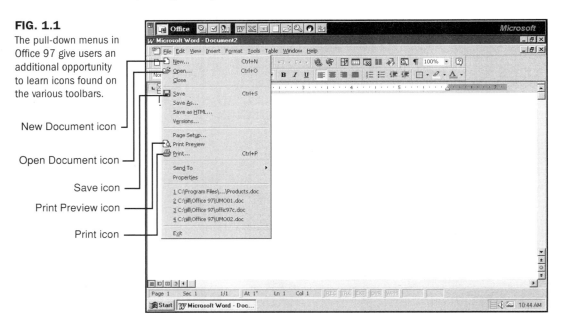

▶ **See** "Common Menus and Menu Options," **p. 22**

# Web Capabilities

Perhaps the biggest change in this version of Office involves its new Web capabilities. These include the following enhancements:

- *Web toolbar.* From within any Office 97 application you can choose View, Toolbars, and then select Web to launch a Web browser installed on your system. This gives you instant access to the Internet or your office's intranet.

- *Hyperlinking.* You can now insert a highlighted link from any Office document to another section of the same document, another document on your hard disk or network drive, or to a specified URL address for an Internet or intranet Web page.

  ▶ **See** "Creating a Hyperlink," **p. 276**

- *Web publishing.* For the first time, you can publish Office documents as attractively formatted Web pages.

  ▶ **See** "Readying Word Documents for the Internet or Intranet," **p. 296**

- *Microsoft on the Web.* This direct link to Microsoft (accessible by clicking Help and choosing Microsoft on the Web in any of the applications) takes you to a variety of application-specific Web pages, offering everything from online help to new templates to sound and video files. Check back often as the selection is always changing and growing.

  ▶ **See** "Enhancing Your Productivity with Freebies from the Web," **p. 70**

**N O T E**   When visiting Microsoft on the Web for the first time, have your Office product ID ready because you will be asked to register for this free service. ■

# New Office Assistants

Replacing the previous version's Answer Wizard, Office 97's Office Assistants appear in an on-screen box, awaiting your questions (see Figure 1.2). You can select from a variety of animated personalities—for example, a paper clip named Clippit, a cat named Scribble, and more—or turn them off altogether. To call for help, click Help and select (application) Help, press F1, or click the Office Assistant button on the standard toolbar.

▶ **See** "Getting Help," **p. 40**

# Integrated Drawing Tools

OfficeArt replaces the separate drawing tools formerly found in Word, Excel, and PowerPoint. Offering consistency and increased capabilities, OfficeArt (accessed by choosing View, Toolbars, Drawing; or by pressing the Drawing button) includes WordArt, 3-D Effects, and AutoShapes, among others. You can also download additional clipart from Microsoft's Web site.

▶ **See** "Creating a WordArt Graphic Hyperlink," **p. 278**

**FIG. 1.2**
Meet Scribble the cat, just one of the many new Office Assistants in Office 97.

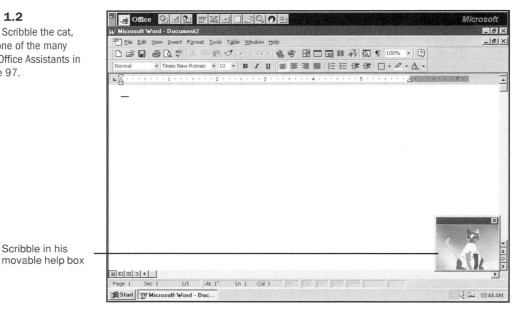

Scribble in his movable help box

## Office Binder 97: A New Way to Get Organized

Word, Excel, and PowerPoint documents pertaining to a given project can now be stored together in a single file to simplify printing, file sharing, and archiving. Even though this feature does not support Outlook and Access, it can still be an excellent way to keep project files in one place.

▷ **See** "Putting It All Together in a Binder," **p. 284**

## Multiple-Level Undo

Once only available in Word, Undo has now expanded to include Excel and PowerPoint. This command can be invaluable for recovering from typing or formatting errors.

## Support for Comments and Changes Made by Multiple Reviewers

Multiple reviewers can now insert their comments into a Word or Excel document. This feature codes edits made by multiple reviewers so that each change can be incorporated or rejected. Track Changes is an improved version of the old revision-marking feature found in the previous version of Word.

▷ **See** "Using In-Place Comments to Synthesize Reviewer Feedback," **p. 288**

## Customized Applications Using Visual Basic for Applications

It's now easier than ever for the advanced programmer or software developer to design custom applications in Office 97. Visual Basic for Applications (VBA) is an improved version of

Part

I

Ch

1

WordBasic that has been standardized for use with Word 97 as well as with Excel, PowerPoint, and Access.

▶ **See** "Macros and Visual Basic for Applications," **p. 310**

# Word 97 Enhancements

In addition to the suite-wide enhancements just described, a number of improvements have been made to Word in its latest version.

## Summarize Your Documents with the Click of a Mouse

Word 97's new AutoSummarize feature can generate an executive summary or abstract for your document and then insert it into the front of the document or save it to its own file.

▶ **See** "Auto Features at a Glance," **p. 124**

## Enhanced Document Navigation

The Select Browse Object button gives you a quick way to navigate to key areas in a document. You can browse a document by heading, by edits, or by graphic, or you can specify search criteria.

The second feature is the Document Map option (see Figure 1.3), which allows you to display a map of your document on the left side of your screen. This gives you an overview of the headings in your document.

**FIG. 1.3**
Click any section in the Document Map to be instantly transported to that part of the document.

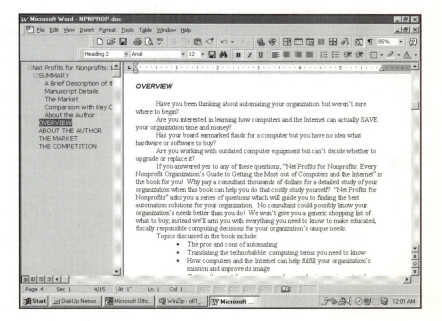

## Improved Formatting Flexibility

Word gives you two new ways to solve formatting headaches: the ability to add a border to a page, and a way to draw tables using a mouse.

## Automatic Typing and Grammar-Checking

Improve your typing speed by putting the new AutoComplete feature to work. Word 97 allows you to program in frequently typed phrases and bits of text so that the program can literally finish your sentences for you.

There's also an Automatic Grammar Checker that will mark incorrect grammar as you type.

▶ **See** "Spell Checking," **p. 36**

▶ **See** "Programming AutoText Entries," **p. 125**

## New Letter Wizard Ensures Consistency

Word 97 gives you a new wizard to help keep business letters uniform in format and content. The Letter Wizard will see to it that your correspondence looks the same time after time, and you'll never have to worry about forgetting a critical element again.

## Version Tracking

The days of having to rename files to maintain copies of a document's various versions are over! With Word 97's Version Tracking feature, you can save multiple versions of a document in one file, and you can include comments regarding each revision. Not only does this make finding the various versions easier, but it also saves disk space.

▶ **See** "Saving Versions of a Document," **p. 291**

# Excel 97 Enhancements

Like Word 97, Excel 97 includes a variety of new features to increase your productivity while making your job easier. Some of the enhancements are minor, while others represent a major upgrade from previous versions.

## Formatting Flexibility

Formatting can make a big difference in data presentation. It can also make scanning a worksheet for specific information easier by off-setting critical numbers. Some of the things Microsoft has done to increase flexibility in Excel formatting include:

- *Conditional formatting*. You can now tell Excel to format data based on whether or not it meets specified criteria.
- *Circle invalid data*. This feature will circle data not meeting your criteria, making it easier to spot.

■ *Page break preview.* This feature enables you to use a mouse to move page breaks.

■ *Rotate cell text.* Use this feature to align text vertically so that you don't have to resize cells based on header length (see Figure 1.4 for an example).

**FIG. 1.4**
Angled headers can make a worksheet much more readable and professional-looking.

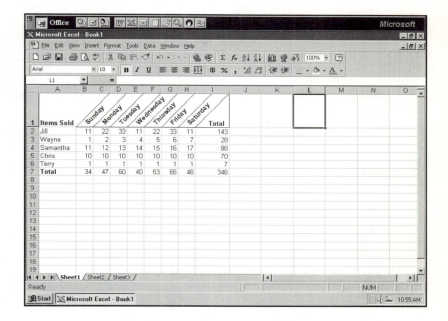

■ *Indent cell text.* This new capability gives you yet another way to format text within a cell to make it distinctive.

▶ **See** "Editing Cell Contents," **p. 134**

## Enhanced Collaboration Capabilities

With people's increasing workloads and the advent of the intranet came the need for workgroup-friendly applications. Excel 97 is one of those applications. Not only does its Share Workbook feature allow multiple people on a network to edit a document simultaneously, but its Data Validation setting can help reduce data entry mistakes by specifying valid data criteria.

▶ **See** "Protecting Workbook Cells Before Sharing It with Others," **p. 292**

## Simplified Formula Programming

Excel's new Formula Palette and Range Finder buttons make applying a function to a new range of cells a snap. And Excel finally supports Natural Language Formulas, which enable you to use row and column header names in place of range references.

▶ **See** "Working with Natural Language Formulas and Ranges," **p. 166**

## Improved Data Capturing and Querying

In addition to being able to create forms to compile data from Web users, Excel 97 comes with enhanced Get External Data features. Not only can you query Access and other databases on your system or network, but you can now query Internet and intranet resources as well.

▶ **See** "Capturing Live Data from the Web," **p. 168**

## Additional Chart Options

Excel 97 comes with a variety of new chart types and options, such as the capability to include chart tips, data tables in charts, and a number of new formatting options.

▶ **See** "Using Chart Wizard to Visualize Your Data," **p. 156**

# PowerPoint 97 Enhancements

True multimedia presentations are no longer a luxury, they're a necessity. PowerPoint 97 lives up to that demand by offering a host of multimedia possibilities along with increased ease of use.

And the new Common Tasks toolbar automatically appears to help you access frequently used features with ease.

## Adding Sound to Presentations

Tired of the same old sound files? With PowerPoint 97, you can now record a voice-over explanation of each of your slides, or you can incorporate a track from a favorite audio CD.

▶ **See** "Adding Basic Sound Clips to Your Presentation," **p. 194**
▶ **See** "Using Audio CD Tracks for Background Sound," **p. 195**
▶ **See** "Recording a Voiceover for Your Presentation," **p. 196**

## Customizing Slide Shows

PowerPoint's new Expand Slide feature allows you to insert backup slides after a primary slide to elaborate on key points. With the Slide Finder, you can preview slides from another presentation and insert them into the current presentation. Finally, you can customize a show to print handouts of a particular combination of slides.

## Simplifying Navigation Through Your Presentation

Adding PowerPoint's new Action Buttons (see Figure 1.5) to your presentation can help your audience find their way around the various slides, and best of all, they're easy to add.

▶ **See** "Simplifying Navigation Through Your Presentation by Adding Action Buttons," **p. 193**

**FIG. 1.5**
Adding Action Buttons to your slide show can enhance the audience's experience by helping them make their way through the entire show.

Previous Slide Button

Next Slide Button

## Animating Your Presentation

Add that extra touch to your slide show by animating charts or including enhanced custom animations. These, more than anything else, will be the things people remember most about your presentation.

▶ **See** "Animating Objects to Grab Attention," **p. 193**

## Always Something New

PowerPoint Central connects you to a variety of resources for additional sound clips, animation, templates, and more. And they're all free!

## Presentation Enhancements

Before giving your presentation, you may want to draft some notes to accompany each slide. In PowerPoint 97, you now have the ability to type notes into Speakers Notes in the Notes Page View. You also have some new presentation options/modes. You can opt to control a presentation from one computer and show it on another, or you can put it in Kiosk Mode, which will keep it cycling though over and over again.

▶ **See** "Adding Speaker Notes to Your Slides," **p. 182**

▶ **See** "Viewing the Presentation from One Computer While Controlling It from Another," **p. 200**

# Access 97 Enhancements

Like the other applications, Access 97 comes with a number of new features, many of them dealing with Office 97's new Web capabilities.

## Improved Year 2000 Support

This version of Access is equipped to deal with the Year 2000 issue. To enter dates in the $21^{st}$ century, enter a date in the range from **1/1/00** to **12/31/29**.

## New Web Capabilities

The new Publish to the Web wizard converts your Access information to a dynamic Internet or intranet site, including query pages and a home page, among others. You can also apply an HTML template to all the pages and automatically post updates to the pages on your Web server. Access also supports a new Hyperlink data type that enables you to link Access data to other sources of information on your intranet or the Internet.

## Complex Form Construction and Handling with ActiveX Controls

Access 97's improved design features now allow you to create complex forms with tabs. Even these complex forms can load without loading Visual Basic for Applications (VBA), which greatly improves their performance. In fact, all Access forms and reports are treated as lightweight unless you specify otherwise. And now you can use ActiveX Controls to enhance your forms and make them even more interactive.

▶ **See** "Using Forms," **p. 224**

▶ **See** "Building Forms with the Form Wizard," **p. 234**

## Securing a Database

You can use the new User-Level Security wizard to create a secure copy of the database. This protects designated fields from being destroyed or corrupted. In order to access the database, users must log in with their ID and password. This information is linked to a security level designation.

# Introducing Outlook 97

Outlook 97, the newest member of the Office suite family, is a number of things. It's a Personal Information Manager (PIM); it's a desktop manager; and it's an e-mail client. As such, it is capable of scheduling appointments, maintaining contact lists, organizing journal entries, and more. Because it is so new and contains so many features, Outlook 97 is explored in great detail in Chapters 14 and 15.

▶ **See** "Sending a Simple E-Mail Message with Outlook," **p. 243**

▶ **See** "Building an Address Book," **p. 250**

▶ **See** "Blocking Out Appointments and Events on Your Schedule," **p. 258**

▶ **See** "Creating a Task List," **p. 262**

▶ **See** "Tracking Items with the Journal," **p. 264**

# The New Small Business Edition of Office 97

Microsoft created a special bundle of its software, targeting the special needs of small businesses. This bundle is also frequently shipped with new computers purchased from many of the leading mail-order vendors.

## Publisher 97

This desktop publishing application has consistently been a top selling software title. Now many Office users will have its powerful publication design wizards, templates, and Web capabilities at their fingertips. See Chapter 17, "Getting Professional Results with Publisher 97," for detailed information about Publisher 97.

## Small Business Financial Manager

The Small Business Financial Manager works with Excel to provide advanced financial analysis capabilities with the help of wizards. You can import your accounting data, run what-if analyses using the What-If wizard, and produce a variety of nicely-formatted reports.

▶ **See** "Importing Accounting Data," **p. 171**

▶ **See** "Creating a Financial Report with Report Wizard," **p. 172**

▶ **See** "Running What-If Scenarios Using the What-If Wizard," **p. 173**

## Automap Streets Plus

This unique mapping program allows you to plan your delivery route, pinpoint your clients on a map, and create a map to a street address. Best of all, these maps are easily inserted into other Office 97 applications. ●

# CHAPTER 2

# Exploring Common Screen and Editing Features

**M**icrosoft has worked hard to make the Office 97 applications much easier to use. Perhaps the biggest step in that direction is its commitment to making the applications as similar as possible in terms of their common screen and editing features. Getting to know these common elements will give you a head start in learning the Office applications you may be less experienced with.

**Common screen elements, menus, and toolbars**

Get acquainted with elements common to the majority of Office 97 applications to speed up your learning time for applications less familiar to you.

**Working with the Office Shortcut bar**

Customize this toolbar for instant access to your most commonly used applications and documents.

**Switching from one document to another**

Learn how to switch from one document to another while you have multiple Office 97 documents open.

**Manipulating blocks of text**

Learn how to select blocks of text and manipulate or change the attributes of that text in one easy step.

**Working with graphic objects**

Office 97 makes it easy to incorporate a variety of graphic objects into your documents and resize or reallocate them as needed.

# Common Screen Elements

When you open any Office 97 application, there are a number of screen elements you can always count on seeing (see Figure 2.1).

**FIG. 2.1**

As you launch any of the Office 97 applications, you'll notice many shared menu items, toolbar buttons, and other screen elements.

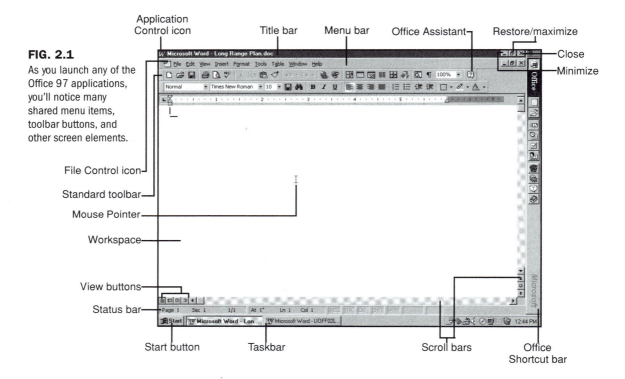

**N O T E**  Applications exclusive to the Small Business Edition (Publisher, the Small Business Financial Manager, and Automap Streets Plus) will be noticeably different, but not beyond recognition. ▨

These common screen elements include:

- ▨ *Title bar*. Contains the name of the program and the name of the document, as well as the Maximize, Minimize, Restore, and Close buttons.
- ▨ *Application Control icon*. Lets you close the application by double-clicking it, or you can click it once to open a pull-down menu that allows you to move or resize the application's window.
- ▨ *File Control icon*. In Word, PowerPoint, and Excel, this icon controls the active file in much the same way that the Application Control icon controls the application—double-click it to close the file, or click once to open a menu of choices.

- *Menu bar*. Allows you to select from a variety of pull-down menus needed to execute commands in Office 97 applications.

- *Standard toolbar*. Holds shortcut buttons that quickly execute common tasks such as printing, opening a new document, and more. This toolbar may be modified to meet your specific needs.

- *Mouse pointer*. Moves on-screen as you move the mouse to assist you in accessing menus and clicking buttons. This element may look different depending on the application you are running and the task you are trying to accomplish.

- *Office Assistant*. Serves as your online helper. Ask the Assistant questions or turn if off as you become more familiar with Office 97.

- *View buttons*. Enable you to adjust your view of a document. In Word, you can choose from Normal view, Outline view, Page Layout view, and Outline Layout view. Other applications offer different views.

- *Status bar*. Displays information about your document, including page count, line number, the task in progress, and so on.

- *Minimize, Restore/Maximize, and Close buttons*. Allow users to quickly resize the window of the current application. All Office 97 applications (except Outlook, Publisher, and Automap Streets Plus) have a second set of these buttons on the Menu Bar to resize the file window within the application window. This is especially useful when multiple windows within an application are open at once.

**TIP** If you resize your windows and find they've gone off the edge of the screen, you can get them back in view. Select the application on the Windows taskbar at the bottom of your screen and right-click its button. The shortcut menu that appears will give you quick access to the elusive Minimize, Close, and Restore/Maximize buttons.

- *Taskbar*. Allows you to toggle back and forth between documents already open, or to launch new applications via the Start button. This is a Windows element, not part of Office 97.

- *Start button*. A Windows button that, when clicked, gives you access to the entire contents of your system via menus. For example, you can click Start and then select Programs to launch your Office 97 applications.

- *Workspace*. Consists of a blank page on which you insert text, numbers, and graphics. Depending on which application you launch, the workspace will have a slightly different appearance.

- *Scroll bars*. Move you quickly around a document. Either slide them with your mouse (point to the scroll box, hold down the left button, and drag), or click on either side of the box for larger jumps. A vertical scroll bar appears at the right side of the document, and a horizontal scroll bar can be found at the bottom of the window just above the status bar.

Part
I

Ch
2

■ *Insertion Point.* Not to be confused with the Mouse Pointer, which moves freely around the screen, the Insertion Point blinks in place to let you know where any inserted text will appear.

■ *Office Shortcut bar.* New to Office 97, this totally customizable toolbar gives you instant access to your most commonly accessed applications and documents.

# Common Menus and Menu Options

Menus organize a number of commands and options into logical categories for easy reference. Just click the name of the menu to open its pull-down menu. In addition to the names of the options, Office 97 displays the appropriate icon where available and lists the keystroke combination needed to execute the same option. Figure 2.2 illustrates a typical pull-down menu in Word.

**FIG. 2.2**

When accessing the File menu in Word 97, you recognize some of the icons from the Standard toolbar, and you see which keys you can press to access the same function.

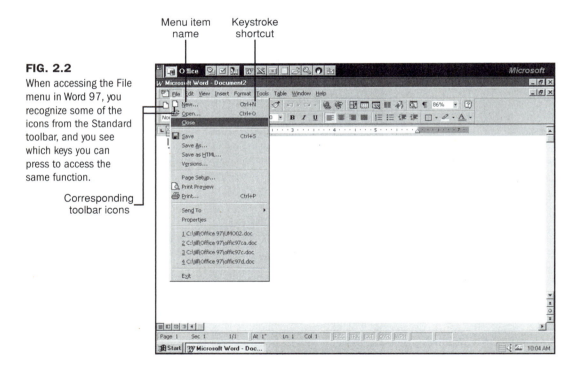

There are a number of menus shared by Office 97 applications that are described in the following list. Application-specific menus are addressed in chapters pertaining to the individual programs.

■ *File menu.* Gives users access to such commands as opening, saving, and renaming a document; setting print properties as well as launching the printing process; specifying file properties; and exiting the application. This is the first item in each application's menu bar.

Part
I
Ch
2

- *Edit menu.* Holds commands for cutting, copying, and pasting, as well as the search and replace option. Options not available in a given circumstance are grayed out (for example, unless a block of text is selected, Copy will be grayed out). Look here first if you need to make a change in a document.

- *View menu.* Presents options needed to alter the screen's appearance. You can add toolbars, turn them off, create document headers and footers, and view your document in Outline mode to name a few. You can also zoom the page in and out to increase print size or reduce it to fit more on-screen.

- *Insert menu.* Allows you to add application-specific objects into a file. For example, in Word you might add clipart; in Access you may insert a new record, and so on.

- *Format menu.* When present, this menu allows you to format text or other objects supported by the application. If you want to change the way your text looks, add a list to your document, or add a border to your work, look here first.

- *Tools menu.* If there's anything you want to customize, the Tools menu is the place to start. Neat gadgets like the Spell Checker, Word Counter, and the AutoCorrect feature reside here in Word 97. Each application has its own subset of tools, so it's definitely a menu worth checking out.

- *Window menu.* While the top half of this menu may change from application to application, the bottom half allows you to switch back and forth between open documents within an application (where available). To access a document listed, simply click its file name.

- *Help menu.* Leads you to a variety of application-specific resources both within Office 97 and on the Web.

**TIP** For speedy access to the pull-down menus, press the Alt key and the underlined letter of the desired menu—for example, to open the File menu, press Alt+F.

# The Shared Standard Toolbar

Just as there are similarities between Office 97 menus, there is a Standard toolbar shared by all the applications that has numerous buttons/icons you'll see no matter which application you're working with (see Figure 2.3).

These buttons are more than just shortcuts to the same option within a menu. When you choose the toolbar button or keyboard shortcut for a menu command, the function is completed with the default. Menus are your best bet for more complex needs.

 Take the New document command in Word 97, for example. You can create a new document by choosing File, New to select a document type from Word 97's library of templates and wizards. You can also create a new document by using a shortcut (clicking the New button on the Standard toolbar, or by pressing Ctrl+N). Using the New document shortcut in this case chooses the default Word template—a blank page referred to as the Normal template.

**FIG. 2.3**

Several buttons included on the default Standard toolbar are shared by the entire Office 97 suite.

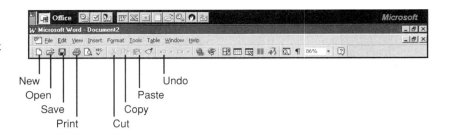

New
Open
Save
Print
Cut
Copy
Paste
Undo

 **TIP** A good rule of thumb: if you want to choose options when executing a command, follow the menu sequence. If the default (a blank page for a new document, one complete copy of the entire document to be printed, and so on) is acceptable, use the method most comfortable to you.

# Tweaking the Toolbar

We all use Office applications differently. As a result, some of the buttons you use most may be missing on the toolbars. Likewise, valuable space may be taken up by other buttons you never use.

To add a button to a toolbar, follow these steps:

1. Make sure that the toolbar you want to modify is in view.
2. Choose Tools, Customize, and select the Commands tab.
3. In the Categories box, click the category of the button you want to add. The command names and icons (if available) are shown in the Commands box.
4. Click the desired icon/command, and then drag it into position on the toolbar.
5. Release the mouse button to set the button in place.

To delete a button from a toolbar, do the following:

1. Make sure that the toolbar you want to modify is in view.
2. Choose Tools, Customize, and select the Commands tab.
3. If necessary, drag the Customize dialog box to another location (click the title bar and drag it) until the button you want to delete is visible.
4. Click the button you want to delete, and then drag it into the Customize dialog box.
5. Release the mouse button to complete the deletion.

# Keystrokes: The Third Way to Get the Job Done

In addition to menus and toolbars, Office 97 offers a host of shortcuts to access commands using the keyboard. Table 2.1 highlights some of the more common functions.

**Table 2.1   Office 97 Keyboard Shortcuts**

| Function/Command | Shortcut |
| --- | --- |
| New | Ctrl+N |
| Open | Ctrl+O |
| Save | Ctrl+S |
| Print | Ctrl+P |
| Cut | Ctrl+X |
| Paste | Ctrl+V |
| Copy | Ctrl+C |

Part

I

Ch

2

# Using the Office Shortcut Bar

The Office Shortcut bar resides on your Windows desktop for quick, easy access to your favorite Office 97 applications. Putting the Shortcut bar to work for you is as simple as clicking on the icon of choice. If you need a reminder of what an icon represents, simply place your mouse pointer over the icon and wait a couple of seconds for the yellow ScreenTips box to furnish your answer.

If you don't see the application you're looking for on the default Shortcut bar, click the New Office Document icon to browse templates from all applications, or launch the desired application from the Windows Taskbar by choosing Start, Programs, and then selecting your application.

# Moving the Shortcut Bar

If you find the Shortcut bar's presence at the top of the screen bothersome, you can move it by clicking on the empty part of the bar, holding the mouse button down, and then dragging the bar to its new location. The box's outline will turn red to show you where the box is positioned at any given point during the move. Touching the mouse pointer to one of the screen's edges will result in the box shaping itself to fit that edge of the screen. The Office Shortcut bar can be displayed vertically or horizontally for maximum flexibility.

# Changing the Programs and Files Listed on the Shortcut Bar

Only you know which applications and functions are most important to you, which is why Microsoft gives you full control over the new Shortcut bar. You can configure this bar in a number of ways. Add your most frequently used applications, delete the ones you never use, or add an icon linking you to your most current project files.

To customize the Shortcut bar:

1. Right-click the word Office on the Shortcut bar.

2. Click Customize, which opens the Customize dialog box.

3. Select the Buttons tab (see Figure 2.4).

4. In the Show These Files As Buttons box, place a check mark (click the box) by the applications or functions you want to include, and delete the check marks (click the box) next to unwanted buttons.

**FIG. 2.4**

Click the box next to the file of choice to select or deselect that item from the Shortcut bar. In this example, the first six files appear on the toolbar, but the last one, Microsoft Word, doesn't.

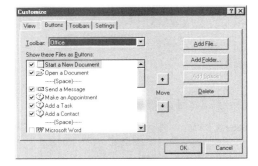

5. If you want to create a link to a folder or file, you may do so by clicking the Add File or Add Folder button. Both options open a dialog box that allows you to browse your files for the proper item. Click Add to complete the link, and then press OK to complete the customization.

# Switching Between Documents

To switch between open documents in an application, do one of the following:

▪ Select the document you want to see from the list on the Windows menu.

▪ Press Ctrl+F6 to flip through the files.

▪ If you've arranged the document windows so you can see bits of each one, simply select the document's Title bar to activate its window.

# Moving Between Applications

After you open an application, a button with an icon representing the application appears on the Windows Taskbar along with a truncated version of the active document's file name. Click the desired button to activate the application. To scroll through the Windows screens, press Alt+Tab.

# Selecting Text

Many commands and operations in Office applications require that you select text before you can make changes to it. For example, to change the font of text or move a block of text, you first have to select it.

Although there are a variety of ways to select items in each application, use the following steps as a starting point. To select desired text/data:

1. Place the mouse pointer at the beginning of the desired text.

2. Click the left mouse button and hold it down while dragging it to highlight a block of text (see Figure 2.5).

3. After the desired area is highlighted, perform your chosen operation on the data as described in the next few sections.

**FIG. 2.5**

Selected text is highlighted on-screen. When resting inside the highlighted text, the mouse pointer takes on a different appearance depending on the application you're working with. In Word, the mouse pointer turns into an arrow.

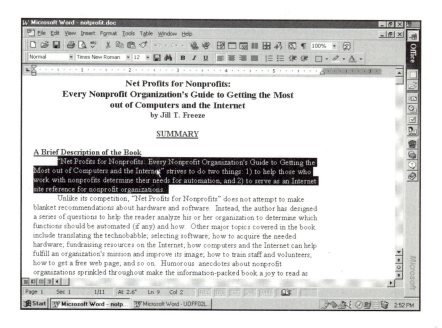

 **T I P**   If you find you need to adjust the selected text area after you've released the mouse button, there's no need to start from scratch. You can hold down the Shift key and use the arrow keys to highlight the exact area you want.

# Deleting Selected Text and Data

To delete a block of text, select the area and press the Delete button on your keyboard.

# Moving a Selected Block of Text

Moving a block of text from one location to another is a simple process:

1. Select the text you want to move as described in the previous section "Selecting Text."

2. Cut the text from its current location using one of three ways: click the Cut button on the toolbar; use Ctrl+X; or choose Edit, Cut. The text will disappear as it is copied to the Clipboard.

3. Move the mouse pointer to the desired location of the text and single-click to set the insertion point in place.

4. To paste the block of text into the new location, click the Paste button on the toolbar; use Ctrl+V; or choose Edit, Paste.

 Right-clicking selected text will also give you access to the Copy, Cut, and Paste functions.

**N O T E** Selected text is copied to the Clipboard. You can Paste or Copy the same item (selected text or object) as many times as you want, until you cut or copy another item. Additionally, after you shut down your system, the Clipboard's contents will be lost.

# Copying Selected Text

Copying a block of text to another location can save a lot of time, even if you have to make minor edits. To do this:

1. Select the text you want to move as described earlier.

2. Copy the text using one of three ways: press the Copy icon on the toolbar; press Ctrl+C; or choose Edit, Copy.

3. Guide the mouse pointer to the desired location of the text and single-click to set the insertion point in place.

4. To paste the block of text into the new location, press the Paste icon on the toolbar; press Ctrl+V; or choose Edit, Paste.

 If you want to place the copied text in more than one location, simply execute steps 3 and 4 as many times as needed. There's no need to reselect the text.

# Changing the Text Font

Perhaps the best way to enhance the appearance of your documents is to choose a distinctive font that fits the message. Whether it's script for the body of an invitation or a more playful style for your kids' Web page, you can find the font for the job. You can select a font one of two ways: by choosing it before you begin typing the input, or by selecting the text and then applying the change to the selection.

To select a font before inputting text, click the arrow next to the Font window of the Formatting toolbar to open the drop-down list box. Choose from the fonts listed.

# Adding Bold, Italic, Color, Underline, and Other Text Attributes

The Font tab of the Font dialog box (see Figure 2.6) gives you countless ways to change the appearance of your text. Start by following these steps:

1. Choose Format, Font to call up the Font dialog box.

2. Select the Font tab (see Figure 2.6) to choose a style or special effect for your text and see it in the Preview window before applying it.

3. Click OK to apply the selected type attributes.

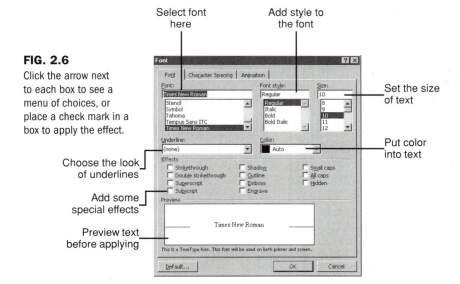

**FIG. 2.6**
Click the arrow next to each box to see a menu of choices, or place a check mark in a box to apply the effect.

You can incorporate any of these attributes into your text (see Figure 2.7) by selecting them from the beginning, or by following the steps for selecting a complex font as described in the preceding steps.

**FIG. 2.7**

The text in the figure was formatted in 26-point Times New Roman and altered as indicated.

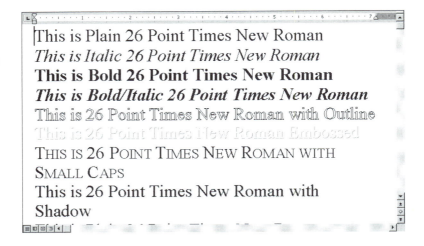

# Changing the Size of the Text

One way to emphasize certain parts of your document is to change the type size. Again, you can either specify the size from the beginning, or select the text and change its size later. To change type size:

1. Click the arrow next to the Font window of the Formatting toolbar to open the drop-down list box.

2. Choose from the sizes listed, or enter your own.

# Finding Text

In the various application-specific chapters, we will look at how to use Find and Replace (for Word) and data filtering and sorting (in Excel, Access, and Outlook) in more detail. There is also a simple Find function that behaves similarly in several of the applications.

Word, Excel, and PowerPoint give users a way to search for items within a document:

1. Choose Edit, Find, press Ctrl+F, or press the Find icon on the Standard toolbar to call up the Find dialog box.

2. Enter the text you are searching for.

3. Select Find Next.

4. After the word is found, it will be highlighted just as selected text is highlighted.

5. To find additional occurrences of the word, select Find Next.

6. Choose Cancel to end the search.

Some applications allow you to narrow this search based on case-sensitivity and other criteria. These options will be presented in chapters dealing with the various applications.

# Selecting and Deleting a Graphic

Creating graphic objects (charts, graphs, clipart, and so forth) is covered in depth in the chapters that discuss the various applications. It can be a very complicated process, but manipulating these objects is fairly simple, and object manipulation is handled the same way in each application.

To select an object, simply click it. Eight little boxes frame the object to let you know that you were successful. After you select the object, you can press the Delete button to erase it.

# Resizing and Moving a Graphic

To resize a graphic object:

1. Select the object. Object handles appear around the object (see Figure 2.8).

Part
I
Ch
2

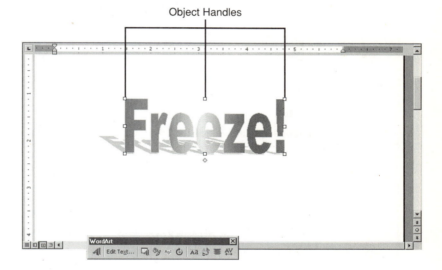

**FIG. 2.8**
Eight handles frame an active object. You use these handles to resize an object.

Object Handles

2. Place the mouse pointer on the handle nearest the direction you want to shift the image.
3. Holding the left mouse button down, drag the frame of the object until it's in the desired position.

   Figure 2.9 shows a graphic that's being resized.
4. This process may be repeated in any number of positions.

**FIG. 2.9**
We've zoomed in extra close on this Publisher screen to show you how graphics are typically resized and moved in Office 97 applications.

To move an object:

1. Select the object.

2. Place the mouse pointer inside the frame until it turns into a cross with an arrow at each point.

3. To move the object, hold the mouse button down and drag the object in the desired direction. The insertion point will show you exactly where the object will be dropped.

**N O T E** An object can only be placed in a "legal" position on the page. For instance, neither Word nor Publisher allows you to drop the object outside of a margin. It will simply place the object up against the margin.

## Cutting and Pasting Graphic Objects

You can also cut, paste, and copy an object just as you can text. Because the object is copied to the Clipboard, you can easily move an object from one application to another. To cut and paste a graphic object:

1. Select the graphic object you want to move.

2. Cut the object from its current location in one of three ways: click the Cut icon on the toolbar; press Ctrl+X; or choose Edit, Cut. The image will disappear as it is copied to the Clipboard for future use.

3. Move the mouse pointer to the desired location of the object and click to set the insertion point in place.

4. To paste the image into the new location, click the Paste icon on the toolbar; press Ctrl+V; or choose Edit, Paste.

 To copy an object from one location to another, repeat the preceding steps, substituting the Copy command for Cut. ●

# Correcting Mistakes, Printing, and Getting Help

The Office 97 suite is designed to help make sure your documents look their best and are error-free. To that end, each application is equipped with powerful, easy-to-use tools that allow you to produce the best-looking (and most persuasive) documents. Spell checking, the ability to easily print documents, and a powerful help system all combine to make your work in Office 97 productive. ■

**Spell checking**

Use Office 97's spell checking feature to avoid embarrassing spelling errors.

**Print a document**

Discover how easy it is to print a finished document from any of the Office applications.

**Accessing the powerful Help system**

From the new Office Assistant to on-line help, Office 97 comes equipped with answers to your questions.

# Spell Checking

Each application in the Office 97 suite (with the exception of Outlook and applications exclusive to the Small Business Edition bundle) shares a common database of stored words. The words added in one application are now reflected in the others, thus increasing accuracy and consistency throughout all your documents.

## Running the Spelling Check

 To run a spelling check from within any of the applications (except Outlook), choose Tools, Spelling and Grammar; press the F7 key on the top of your keyboard; or click the Spelling and Grammar button on the Standard toolbar.

## Dealing with Misspelled Words

When a spelling error is detected, you are presented with a suggested alternative and a few options. These options may include adding the entry to the dictionary, ignoring the word once or many times, accepting the suggestion, or changing all occurrences of the misspelling.

# Using AutoCorrect

AutoCorrect is a tool shared by Word, Excel, PowerPoint, and Access that allows you to store an abbreviation for an often-used chunk of text or image. When you type the programmed abbreviation, AutoCorrect inserts the designated text or image. This feature is particularly useful if you have a "wordsmithed" mission statement for your organization, a biography of your company's president, or some other frequently used paragraph or phrase.

 **TIP** Consider using AutoCorrect for e-mail and Web addresses that are prone to keystroke errors. Think of all the time you'll save just by not having to hunt for the tilde (~) key needed for many Web URL's.

Furthermore, you can even program it to recognize typos you make regularly (like *teh* for *the*), and AutoCorrect will fix them for you.

▶ **See** "Auto Features at a Glance," **p. 124**

## Disabling AutoCorrect

Office 97 comes loaded with predefined corrections. For example, (c) is automatically turned into a copyright symbol, and the smileys you find in your e-mail box are turned into right-side up smiling faces. Because AutoCorrect is turned on by default, you may want to know how to shut it off. To disable the AutoCorrect feature from within Word, Excel, Access, or PowerPoint:

1. Choose Tools, AutoCorrect. You see the AutoCorrect dialog box (see Figure 3.1).
2. Select the AutoCorrect tab.
3. Unselect the check mark next to the Replace Text as You Type box.

**FIG. 3.1**
By default, the
AutoCorrect options are
set to replace text as
you type.

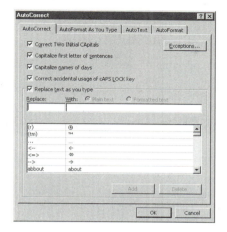

4. Click OK to complete the request.

# Programming AutoCorrect

There are two ways to program AutoCorrect. From within Word, Excel, PowerPoint, or Access:

1. Pull up a document containing the text you want to include, and then highlight the text for which you'd like to program the entry.

2. After the text is highlighted (or if you'd like to enter the text directly), choose Tools, AutoCorrect to open the AutoCorrect dialog box.

3. If you've selected text, it will appear in the With box. If not, you may enter the desired text at this point.

4. Because Microsoft has preprogrammed a number of common spelling and typing errors, you may want to scroll down their list before making your own entry. If you find you do need to make an entry, type a set of characters that will set off AutoCorrect and enter them in the Replace box.

5. Select Add, then click OK to complete the process.

**CAUTION**

Use extreme caution when selecting the set of characters to *trigger* AutoCorrect because it's that set of characters that will retrieve the text you programmed in to AutoCorrect. For example, you may not want to use the word boss to call up her biography because that biography will appear every time you type the word **boss**. Of course, you can edit either the Replace or With text at any time.

Part

I

Ch

3

### Editing an AutoCorrect Entry

Should you need to edit an AutoCorrect entry, follow these steps:

1. Click Tools, AutoCorrect to bring up the AutoCorrect dialog box.
2. Scroll through the list of entries until you find the one you want to edit.
3. After you locate the entry, click it to activate it. This will bring it into the Replace and With boxes, where it can be edited.
4. When you've finished with the edits, press the Replace button.
5. AutoCorrect will tell you that the entry already exists and will ask whether you want to redefine it.
6. Choose Yes or No, and then click OK to complete the change.

# Preview Before You Print

 To make sure you'll get the output you expect when printing your documents, use Print Preview. To do this, choose File, Print Preview, or select the Print Preview button on the Standard toolbar. To close the preview, simply click the Close button on the Print Preview toolbar. Figure 3.2 shows an example of print preview in Word.

**FIG. 3.2**
With Print Preview, you can see what you'll get before you print it.

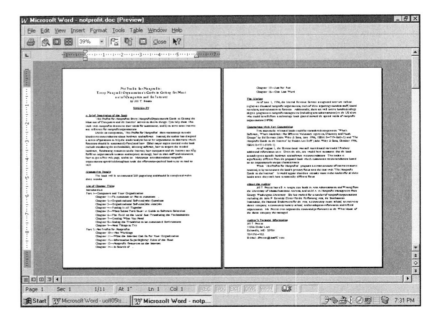

While in print preview, you have some special display options:

 *One Page.* Shows only the current page in print preview.

■ *Multiple Pages*. Shows a grid of three columns and two rows of pages. Drag your mouse to highlight the desired number of pages, and then release it to see the number of pages you selected in print preview.

■ *Zoom Control*. Use this drop-down box to select the zoom percentage of the display. Obviously, you won't be able to see much detail with six pages displayed, and zooming in would defeat the purpose of having so many pages displayed.

■ *Shrink to Fit*. Instructs the application to squeeze stray lines of text or a table onto one less page if possible.

■ *Close Preview*. Returns to the current page in normal view.

# Printing a Document

You can quickly print a basic Office 97 document from within the document by pressing Ctrl+P or by clicking the Print icon on the toolbar.

For more complex documents or to set advanced print options, see the chapter about the application with which you are working.

Part
I

Ch
3

# Setting Programs to Launch Automatically When Windows Starts

If you have an application you use constantly, you may want to consider programming it to launch automatically with Windows. You can follow these steps for any of the Office 97 programs:

1. Click the Start button in Windows, and then choose Settings, Taskbar.
2. When the Taskbar Properties dialog box appears (see Figure 3.3), select the Start Menu Programs tab.

**FIG. 3.3**
The Taskbar Properties dialog box.

3. Click the Add button to launch the Create Shortcut Wizard.

4. The Wizard prompts you for the name of the program you want to create a shortcut to.

5. To ensure that the proper name is inserted, click the Browse button and search for the folder where Office 97 is installed. By default this will be the C:/Program Files/ Microsoft Office/Office folder, but yours may be different. Then select the name of the desired application and click Open.

6. This will return you to the Create Shortcut Wizard. The proper path (address) of the application's program/shortcut link file will be inserted in the command line. Press Next to continue.

7. You are then asked where you want to place your shortcut. Scroll to the Startup folder in the Program folder of the Start menu, and then click the Startup folder. Click Next to proceed.

8. When asked for the title you want to give the program, choose the default for now. Click Finish, and then click OK.

You can test the program by clicking the Start button, and then selecting Programs, Startup to see which programs will be started automatically with Windows 95. The application you chose should now appear on that list.

# Getting Help

No matter what your learning style or preferred research method is, there's a Help tool just right for you. For example, choose from the animated Office Assistant, online documentation, and support available on the Internet. The options are seemingly endless.

# Using an Office Assistant to Get Help

This animated helper (see Figure 3.4) is prepared to answer any questions you may have. Just enter your question in the text box and press Search. He even attempts to guess what you may need help with. Even if animated helpers aren't your thing, you may want to see some of the personalities Microsoft has created (see the "Setting Office Assistant Options" section below).

## Turning the Office Assistant Off and On

To turn off the Office Assistant, click the Close button in the Office Assistant window. If a talk bubble is present, click on the center of the Office Assistant window to close it, and then close the Office Assistant window.

When you launch an application, the Office Assistant will automatically appear unless you remove the check mark next to the Show Me These Options At Startup option.

To call the Office Assistant back to work, click the Office Assistant button on the Standard toolbar, choose Help, Microsoft (application) Help, or press F1 at the top of your keyboard.

**FIG. 3.4**

When you call your animated Office Assistant into action, a yellow talk bubble appears. The Assistant offers some help topic options and gives you access to additional tips and help options.

Help Topic Options

Type Question Here

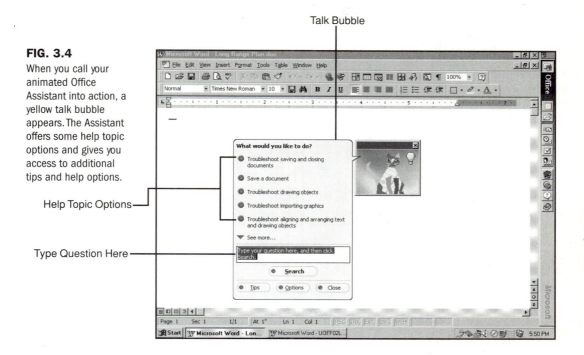

Talk Bubble

## Setting Office Assistant Options

To access Office Assistant options:

1. If the Office Assistant is not visible, click the Office Assistant talk bubble icon on the Standard toolbar.

2. To access the Office Assistant options, choose options in the talk bubble. If no talk bubble appears, click in the middle of the Office Assistant box to open one.

3. Select the Options tab to set the Office Assistant's behavior (see Figure 3.5). Click OK to complete the change.

**FIG. 3.5**

Select the kind of material you want the Office Assistant to present.

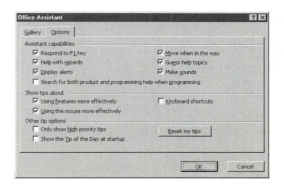

4. Select the Gallery tab to search for a new Office Assistant (see Figure 3.6). Press Back and Next to see each of your choices come to life. Click OK to process your selection.

**FIG. 3.6**

Meet the Genius, another of the Office Assistant personalities.

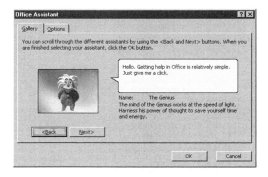

# Using Online Help

A variety of online resources designed to help you are already loaded on your PC. To locate them, choose Help, Contents and Index. The Help Topics: Microsoft (application) dialog box appears. Select one of the tabs, which are described in the sections that follow.

## Using the Contents Tab

The Contents tab (see Figure 3.7) is a great resource for the beginning to intermediate user who has an idea of what he wants to do, but maybe isn't totally up on all of the technical terms. You can browse general topics, and then click one for a further breakdown of that topic.

**FIG. 3.7**

Use the Contents tab to browse general help topics. You can work your way to more narrow topics by clicking a topic of interest.

## Looking Up Topics Using the Help Index

For intermediate to advanced users who know exactly what they want, the Index tab in the Help Topics dialog box is an excellent resource (see Figure 3.8). In the first box, type the first few characters of the item you're searching for, and then move to the second box to highlight the specific term. Click the Display button to jump directly to the topic.

**FIG. 3.8**
Get where you need to go quickly using the Index tab.

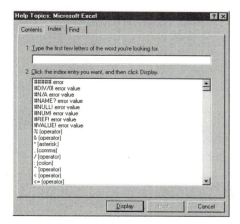

## Searching for Words or Phrases in Help

If you can't find it anywhere else, check the Find tab in the Help Topics dialog box. The Find tab allows you to search for any word or phrase—not just those in the help file index.

Before you use this feature for the first time, Windows must create a list (or database) of all the words in your Help files. For most people, Minimize Database will be the best option because it conserves system resources by selecting an application's primary help files only. Building the list will take awhile, but you only need to do it once to gain access to these powerful tools.

If you're someone who constantly pushes applications to their limits, you may want to Maximize the Database. A third option, Customize Database, is also available. With this option, you can specify which help files Windows uses to create your database.

# Using What's This?

Ever wonder what a certain screen element does? Pop into What's This? for a quick answer. To access What's This?:

1. From within any Office 97 application, choose Help, What's This?; press Shift+F1; or click the Help button within a dialog box (see Figure 3.9).

2. The mouse pointer changes to an arrow with a question mark beside it.

3. Click the item in question to see its pop-up definition.

**FIG. 3.9**
A pop-up definition box accessed in What's This? mode.

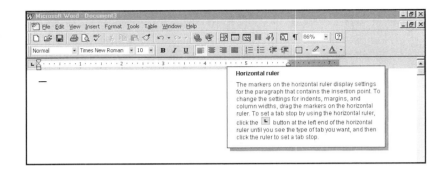

4. Press Esc, Enter, or click on the application's workspace to close the definition box.

 **T I P** To learn the identity of an icon on any of the toolbars, rest the mouse pointer on top of it. In a few seconds a yellow ScreenTips box will appear with the name of the icon.

# Using Microsoft on the Web

Microsoft has made getting the latest and greatest features much easier in Office 97. If you have a link to the Internet, you can explore these Web sites full of free goodies by choosing Help, Microsoft on the Web from within any application. In Microsoft on the Web, you'll find many application-specific templates, drivers, new product information, and the like. Microsoft on the Web works by bringing up your default Web browser and pointing you to a special Microsoft Web site.

▶ **See** "Enhancing Your Productivity with Freebies from the Web," **p. 70**

# Installing the IntelliMouse

Few people can resist playing with a new toy, and some Office 97 owners were lucky to get one in the bottom of their Office 97 box. The mouse, which looks like a standard two-button Microsoft mouse with a small gray wheel between the buttons, gives users additional document navigation options.

Before you can reap the rewards of these new options, however, you'll need to install the IntelliMouse. To do so, follow these steps:

1. Exit all your applications, shut down Windows, and then turn off your computer.
2. Unplug your old mouse, and then plug in the IntelliMouse.
3. Boot your computer, and then insert the floppy disk that came with the mouse.
4. Use the Start, Run Windows 95 command to run the setup program.

▶ **See** "Using IntelliMouse for More Accurate Scrolling in Word," **p. 80**

# CHAPTER 4

# Opening and Saving Files

**Create and open a document**

Learn to create a new document and open an existing document.

**Save a document automatically**

Use AutoRecover and automatically generate backup files to protect your hard work from power surges and other unforeseen data disasters.

**F**ile management capabilities in Office 97 are more powerful and versatile than ever. With increased file name size and the ability to edit and search a number of new and expanded file properties, you can find exactly what you want right when you need it.

The Save As and Open dialog boxes now have their own toolbars that allow you to view and find other files on your system or network. This helps you when it comes to selecting the best placement for your documents because you can quickly see where similar documents have been placed. And if the perfect spot doesn't exist, you can create it on-the-fly from within the File dialog box.

**N O T E**  The items in this chapter refer only to the core Office 97 applications (Word, Excel, and
PowerPoint) unless otherwise specified. Because Access, Publisher, AutoMap Streets Plus,
and Small Business Financial Planner 97 all behave differently, you will learn more about them in later
chapters.

# Creating a New Document

Obviously, you need to create a document (or at least view someone else's) before you can save
it. To create a new document, try one of the following:

- Click the New Office Document button on the Office Shortcut bar. You see a New Office
  Document dialog box like the one in Figure 4.1.

**FIG. 4.1**

The New Office
Document dialog box
gives you access to a
huge variety of Office 97
templates and wizards.

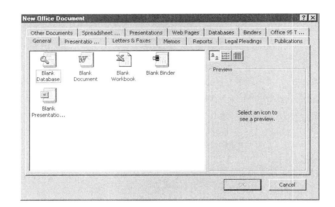

- Click Start on the Windows Taskbar and choose New Office Document, which gives you
  a dialog box similar to the one in Figure 4.1.
- Launch the application you want to use to create the document. Choose File, New to
  access the application's templates and wizards; or click the New Document button on the
  toolbar; or press Ctrl+N to open a blank workspace.

  ▶ **See** "Viewing Available Templates," **p. 64**

# Opening a Document

To open an existing Office document, use any of the following options to access the Open
dialog box:

- Click the Open Office Document button on the Office Shortcut bar.
- From the Windows Taskbar, click Start and then choose Open Office Document.
- Open the desired application. Choose File, Open; click the Open button on the toolbar;
  or press Ctrl+O.

Now select the document you want to open, and click Open to retrieve the document.

**TIP** If you're in a hurry to access a document, consider pressing the Start button on the Windows 95 Taskbar, and then selecting <u>D</u>ocuments to see a list of recently edited documents. Double-click the desired file to launch the application along with the selected file.

If you use the <u>F</u>ile, <u>O</u>pen command to open a file from within an application, you can use any of the following views to make finding the desired document that much easier:

 ▦ *List button.* The default view for the file display window, the List button merely shows the names of folders and files held in the specified folder.

▦ *Details button.* Click this button to see a folder's contents displayed in four columns. These columns include document name, size, type of file, and date and time modified (see Figure 4.2).

**FIG. 4.2**
The Details view gives you the chance to sort each column of data in ascending or descending order with a single mouse click.

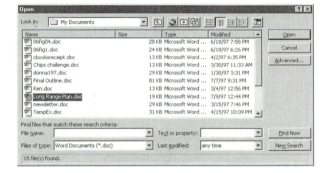

Part

I

Ch

4

 ▦ *Properties button.* Select a file in the file display window and click the Properties button to see all of the file's vital statistics like title, author, template used, revision number, print history, date of creation, and so on.

 ▦ *Preview button.* Get a sneak peek at a file's contents by clicking this button.

# Opening Local Area Network Documents

To view an Office document residing on a network, follow these steps:

1. Access the Open dialog box using one of the following methods:
   - Click the Open Office Document button on the Office Shortcut bar.
   - Click Start on the Windows Taskbar and select <u>O</u>pen Office Document.
   - From within an application, choose <u>F</u>ile, <u>O</u>pen; click the Open button on the toolbar; or press Ctrl+O.

2. In the Look <u>I</u>n box, click the arrow to browse through the network files as described in "Saving a File to Your Network" later in this chapter.

3. When the desired document is found, click the <u>O</u>pen button.

# Saving a Document for the First Time

Even though Office 97 gives you a host of safety features to help minimize data loss (see the later section "Selecting Advanced Save Options"), it's still wise to save your documents on a regular basis. But there's much more to it than merely clicking Save. You'll want to select a folder in which to store the document, give it a name that provides some clue as to its contents, and place frequently used files in a Favorites folder or maybe even create a shortcut to it on your Office Shortcut bar. Let's start, however, by learning how to save a document.

 **T I P** Putting all your documents in the same directory or folder would make it nearly impossible to find what you're looking for in a reasonable amount of time. Don't be afraid to add folders to make things easier to find.

From within any of the Office 97 applications, do one of the following:

- Click the Save button on the Standard toolbar.
- Use the Ctrl+S shortcut.
- Choose File, Save.
- Exit the document, and the application will prompt you to save your work.

Because you are saving the document for the first time, the Save As dialog box opens, asking you to name the document in the File Name box and select its placement in the system hierarchy. After you've selected the location (see the section titled "Searching for a Location to Save Your Files" later in this chapter), click Save to save the document or Cancel to cancel the transaction.

# Saving Changes to an Existing Document

Use one of the preceding methods to save changes to an existing document, where the document is saved with the same file name. If you want to track each version or revision of the document, consider using the Save Version option in Word or renaming the file by using Save As so that both versions remain intact.

> **CAUTION**
>
> Before clicking Save, make absolutely sure you want to replace the existing file with the changes you've just made. If so, simply click Save. If not, choose File, Save As to rename the new file.

 **T I P** You can have more than one file open in each application at once. To see if this is the case, choose Window and look under the horizontal line. Each open document is named and a check mark appears beside the active file name. In Word, you have the ability to save all open documents with one command. To do so, hold the Shift key and choose File, Save All.

# Saving a File to Your Network

Assuming you have the network administrator's permission, you can upload files to common folders on your local area network (LAN) by doing the following:

1. When saving a new document for the first time, the Save As dialog box appears.

2. In the Save In box, click the arrow to open the drop-down list box.

3. Select Network Neighborhood. After a few seconds you will see an Entire Network icon. Click this to see a view of all the computers linked to yours.

**N O T E**  Assuming you are connected to the network, have drives mapped, or have logged into these machines before, you don't have to go through step 3. You will have a list of connected machines already in view. ▓

4. Select the name of the network or computer on which the common folders reside.

5. If you have permission to access that system, you will be allowed to specify that network path to save your document.

There are a number of security measures you can take to ensure the integrity of your Word and Excel network documents. In the Save As dialog box, click the Options button to see a file-sharing options box. From here, you can create a password to open the document, a password to modify it, and a button you can enable to make the document Read Only. Consider using these options for documents containing critical data.

# Selecting Advanced Save Options

It's easy to lose track of time when you're working on a major report or running a complex financial analysis, which is why Office 97 offers multiple save options to help protect your work even if you forget. You'll want to set these options from the very beginning, so we'll cover them before moving on to simple save procedures.

 **TIP**  Always save your work after each major change you make to a document even if AutoRecover or AutoSave are enabled. The default AutoRecover and AutoSave times are ten minutes between saves, and though that may not seem like a long time, it's enough to have applied new fonts, gone through a complete grammar and spell check, and polished some key sentences.

## Using AutoRecover in Word and PowerPoint

To enable AutoRecover in Word or PowerPoint, do the following:

1. On the menu bar, choose Tools, Options to bring up the Options dialog box. (In Word you can also set this by choosing File, Save As, and then clicking the Options button.)

2. Select the Save tab.

3. Select the Save AutoRecover Info check box.

4. In the <u>M</u>inutes box, either click on the box and then enter the desired number of minutes or use the arrow buttons to scroll up and down in one-minute increments.

5. Press OK to complete the change.

You can also follow these steps to adjust the time that lapses between saves by tweaking the <u>M</u>inutes box as shown in step 4.

## Setting AutoSave in Excel

Enabling AutoSave in Excel is a little more complicated:

1. Choose <u>T</u>ools to open the menu and verify AutoSave's installation.

2. If you do not see the term AutoSave in the <u>T</u>ools pull-down menu, insert your Office 97 disk and click <u>A</u>dd-Ins to open the Add-Ins dialog box as shown in Figure 4.3.

**FIG. 4.3**

The Add-Ins dialog box in Excel allows you to install a number of useful tools.

3. Select the check box next to AutoSave and then click OK to complete the request.

4. To confirm that the AutoSave Add-In has been installed successfully, choose <u>T</u>ools. You should now see AutoSa<u>v</u>e listed in the pull-down menu.

5. Excel AutoSave defaults are every 10 minutes for the open workbook only, but by choosing <u>T</u>ools, AutoSa<u>v</u>e, you can change this number. You can also specify to save all open workbooks as an option by selecting the radio button next to Save <u>A</u>ll Open Workbooks. You can also request that Excel prompt you before saving your work.

## AutoSave in Access

Because Access saves data each time you move from one record to another, there is no AutoRecover/AutoSave counterpart. You may want to save your forms as they're under development, however.

## AutoSave in Publisher

Although Publisher has an option referred to as AutoSave, it merely reminds you to save your publication; it doesn't save it like many other applications do. You do, however, need to decide whether or not to save the document at that point (see Figure 4.4), which can be just as effective and in many cases more controlled than a true AutoSave.

**FIG. 4.4**
When enabled,
Publisher's AutoSave
option reminds you to
save your publication at
intervals you select.

To set Publisher's AutoSave timer:

1. Choose Tools, Options to open the Options dialog box.
2. Select the Editing and User Assistance tab.
3. In the User Assistance box, place a check mark next to Remind to Save Publications, and then enter the number of minutes you want to pass before Publisher prompts you to save your work.

## Automatically Generating Backup Files

Another safety feature included in Word and Excel is the automatic creation of a backup file. It gives you another document to fall back on in case something should happen to the original.

To create these backup files:

1. Choose File, Save As and click the Options command button.
2. Select the Always Create Backup check box. (In Word, you can also locate this box by choosing Tools, Options, and then selecting the Save tab.)
3. Click OK to complete the request.
 4. To access these backup files, choose File, Open to bring up the Open dialog box (or click the Open Office Document on the Office shortcut bar).
5. Change the Files of Type box to read All Files (*.*).
6. Browse for files with the backup prefix followed by the original document name.

# Searching for a Location to Save Your Files

In order to find the best location for your files, you may want to browse your system's hard disk and any network storage resources you may have available to you. Start by calling up a Save As dialog box in any Office 97 application (choose File, Save As) similar to the one in Figure 4.5.

 **TIP** If you are creating files to be shared or accessed by other members of your workgroup, make certain the document is filed in an easy-to-find common folder on your network, not on your personal hard disk. That is unless, of course, you are sharing your hard disk with other users via Windows file sharing.

Up One Level button       Look in Favorites button       Create New Folder button

**FIG. 4.5**

The Save As dialog box is just one way to browse your Office 97 files.

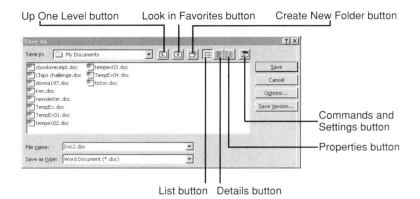

Commands and Settings button

Properties button

List button   Details button

The Save As dialog box is the logical place to conduct your search. From here, you can get a bird's-eye view of every file on your system or on the network to which your machine is connected. Use the following elements to make your way through folders and directories:

- *Save In box.* This box displays the current file folder. By default, Office 97 saves documents in the My Documents folder on Windows 95 systems. To specify a different directory, click the arrow next to the Save In box to open the drop-down list. You will see an outline of your system with corresponding icons, as shown in Figure 4.6. Click each device to see folder/directory options available, or create a new folder on your hard disk by pressing the Create New Folder button. You can also move up the system hierarchy one level at a time by clicking the Up One Level button.

**FIG. 4.6**

The Save In drop-down list box allows you to jump quickly to the section of your system or network in which you want to save the current document.

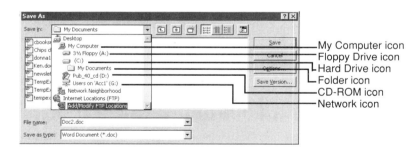

My Computer icon
Floppy Drive icon
Hard Drive icon
Folder icon
CD-ROM icon
Network icon

- *Up One Level button.* Click this button to make your way up the system hierarchy one level at a time.

- *Look in Favorites button.* If you've placed your frequently accessed documents in the Favorites folder, click this button to get there instantly.

- *Create New Folder button.* One way to keep related files together is to create a new folder in which to keep them. (Binders, another option, is covered in Chapter 23, "Sharing Data Between Documents and Applications.") Click this button to call up the New Folder dialog box, which will prompt you for the name of your new folder.

# Viewing File Information When Saving

There are multiple ways you can view your files before choosing a location for the current document. Use the following buttons in the Save As dialog box to achieve the described views:

 ■ *List button.* The default view for the file display window, the List button shows just the names of subfolders and files held in the specified folder.

 ■ *Details button.* This view shows a folder's contents displayed in four columns. These columns include document name, size, type of file, and date or time modified.

 ■ *Properties button.* Select a file in the file display window and then click the Properties button to see all of the file's vital statistics like title, author, template used, revision number, print history, date of creation, and so on.

# Setting Default Save Options

The following buttons in the Save As dialog box allow you to set save options ranging from defining an FTP site to saving a new version of a document.

 ■ *Commands and Settings button.* Click this button to access a menu for editing file properties, sorting files, mapping a network drive, or adding or modifying an FTP site.

■ *Options button.* This button allows you to set save options from within the Save dialog box.

■ *Save Version button (Word only).* This option allows you to track versions of a Word document by date, time, and who saved it. You can also insert comments designed to help you differentiate one version from another or to note major changes in the document.

# Saving Files in a Different File Format

If you're working with colleagues using other versions of Microsoft applications, or even people using other applications altogether, you'll want to use the Save as Type box in the Save As dialog box to save your document to a different file format. This box provides a drop-down list box giving you the opportunity to save a document in a variety of formats. Table 4.1 lists default file extensions used by Office 97 applications.

**Table 4.1   Default File Extensions in Office 97**

| Application | File Extension | Application | File Extension |
|---|---|---|---|
| Word | .doc | Outlook Address Book | .olk |
| Excel | .xls | Publisher | .pub |
| PowerPoint | .ppt | Binders | .obd |
| Access | .mdb | | |

In addition to seeing options for various versions of the current application, you may see special extensions for WordPerfect when using Word, Lotus when using Excel, and so on.

# Naming a Document

Back in the days of DOS, file names could be only a maximum of eight characters in length followed by a three-character extension. With Windows 95 and Office 97, the possibilities are nearly endless:

- File names can now be as long as 255 characters.
- Spaces may now be included in a file name.
- Any characters except /, \, [, ], ;, :, <, >, " may be used.

With all these options, it's now possible to give your documents meaningful names that will help you find what you need in less time.

**N O T E** Although Windows 95 shortens long file names when converting to older file formats, older versions of Windows or DOS cannot use files with long names. If you exchange files with someone running an older operating system, you need to stick to the 8.3 file-naming convention.

# Closing a Document

After you finish working in an application, you may want to close it to free up system resources for other applications. You can do this in any of the following ways:

- Click the X at the far right end of the application's Title bar.
- Double-click the upper-left corner of the application's window.
- Choose File, Exit on the menu bar.
- Press Alt+F4.

If any documents open in the application have not been saved, the Save As dialog box will appear, asking you to name the file.

To close only the document while leaving the application open, choose File, Close. ●

# CHAPTER 5

# Finding and Managing Files

**A**fter you've created and saved a document, it's important to know how to find and manipulate that file at a later time. Not only will good file-management skills save you much frustration, they will also help you organize your work more effectively and make you more productive. Each Office 97 application makes it easy to quickly find and work with all your documents. ■

**Finding anything anywhere**

Learn how to use Office 97's powerful search features to find any file, no matter where it's located on your hard disk or network.

**Moving and Copying Files**

Discover the most effective, time-efficient ways to organize your files more logically and productively.

**Customizing file properties**

Use the new and extended file property fields to make important documents even simpler to find.

**N O T E**   The items in this chapter refer only to the core Office 97 applications (Word, Excel, and
         PowerPoint) unless otherwise specified. Because Access, Publisher, AutoMap Streets Plus,
and Small Business Financial Planner 97 all behave differently, you will learn more about them in later
chapters. ▨

# Finding Files

   From the Windows desktop, you can begin your file search by clicking the Open Office Document button on the Office Shortcut bar (see Figure 5.1). If you want to find a file from within an
application, click File, Open to call up the Open Office Document dialog box. From this box,
you have numerous ways to find files.

**FIG. 5.1**

The Open Office
Document dialog box
gives you countless
ways to search your
files.

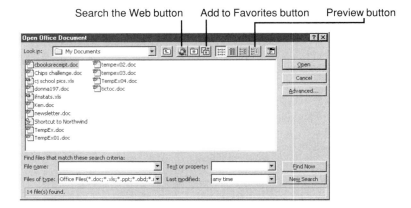

## Sorting the File List

   Click the Details button on the Open dialog box toolbar, and then click the column headers to
perform basic sorts on your chosen file list. Click the column header once to sort in ascending
order, then click again to sort in descending order. For example, to sort the files by size, click
the Size column header once to view the smallest to the largest; click a second time to reverse
the view to the largest to the smallest.

## Finding a File by Date

If you need to locate a document you recently worked on but can't remember its name, try
searching by date to narrow the possibilities.

1.  Call up an Open dialog box as described earlier.

2.  Select the directory/folder you want to search in the Look In box.

3.  Click the arrow next to the Last Modified box to open the Last Modified drop-down
    list box.

4. Select the time period you want to see displayed. Your choices in this menu include Today, Yesterday, Last Week, This Week, Last Month, This Month, or Any Time.

5. If you're still not sure which file you really need, select one, and then click the Preview button to see its contents.

6. After the desired file has been found, confirm that it's selected and then click Open to open it.

## Finding a File by Contents

To search for a string of text in a file, start at the Open dialog box. In the Text or Property box, enter the text you want to search for, and then press Find Now to perform the search. All files containing the specified text will be displayed in the window. This is a great way to search files for a person's name or other pertinent information.

## Narrowing Your Search Using Wild Cards

If you think you know at least part of the desired file's name, use wild cards to narrow your search. There are two characters that can help you limit the list based on characters in the file name: the * (asterisk) and the ? (question mark). Some examples follow in Table 5.1.

**Table 5.1   Sample Wild Card Searches**

| Use This | To Get This |
| --- | --- |
| C* | All files that begin with C |
| Vol?? | Vol10, Vol11, Vol12 |
| *cat* | Cat Care Tips, Catalog Text, Cathy's Recipes |

To use these wild card searches in the Open dialog box, enter text similar to the examples shown in Table 5.1 in the File Name box and then click Find Now to see the results.

## Expanding the Search

To broaden your search, try the following:

1. In the Open dialog box, click the arrow next to the Look In box to browse the system hierarchy.

2. Select the highest level you want to search (for example, the C drive).

3. Click the Commands and Settings button to open the pull-down menu. Select Search Subfolders.

4. Proceed with your search.

Part

I

Ch

5

# Advanced Search Options

Still can't find what you're looking for? Using the Advanced Find dialog box, you can perform And or Or searches, specify case sensitivity, and search multiple file properties.

To search for specific or nontext file properties, follow these steps:

1. Choose File, Open, and then click the Advanced button in the Open dialog box. The Advanced Find dialog box appears (see Figure 5.2).

**FIG. 5.2**

In the Define More Criteria portion of the Advanced Find dialog box, you can use drop-down arrows to select a variety of search elements.

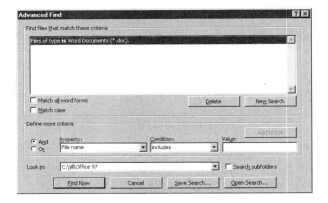

2. To clear the existing search criteria and use default search values, click New Search.
3. Under the Define More Criteria section, specify search criteria by selecting the options you want in the Property, Condition, and Value boxes.
4. Click Add to List.
5. To create additional search criteria, click And or Or, and then repeat steps 3 and 4.
6. To save your search, click Save Search. (You can recall it later by clicking Open Search.)
7. To perform the search you just described, click Find Now.
8. To cancel your work at any point, click the Cancel button.

# Selecting Files

Before you can perform an operation on a file or multiple files, you'll need to select the files you want to include in the transaction. You may select files from within a standard file dialog box in one of three ways:

- Click one file's name.
- Press Ctrl while clicking files you want to select. (You need not select them in any particular order.)
- To select adjacent files as a group, click the first file, hold the Shift key, and then click the last file in the group to select all files in between.

# Managing Files from the Open and Save As Dialog Boxes

While in the Open or Save As dialog box, you have a number of hidden commands you can perform. To execute them, select files as directed in the section "Selecting Files," and then right-click the highlighted area to see these options. Table 5.2 lists these options and the resulting action.

**Table 5.2    List of Hidden Commands**

| Select This | To Do This |
| --- | --- |
| Open | Open the selected files. |
| Open Read Only | Open the selected files as read-only. You must rename them to save any changes. |
| Open as Copy | Create a copy of all selected files, which you can edit and save as new files. |
| Print | Print one complete copy of each file (except files created in Access). |
| Show | Present PowerPoint files as a slide show. |
| Save | Save all selected files (this command replaces those above in the Save As dialog box. |
| Send To | Move or save copies of a file as indicated in Table 5.3. |
| Cut | Move selected files to the Clipboard and replace existing Clipboard files. |
| Copy | Copy selected files to the Clipboard in addition to items already in the Clipboard. |
| Create Shortcut | Create another icon in the directory to act as a shortcut to the specified files. |
| Delete | Remove the files from their current location and place them in the Recycle Bin. |
| Rename | Give the file a new name. |
| Properties | Program a keyboard shortcut to the file, or view the file properties, as described later in this chapter. |

Part

I

Ch

5

As noted in Table 5.2, the Send To command has a number of options within it. These are listed in Table 5.3.

**Table 5.3   The Send To Hidden Commands**

| Select This | To Do This |
|---|---|
| A floppy or removable drive | Create copies of the selected file(s) on the chosen device. |
| Any Folder | Move or copy the selected files to another location. |
| Clipboard as Contents | Replace any Clipboard content with the selected files. |
| Clipboard as Name | Add selected files to existing Clipboard content. |
| Fax Recipient | Fax the selected files to a specified recipient. |
| Mail Recipient | Send the selected documents to a person via e-mail. |
| My Briefcase | Place the selected files in a briefcase for easy transport and synchronization. |

**N O T E**  Because Send To is really a Windows feature, the options you see in this menu will vary, depending on your system configuration and the software installed on your machine.

# Moving and Copying Files to a New Location

As the number of files on your system continues to grow, you may need to reorganize the contents of your system by adding new folders. This reorganization may require you to relocate some of your files. To do so, follow these steps:

1. Bring up an Open or Save As dialog box.
2. Select the files you want to copy or move.
3. Right-click the highlighted area to bring up the hidden menu.
4. Choose Se_n_d To, Any Folder to bring up the Other Folder dialog box, pictured in Figure 5.3.

**FIG. 5.3**

The Other Folder dialog box helps you organize the file moving and copying procedure.

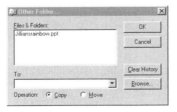

5. Confirm that all the files you want to include are listed in the Files & Folders window.
6. Click Browse to locate the targeted folder, or insert its name into the To box.

7. Select the option button next to the operation you want to perform. You can select from Copy or Move.

8. Click OK to complete the request.

# Placing a Document in Your Favorites Folder

If you work on a specific file regularly, you may want to place it in a Favorites folder for instant access. To do this:

1. Call up an Open or Save As dialog box from within any application.

2. Locate the file you want to move to the Favorites folder and select it.

3. Click the Save in Favorites button.

4. Click OK to save the transaction.

**TIP** Try to be judicious about which files you place in the Favorites folder. Placing too many documents in it will defeat the purpose of quick, easy access to the files.

To open the documents in your Favorites folder, you have a couple of options:

- If you've customized your Shortcut bar to include a Favorites button, press it to see the contents of your Favorites folder.

- Bring up an Open dialog box from within any application, click the Look in Favorites button, select the desired file, and then click Open.

 You may view the contents of your Favorites folder by using either of the preceding options, or by accessing the Favorites folder from within a Save As dialog box. Just click the Look in Favorites button to take a peek.

# Working with File Properties

Use the file property options to track information about a document. File properties can be invaluable for conducting advanced searches to find exactly what you're looking for.

## Viewing and Editing File Properties

To view and edit file properties, follow these steps:

1. With the file open in Word, Excel, or PowerPoint, choose File, Properties (in Access, choose File, Database Properties) to bring up the Properties dialog box shown in Figure 5.4.

2. Select the properties tab that you want to edit.

3. Enter the desired information.

4. Click OK to complete the changes.

Part

I

Ch

5

**FIG. 5.4**

The Properties dialog box organizes document information in five tabs: General, Summary, Statistics, Contents, and Custom.

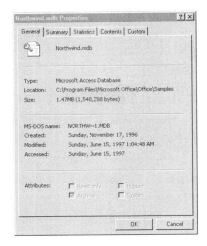

# What Can You Track in a File Property Tab?

Here is some of the information that can be tracked in each File Property tab:

- *General tab.* This tab, which is completed by the application, includes such information as the file name, file type, location, size, MS-DOS name (six characters plus a three character file extension), document creation date, date last saved, and more.

- *Summary tab.* You can fill in the information on this page to help you search for the file down the road. Fields include author, manager, company, category, keywords, and comments, along with a few others.

- *Statistics tab.* The contents of this tab vary according to the document's native application, but some of the fields may include the date and time the file was created, modified, and accessed; print history; who saved the document last; how many times it's been revised; time spent editing the file; along with a host of application-specific statistics (for example, in PowerPoint, statistics include total number of slides and the number of multimedia clips, among others).

- *Contents tab.* This tab also contains application-specific information; for example, an Access database shows a list of all object types and names on this page.

- *Custom tab.* In this customizable tab, you can track any information about a file you want.

# CHAPTER 6

# Templates and Wizards: An Overview

**T**emplates and wizards can go a long way toward helping you create professional looking documents whether you're a manager for a major corporation, a high school student wanting to submit high quality college application materials, or a grassroots nonprofit organization seeking funding.

*Templates* are documents or worksheets that contain the text, graphics, macros, customized toolbars, and formulas you can use to create standardized documents. For instance, a business may create a letterhead in Word that contains a font style and size that they want to use in other documents. This document is saved with a special file extension (.dot in Word) so that it can be applied to other correspondence to create a consistent, professional image.

*Wizards* are interactive help utilities that guide you step-by-step through a multi-step operation offering explanations and tips along the way. Wizards will also ask you questions to help customize the document. ■

### Accessing templates

Click the New Office Document button on the Office Shortcut bar to browse through countless template options.

### Applying a template to an existing document

Learn how to apply templates to existing files to ensure a consistent, professional look.

### Using wizards

Browse the New Office Document dialog box for the .wiz file extension to choose from a number of preinstalled wizards.

### Finding more templates and wizards

Link to Microsoft on the Web to download a constantly growing number of new templates and wizards.

# Viewing the Available Templates

To see a list of templates available from within an application, choose File, New and look through your choices. When you select a template in this list, a preview of what the document will look like is shown in the Preview box (if a preview is available for that template). You can start a new document based on a selected template by clicking OK. Watch for the special template file extensions, as noted in Table 6.1. Knowing these extensions will help you distinguish between a template and a wizard's step-by-step document creation.

▶ **See** "Creating a New Document," **p. 46**

**Table 6.1   Template File Extensions**

| Application | Template File Extension |
|---|---|
| Word | .dot |
| Excel | .xlt |
| PowerPoint | .pot |
| Outlook | .oft |

You can also call up most Office 97 (and Office 95 if you installed this version over the previous version) templates by clicking the New Office Document button on the Office Shortcut bar, or by clicking Start on the Windows Taskbar and selecting New Office Document. The New Office Document dialog box presents all available Office templates and wizards, as shown in Figure 6.1. The templates and wizards are organized into different tabs in the dialog box according to the kinds of documents that you create with them. Outlook also houses a few templates that do not show up in the New Office Document dialog box. These can be found from within Outlook by choosing File, New, Choose Template.

**FIG. 6.1**
By selecting a tab on the New Office Document dialog box, you'll notice the special file extensions that identify templates and wizards. This figure shows the Letters and Faxes tab.

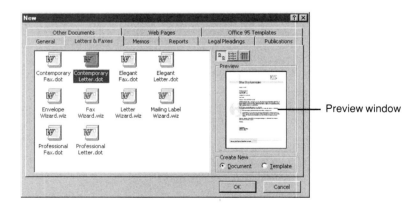

Preview window

# Add Style to Your Documents from the Start Using Templates

If you know the basic editing techniques used by the application that created the template, you're in luck. (If you don't know them, you will by the end of this book.) Take Word's Professional Resume template as an example. Creating a nice-looking resume is as easy as entering and deleting text. No need to worry about formatting or font selection—it's all done for you.

Templates can save you a lot of time, enabling you to focus on content instead of formatting issues.

After you've chosen the desired template, move your mouse pointer to the area where you want to begin working first. Click on the area to set the insertion point in place, and then manipulate the text as you would any other text in the application.

Because the text of a template is already formatted, you can use the template's formatting as a cue for determining appropriate content. For example, larger fonts indicate titles or section headings, which are worded differently than body text.

There is a downside to templates, however. If the chosen font doesn't work for you, it can take time to go through the entire document and alter the formatting and text attributes. Instead, you may opt to modify an existing template and then save it under your own name, or you may decide to create your own template from scratch. We show you both methods later in the chapter.

## Switching Templates On-the-Fly

Suppose that you spent hours inserting text into a template only to find at the end you're not as happy with it as you could have been? You may want to consider switching templates to see whether the results are any better.

**N O T E** Switching templates works best in Word because you can select from a number of similar templates. But if your company has designed its own set of templates or if you've downloaded additional templates from the Internet, you may have choices in other applications as well. ■

Although technically you can apply any template to a document (for example using the Elegant Letter.dot template on your resume), doing so can have unpredictable results in formatting. To save time (not to mention your sanity), select only templates designed for documents similar to the one you are working with. To apply a template to a document using a similar template, do the following:

1. Open the document in which you want to change the template (see Figure 6.2).
2. Choose Tools, Templates and Add-Ins to bring up the Templates and Add-Ins dialog box (see Figure 6.3.).

**FIG. 6.2**
You can use Word's Professional Resume.dot template to get a jump-start on creating a resume.

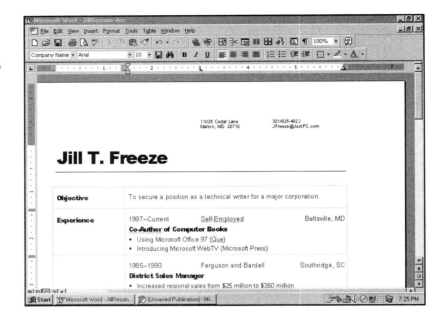

**FIG. 6.3**
The Templates and Add-Ins dialog box allows you to dramatically alter the appearance of a document in a few short steps.

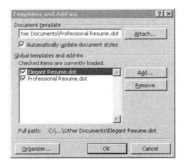

3. If the template you want to use does not appear on the list, click the Add button to open the Add Template dialog box.

   If the template does appear on the list, place a check mark next to it and deselect any other templates checked. Skip ahead to step 7 to attach the template.

4. Browse through the folders to find the desired template, and then select it.

5. Click OK to return to the Templates and Add-Ins dialog box.

6. Confirm that the file you selected is currently loaded. (It will appear in the Global Templates and Add-Ins box.)

7. Click Attach to open the Attach Template dialog box.

8. Select the desired template again, and then press Open to return to the Templates and Add-Ins dialog box.

9. The path to the template you just selected should appear in the Document Template box.

10. Select the Automatically Update Document Styles box to change the styles displayed by the current template.

11. Click OK to attach the new template to the active document (see Figure 6.4).

**FIG. 6.4**
The contents of the resume are still the same as in Figure 6.1, but the formatting has changed to the styles of the new template.

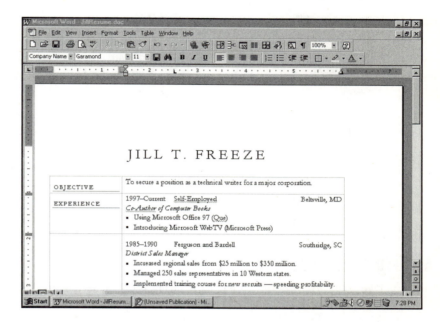

## Achieve the Results You Want by Modifying a Template

If you like the formatting of an existing template but aren't crazy about the fonts used in it, you can modify it and save it under a different name for use with other documents. Here's how:

1. Choose File, Open, and then open the template you want to modify. If there aren't any templates listed in the Open dialog box, click Document Templates (*.dot) in Word or the respective template extension of the active program in the Files of type box.

2. Change as much or as little of the template as you want—its text and graphics, styles, formatting, macros, AutoText entries, toolbars, menu settings, and shortcut keys can be customized to meet your needs.

3. Click Save and rename the template to preserve the original. Be sure the appropriate template extension is specified. It should match that of the template you modified.

Part
I
Ch
6

# Creating Your Own Template

Maybe you spent a lot of time formatting a report in the past and you liked the results. You can turn your hard work into a template you can use again and again. To create a new template based on an existing document, do the following:

1. Choose File, Open, and then open the document you want.

2. Choose File, Save As.

3. In the Save As Type box, select the appropriate template extension for the document.

4. The application suggests a Templates folder in the Save in box. To save the template in another folder, switch to the corresponding subfolder within the Templates folder.

5. In the File Name box, type a name for the new template, and then click Save.

6. In this new template, add the text and graphics you want to appear in all new documents based on the template, and delete any items you don't want to appear.

7. Make the desired changes to the margin settings, page size and orientation, styles, and other formats.

8. Choose File, Save, press Ctrl+S, or click the Save button.

9. Choose File, Close.

# Using Wizards

Like templates, wizards result in high quality, professional-looking output. The main difference between wizards and templates is that wizards help you create a customized document, whereas templates create standardized documents. For example, in Publisher you can use the PageWizard to create a newsletter. The wizard asks you questions about the number of columns you want your publication to have, how many articles you want to appear on the front page, and so on. (Word, PowerPoint, and Access also have wizards you can call on for help.) A template, on the other hand, simply produces a four-column boilerplate into which you insert text.

In the following example, Publisher's PageWizard is used to create a newsletter. This example will give you a better feel for the kinds of questions a wizard asks.

1. Start Publisher.

2. From the PageWizard tab, select Newsletter, and then click OK.

3. The Newsletter PageWizard Design Assistant (see Figure 6.5) asks you a number of questions beginning with "What style do you want?" Click the More arrow at the right side of the PageWizard box to see previews of the styles available. Click a style, and then click Next.

4. You are asked how many columns you want your newsletter to have and how many stories you would like on the first page. The preview box reflects your selections.

5. Type the title of your newsletter. Although you can change it later, Publisher will use this information to produce the title page of your newsletter.

**FIG. 6.5**
Use the More arrow at the right of the screen to view all the options available.

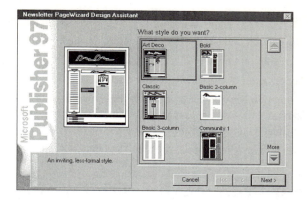

6. Choose other options you want to include. You can choose a table of contents, the date, and volume and issue numbers.

7. How many pages do you want? Again, you can always add or delete pages later, but this just gives you a set number of pages to begin working with without having to create more right away.

   Other options you are asked about include "Do you want room for a mailing label on the back?" and "Will you be printing on both sides of the paper?" which affects how the headers on each page are laid out.

8. After all the questions have been answered, you're asked to choose Create It! to have Publisher build your newsletter based on the selected options. Within seconds, you'll see the publication you designed, ready for you to fill in with text and graphics.

▶ **See** "Designing Professional-Looking Documents Using PageWizard," **p. 206**

Although the thought of customized wizard documents may seem appealing, there is a downside to using them. Unlike templates, which you can switch, you can't easily alter the results of a wizard. Making adjustments requires a lot of hard work either by manually adjusting style and formatting elements as you normally do within the application, or by running through the wizard's steps again and using cut and paste to achieve the desired results.

**N O T E** Even though Publisher wizards don't show up on the New Office Document dialog box, this application is a tremendous source for Web page, brochure, and business form wizards. Additionally, Publisher is a bit more flexible than Word when it comes to producing a newsletter. ▪

To locate these wizards, click the New Office Document button on the Office Shortcut bar, or click Start on the Windows Taskbar and choose New Office Document. Look for Word files with the .wiz extension, with the word *wizard* in their name, or Access files with .mdz extensions. A number of wizards reside in the New Office Document tabs, but you'll definitely need to do some scrolling and browsing to find them.

Other places to check for wizards include:

- Launch PowerPoint and select the AutoContent Wizard.
- Launch Publisher and browse PageWizard.
- Launch Access and choose the Database Wizard.
- Advanced function wizards are available within an application such as Excel's ChartWizard and the Labels, Forms, and Control wizards within Access, among others. We look at these in detail later on.
- Look for wizards on Microsoft on the Web (see details in the next section).

# Enhancing Your Productivity with Freebies from the Web

If you have a connection to the Internet, you can get many neat templates, wizards, and tools free from Microsoft on the Web.

**N O T E**    If you purchased Office 97 on CD, you may very well have many of these freebies already available to you on the accompanying ValuPack. If you haven't worked with ValuPack before, you may need to insert your Office 97 disk, and then use Windows Explorer on your CD-ROM drive to access ValuPack's Overview section. The resulting PowerPoint presentation will give you a closer look at everything available in your ValuPack.

The selection of goodies is constantly growing, but here's a sampling of some things you might find:

- An Avery Wizard Value Pack for Word that helps you print your labels and other Avery products right the first time.
- Word Web Page Wizard Accessories featuring new visual styles and layouts to make your Web pages look even better.
- Web Query Tools for Excel that increase and simplify your ability to capture and analyze Web data.
- An Excel Loan Manager template to help you calculate loan payments and equity in your home.
- Outlook e-mail fixes and enhancements.
- Crystal Reports Designer gives you a way to analyze your Outlook data.
- Download a host of animated cursors, Windows sounds, and new Office Assistants.
- More PowerPoint AutoContent templates to give you even more presentation design options.

So how do you find all of these treasures?

1. From within any Office 97 application, choose Help, About Microsoft (application).

2. On the About screen, you'll find a long Product ID number. Write it down before proceeding to the next step.

3. Click on the X in the upper-right corner of the About Screen to close it.

4. Make sure you have an active connection to the Internet.

5. Choose Help, Microsoft on the Web to open the submenu illustrated in Figure 6.6.

**FIG. 6.6**
The Microsoft on the
Web submenu points
you to a variety of
online resources,
including product news
and online support.

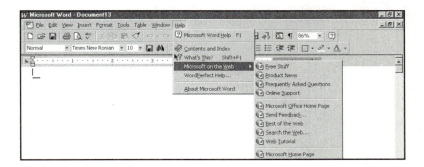

6. Choose Free Stuff to get to all the free tools, templates, and wizards.

**N O T E** Because this feature works by launching your default Web browser, you may have trouble if there is no Web browser installed on your system. Many Office 97 owners received Internet Explorer with their Office 97 software, so it can be installed with minimal hassle. You can reach Microsoft on the Web with most any popular Web browser. ▪

7. After you've selected an item to download, you'll be invited to register for the free service, which gives you full access to all the software as it becomes available. This is where you'll need your product ID number, and you can even decline any further mail— snail mail or e-mail—from Microsoft or any of its partners.

**N O T E** Need more information on using the Internet? Check out Que's *Special Edition Using Microsoft Internet Explorer* or *The Complete Idiot's Guide to Microsoft Internet Explorer.* ▪

**N O T E** The Web address for the main Microsoft Office Free Stuff page is **http://www. microsoft.com/officeFreeStuff**. You can enter this address in Internet Explorer to open a Web page with links to the Free Stuff pages for each application. Remember that each application has its own page of free stuff, so check them all regularly so you don't miss anything! ▪

Part

I

Ch

6

# Getting the Most from Each Application

# Creating and Editing Text in Word 97

**Working in Word**

Understand the layout of the Word workspace and the default settings of new documents.

**Finding your place in a document**

Use shortcut keys, the new IntelliMouse, and other functions to quickly get to where you want to be.

**Find and replace text**

Learn ways to find and manipulate text to drastically cut your time spent editing documents.

Technically, Word is considered a word processor. Although it does a superior job at that, it's really so much more than a word processor. Word can create Web pages loaded with hyperlinks, and it can even produce newsletters that would push the capabilities of many small desktop publishing programs.

Word 97 brings with it many enhancements and improvements over its previous version. And with such busy work schedules, few people have time to play with these new features, let alone master them. In this chapter and the next, you learn all kinds of ways to share your workload with Word. ■

# Anatomy of the Word 97 Workspace

Knowing Word 97's screen elements will go a long way toward helping you unleash its power. Figure 7.1 points out all of the critical elements.

Title bar    Menu bar    Standard toolbar    Formatting toolbar    Ruler     Office Assistant

**FIG. 7.1**

Knowing the critical Word 97 screen elements will help you move through the document efficiently.

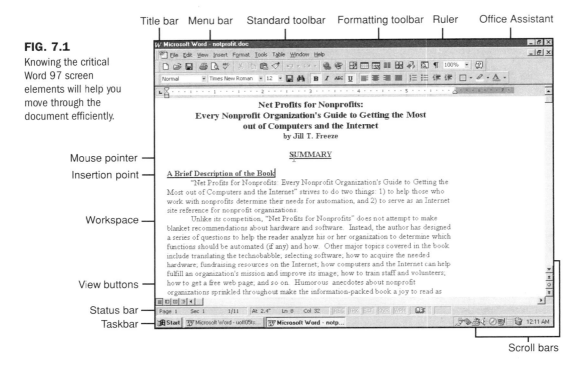

Mouse pointer

Insertion point

Workspace

View buttons

Status bar

Taskbar

Scroll bars

These elements are described briefly in the following list, but many of these functions will be explored in greater detail in the pages to follow.

- *Title bar*. Contains the name of the program and the name of the document, as well as the Maximize, Minimize, Restore, and Close buttons.

- *Menu bar*. Allows you to select from a variety of pull-down menus needed to execute commands in Word 97.

- *Standard toolbar*. Holds shortcut buttons to quickly execute common tasks such as printing, opening a new document, and so forth. This toolbar may be modified to meet your specific needs.

   ▶ **See** "Tweaking the Toolbar," **p. 24**

- *Formatting toolbar*. Presents buttons to quickly format text as you work. Selections include font style, font size, text alignment, and text traits (for example, bold, italic, underline).

- *Ruler*. Provides a quick and easy way to guide the setting of tabs and indents in your documents.

- *Insertion point*. Shows you where the text or graphics will be placed. In other programs, it is referred to as a cursor.

- *End of Document marker*. Indicates the end of a document with a short, horizontal line. You cannot move past this point.

- *Mouse pointer*. Moves on-screen as you move the mouse to assist you in accessing menus and clicking buttons.

- *Office Assistant*. Serves as your online helper. Ask it questions or turn it off as you become more familiar with Word 97.

- *View buttons*. Enable you to adjust your view of a document. Choose from Normal View, Outline View, Page Layout View, and Outline Layout View.

- *Status bar*. Displays information about your document including page count, line number, and so forth.

- *Taskbar*. Allows you to toggle back and forth between applications already open or to launch new applications via the Start button.

- *Workspace*. Consists of a blank page on which you insert text and graphics.

- *Scroll bars*. Move you quickly around a document. Either slide them with your mouse (point to the scroll box, hold down the left button of your mouse, and drag), or click either side of the box for larger jumps.

# Word 97 Document Defaults

When you create a new document without choosing a special template or wizard, Word 97 applies a predefined template to that document referred to as normal.dot. Unless you tell it otherwise, Word will assign the attributes listed in Table 7.1 to the document.

**Table 7.1   Word 97 Document Defaults**

| Setting | Value |
| --- | --- |
| Left/Right Margins | 1.25 inches |
| Top/Bottom Margins | 1 inch |
| Tab Stops | Every 0.5 inch |
| Page Orientation | Portrait |

**N O T E**  If your new blank documents are being created with settings other than these, chances are your normal.dot template was modified at some point. You can use the preceding settings to restore it to its original condition if necessary.

Part

II

Ch

7

# Viewing Your Documents with Word

Word 97 offers a variety of document views that facilitate document editing and formatting, and in some cases even enhance navigation within your document. These views are easily changed by pressing the view icons pictured in the list that follows. To return to Word's Normal view at any time, simply press the Normal view button.

These views include the following:

- *Normal view.* Word 97's default document view, the Normal view, is the standard view used for document editing and formatting. While it shows document layout pretty much as it will appear on the printed page, the workspace remains uncluttered for quick and easy editing.

- *Online Layout view.* This view optimizes text for easier viewing online. For example, text appears larger and it wraps to fit the viewing window rather than the way it would actually print. While in this view, Word also displays the document map, a separate pane on the left side of the screen that allows you to navigate through your document with the click of a mouse.

- *Page Layout view.* In this view, you can see how objects will be arranged on the page. This view is especially good for editing headers and footers, for working with margins and columns, and for drawing objects and frames.

- *Outline view.* The Outline view makes it easy to move or copy entire sections of text because it gives you customizable views of your document. You can see the relative importance of each section title, but only if you apply style codes or build the outline from scratch.

  ▶ **See** "Building an Outline," **p. 109**

- *Document Map view.* A vertical pane on the left side of the screen that shows all the headings of your document. You can customize which headings are viewed; you can see where you are in a large document at any given time; and you can move to the desired section in the document by simply clicking its title in the document map.

  ▶ **See** "Viewing the Outline While You Write," **p. 111**

# Jumping to a Specific Page

You can jump to a specific page one of two ways: by dragging the vertical scroll box until the desired page number appears in the yellow ScreenTip box; or by double-clicking the page number in the status bar. This brings up the Go To tab of the Find and Replace dialog box (see Figure 7.2), from which you can jump to a specific page simply by entering its page number. You can jump to specific headers, objects, and so on in a similar fashion.

**FIG. 7.2**
The Find and Replace dialog box allows you to find anything anyplace in your document.

# Shortcut Keys to Find Your Way Around a Document

Word 97 gives you a number of shortcut keys to move swiftly from one location to another. See Table 7.2 for a list of these.

**Table 7.2   Word Navigation Shortcut Keys**

| To Move Here | Press |
| --- | --- |
| One character to the right | Shift+Right Arrow |
| One character to the left | Shift+Left Arrow |
| To the end of a word | Ctrl+Shift+Right Arrow |
| To the beginning of a word | Ctrl+Shift+Left Arrow |
| To the end of a line | Shift+End |
| To the beginning of a line | Shift+Home |
| One line down | Shift+Down Arrow |
| One line up | Shift+Up Arrow |
| To the end of a paragraph | Ctrl+Shift+Down Arrow |
| To the beginning of a paragraph | Ctrl+Shift+Up Arrow |
| One screen down | Shift+Page Down |
| One screen up | Shift+Page Up |
| To the end of a window | Alt+Ctrl+Page Down |
| To the beginning of a document | Ctrl+Shift+Home |
| To include the entire document | Ctrl+A |

Part
II

Ch
7

# Using IntelliMouse for More Accurate Scrolling in Word

If you have the Microsoft IntelliMouse installed, you can use it to move more accurately through Word documents.

▶ **See** "Installing the IntelliMouse," **p. 44**

Here are just a few of the operations made simpler with the IntelliMouse:

- *Scroll Up/Down*. Rotate the IntelliMouse wheel forward/backward.
- *Pan Up/Down*. Click and hold the wheel while moving the mouse in the direction of the text you want to view.
- *Autoscrolling Up/Down*. Click the wheel and then move the mouse in the direction you want to scroll. Text will continue to scroll in the desired direction until the wheel is clicked again.
- *Zoom In/Out*. Hold down the Ctrl key, and then rotate the wheel forward to zoom in or rotate backward to zoom out.

# Inserting Text

To insert text into an existing Word document, move the pointer to the desired location, click once to set the insertion point, and then simply begin typing. If the block of text is long and exists elsewhere, you may want to consider using cut and paste rather than retyping all the data.

▶ **See** "Copying Selected Text," **p. 28**
▶ **See** "Inserting AutoText Entries in a Document," **p. 126**

# Inserting Manual Page Breaks

There are times you'll want to print a partial page on its own piece of paper before moving on to the body of the text. The introduction to a major report or term paper is a good example. You'll want to write your introduction, and then start with the document itself on a fresh page.

To do this, insert a manual page break by setting the insertion point at the end of the page's text, and then pressing Ctrl+Enter. You can remove the page break by placing the insertion point in the first position of the following page, and then backspacing over the page break.

# Deleting Text

You may delete text in one of three ways:

- Use the Delete key to delete characters to the right of the insertion point.
- Use the Backspace key to delete characters to the left of the insertion point.

■ Select a block of text (see "Selecting a Block of Text" in the following pages) and then press Delete.

---

 **T I P**  If you're about to delete a large block of text you may want to use later, consider using the Cut function instead of Delete to temporarily copy the information to the Clipboard. This way, the deletion isn't permanent until you copy something else onto the Clipboard.

---

# Undoing Changes

 If there's one set of keystrokes to memorize in Word, it's Ctrl+Z. Knowing how to undo something in a flash can save hours of reformatting, typing, and so on. Undo can also be accessed by clicking the Undo button on the toolbar.

Word has a multiple level Undo feature; you can click the arrow next to the Undo button to see a list of operations you can undo. However, if you undo an item way down on the list, all the items above it will be undone as well. In this case, rekeying or reapplying the formatting may save you more time than using Undo. If you change your mind after undoing a change, you can always redo it by pressing the Redo button.

# Selecting Blocks of Text

By selecting blocks of text, it is possible to manipulate varying amounts of data at one time. This is useful for applying a new font style or size, a new text attribute, or for rearranging a document's contents. Although some text selection techniques were described earlier, the ones that follow are especially useful in Word.

## Selecting Text with the Mouse

Table 7.3 shows multiple ways to select a block of text with a mouse.

### Table 7.3  Selecting Text Blocks with the Mouse

| To Select This | Do This |
| --- | --- |
| Word | Double-click inside the word. |
| Sentence | Ctrl+click inside the sentence. |
| Paragraph | Triple-click inside the paragraph. |
| Graphic/image | Click the graphic/image. |
| Entire document | Move mouse pointer to the left of the text until it turns into an arrow, as pictured in Figure 7.3, and then triple-click. |

*continues*

Part

**II**

Ch

**7**

**Table 7.3  Continued**

| To Select This | Do This |
| --- | --- |
| Vertical text block | Hold down the Alt key and drag the mouse pointer over the text. |
| Large text blocks | Move the mouse pointer to the left of the text until it becomes an arrow; then click the left mouse button and drag the mouse until the desired block of text is highlighted. |

**FIG. 7.3**

Move the mouse pointer to the left margin of the document to turn it into an arrow, and then select text as directed in Table 7.3.

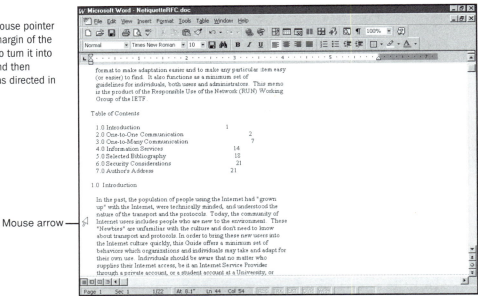

Mouse arrow

## Selecting Text Blocks with the Keyboard

For some reason, there are people who prefer to work with the keyboard instead of the mouse whenever possible. If you're one of those people, you'll be interested in Table 7.4, the listing of shortcut keys for selecting blocks of text.

**Table 7.4  Keyboard Shortcuts for Selecting Text**

| To Select This | Do This |
| --- | --- |
| One character at a time to the left of the insertion point | Press Shift+Left Arrow; repeat until the desired number of characters is highlighted. |

| To Select This | Do This |
|---|---|
| One character at a time to the right of the insertion point | Press Shift+Right Arrow; repeat until the desired number of characters is highlighted. |
| The beginning of the word to the left of the insertion point | Press Shift+Ctrl+Left Arrow; keep pressing the arrow key to select additional words. |
| The beginning of the word to the right of the insertion point | Press Shift+Ctrl+Right Arrow; keep pressing the arrow key to select additional words. |
| The insertion point to the same position in the previous line | Press Shift+Up Arrow. |
| The insertion point to the same position in the next line | Press Shift+Down Arrow. |
| The insertion point to the beginning of the current paragraph | Press Shift+Ctrl+Up Arrow. |
| The insertion point to the beginning of the next paragraph | Press Shift+Ctrl+Down Arrow. |
| The insertion point to the beginning of the document | Press Shift+Ctrl+Home. |
| The insertion point to the end of the document | Press Shift+Ctrl+End. |

# Dragging and Dropping Text

If you only have to move a small chunk of text a short distance, you may want to consider using the drag-and-drop method. This method works best when all of the text and its destination appear on the screen. To use drag and drop:

1. Select the block of text as illustrated in the "Selecting a Block of Text" section earlier in this chapter.

2. Place the mouse pointer in the middle of the highlighted text and hold down the left mouse button.

3. While holding the left mouse button down, drag the text to its new location and release the button (see Figure 7.4).

Part

II

Ch

7

**FIG. 7.4**
As you drag the mouse pointer away from the highlighted text, the insertion point moves with it, showing you where the text would be dropped at any given time.

Mouse pointer

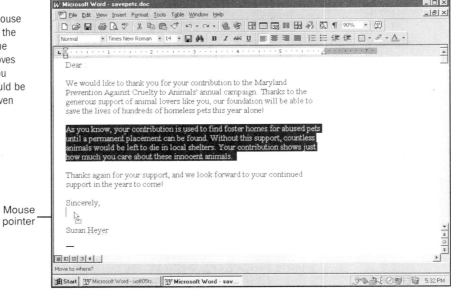

# Finding and Replacing Text in Word

Word 97 makes it easy to replace one word with another. To do so, follow these steps:

1. Choose Edit, Replace; or press Ctrl+H. The Replace tab of the Find and Replace dialog box appears.
2. In the Find What box, enter the text you want to search for.
3. In the Replace With box, enter the replacement text.
4. Click Find Next to move to the next occurrence of the chosen text, Replace to replace that occurrence with the Replacement word, or Replace All without going through and approving each replacement.

# Finding and Replacing Noun or Adjective Forms or Verb Tenses

You can now replace a singular noun with a plural noun, alter adjective forms, and even replace verb tenses. In fact, you can even perform multiple operations at once—for instance, you can change **apple** to **orange** all at one time by following these steps:

1. Choose Edit menu, Replace.
2. If you don't see the Find All Word Forms check box, click More.
3. In the Find What box, enter the text you want to search for.

4. To replace the text, enter the replacement text in the Replace With box.

5. Select the Find All Word Forms check box.

6. Click Find Next, Replace, or All as desired.

**CAUTION**

When replacing text in your document, use Replace All with care because the results may not be what you expect. If you're replacing text, consider selecting Replace instead of Replace All so that you can approve each replacement as it appears.

7. If the replacement text's part of speech could easily be confused, click the word that best matches the meaning you want. For example, because "saw" can be both a noun and a verb, click "saws" to replace nouns, or click "sawing" to replace verbs.

# Finding and Replacing Specific Formatting

Word's advanced Find and Replace feature also lets you find and replace formatting with minimal hassle. You can even replace found text with different text at the same time. Use the following steps to take advantage of this powerful tool:

1. Choose Edit, Replace to open the Replace tab of the Find and Replace dialog box (see Figure 7.5).

**FIG. 7.5**
You have access to several Find and Replace features.

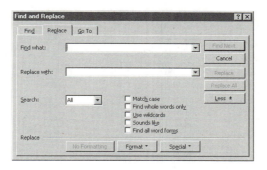

2. To search for text with specific formatting, enter the text in the Find What box. You may also leave the Find What box blank to search for any text with the desired formatting attribute.

3. Click Format, and then select the formats you want to search for. Click OK to continue.

4. In the Replace With box, enter the text you want to replace the found text with.

5. Click Format to define the formatting you want to apply to the found or replaced text.

6. Click Find Next, Replace, or Replace All as desired.

Part
II

Ch
7

# Formatting and Printing Text

**K**nowing how to format and print your documents so that they impact your readers in the most productive, persuasive manner is an essential skill you need to master. Fortunately, Word 97 comes equipped with plenty of tools and options that allow you to easily give your text a polished appearance. And, when it comes time to print, Word's simple, direct instructions and features will have you producing hard copy of your documents as fast as you can click Print.

**Format the page**

From setting margins to using tabs and indentation, you'll learn how to do it quickly and easily.

**Create lists that communicate your points with style**

Use Word's numbered and bulleted lists to add class and clarity to your documents.

**Add headers and footers**

Learn how to add chapter titles to make your document more cohesive.

**Use special Word 97 printing features**

Use Word 97's flexible printing options to print only what you need.

# Aligning Text

Word 97 text can be aligned four ways: flush left (as this book is), centered, flush right, and justified (stretched out to make both margins even). To align your text any of these ways, select the block of text and click the appropriate button on the toolbar, as shown in Figure 8.1.

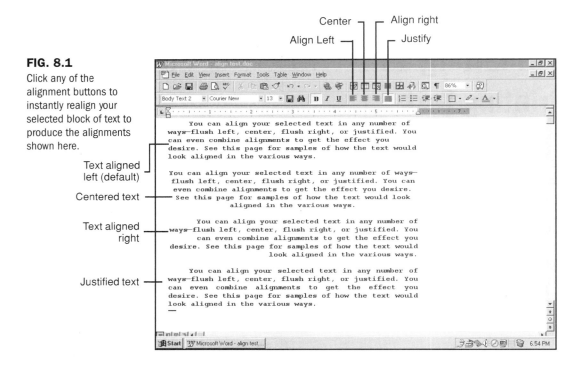

**FIG. 8.1**

Click any of the alignment buttons to instantly realign your selected block of text to produce the alignments shown here.

You can also choose the alignment beforehand and then enter the text to achieve the desired look.

# Compressing or Expanding the Space Between Lines

You can change line spacing in Word documents by following these steps:

1. Select the text for which you want to change the line spacing.

**TIP** You can select an entire document by moving the mouse pointer to the left margin of the document until it turns into an arrow and then triple-clicking. The entire document should be highlighted.

2. Choose Format, Paragraph, and then select the Indents and Spacing tab.
3. Select the desired options in the Spacing section using Table 8.1 as a guide. You can preview your selection in the Preview window before applying it.

**Table 8.1  Line Spacing Options Available in Word**

| Choosing This Option | Gives You the Following Results |
|---|---|
| Single | Line spacing for each line that accommodates the largest font in that line plus a small amount of extra space. The amount of extra space varies, depending on the font used. |
| 1.5 Line | Line spacing for each line that is one-and-one-half times that of single line spacing. |
| Double | Line spacing for each line that is twice that of single line spacing. |
| At Least | Minimum line spacing that Word can adjust to accommodate larger font sizes or graphics that would not otherwise fit within the specified spacing. |
| Exactly | Fixed line spacing that Word does not adjust. This option makes all lines evenly spaced. |

**N O T E**  If you select an entire document, using the Exactly line spacing option can result in some characters in a larger font being cut off. You may want to opt for one of the adjustable line spacing options when multiple font sizes are used, or apply line spacing to selected paragraphs rather than to the entire document.

# Creating Bulleted and Numbered Lists

There are two kinds of lists you can use to draw the attention of the reader: bulleted and numbered lists. Bulleted lists use small icons, or bullets, to indicate each item in the list. Numbered lists use a numbering system for the items. Both types of lists can be modified to use different bullet and numbering styles.

## Entering New Text Formatted as a List

To create either a bulleted or numbered list from the beginning, follow these steps:

1. Type the text leading up to the list.
2. When you're ready to enter the list, place the insertion point at the location you'd like the list to appear.

3. Click the Numbering or Bullets button on the Standard toolbar.

4. Type each section of text, followed by the Enter key, to set up subsequent bullets or numbered sections.

5. When the list is complete, press Enter and click the Numbering or Bullets button again to turn off the formatting. (Samples of the resulting lists are shown in Figure 8.2.)

**FIG. 8.2**
This example shows simple numbered and bulleted lists.

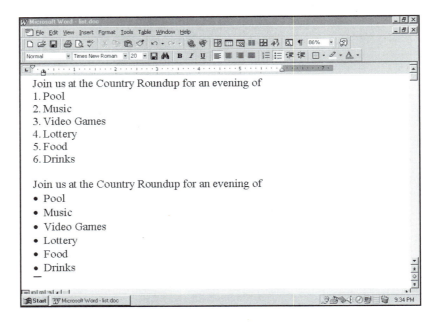

 **TIP**   To set your lists off even further, insert tabs before the list.

## Generating a List from Existing Text

Select the text to be turned into a list and then click the desired list button on the Standard toolbar. Keep in mind that each list entry must be followed by a hard return (pressing the Enter key); otherwise, the items will all be placed on a single list entry. This may require you to insert returns after you have formatted the list.

## Changing the Bullet or Numbering Style

If standard bullets or numbers don't catch your fancy, you can apply something a bit more elaborate. Choose Format, Bullets and Numbering, and then select either the Bulleted or Numbered tab as appropriate. The Bulleted tab gives you access to little black boxes, check marks, and other distinctive bullet styles. The Numbered tab can turn standard numbers into letters or even Roman numerals. Simply choose the style you want, and then press OK to apply it.

## Sorting a List

You can put your lists in alphabetical order or chronological order by running a sort against it. To do this, follow these steps:

1. Select the list you want to sort.
2. Choose Table, Sort to bring up the Sort Text dialog box (see Figure 8.3).

**FIG. 8.3**
Use the Type drop-down list box to choose the kind of sort you want to run against your list.

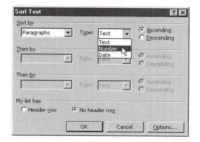

3. In the Sort By box, select Paragraphs.
4. In the Type box, choose Text, Number, or Date as appropriate.
5. Choose Ascending or Descending as desired.
6. Press OK to run the sort.

# Setting Tabs

You can set four different types of tabs in Word: left, right, center, or decimal. Word uses a left tab every half inch by default, which will meet your needs a majority of the time. The center and right tabs are useful for advanced formatting, like centering column headers for a table. Decimal tabs are best used to line up columns of numbers.

To set tabs, do the following:

1. Make sure the ruler is displayed at the top of your Word workspace. If it isn't, you may retrieve it by choosing View, Ruler.
2. Select the text you want to format using the tabs. To have them apply to the whole document, just triple-click in the left margin.
3. Click the Tab button (see Figure 8.4) until you see the icon of the tab you'd like to create (see Table 8.2).
4. Click the ruler to set the location of the selected tab.
5. If the tab already exists, you can move it by clicking it and dragging it to the new location.
6. To delete a tab, click it and drag it onto the workspace.

Part
II

Ch
8

**FIG. 8.4**
Use the Tab button to
select the desired type
of tab.

Tab button

### Table 8.2 Types of Tabs

| Icon | Tab Type |
| --- | --- |
| **L** | Left-aligned tab |
| **⊥** | Centered tab |
| **⅃** | Right-aligned tab |
| **⅃.** | Decimal tab |

Alternatively, you may also set tabs based on an exact measurement by choosing Format, Tabs. Unfortunately, this function's dialog box programming makes it impossible to visualize where the tab stops would fall on the page. Although the ruler may be more cumbersome to work with, it allows you to see your tab stops.

# Setting Indentations

Indentations, by definition, are the spaces between your paragraphs and the margins of the paper. There are essentially three ways to indent:

■ *Tabbed-in indent.* This is the normal indentation, where the first line of a paragraph is indented by one-half inch and subsequent lines are flush against the margin.

■ *Right and left indent.* Most commonly used to offset a quote in the middle of a block of text.

■ *Hanging indent.* The first line of text is flush against the margin and subsequent lines are indented. This format is frequently used for bibliographies.

Setting indentation is a simple process; just follow these steps:

1. Select the body of text you want to modify.

2. To create a paragraph where the first line is always indented, simply drag the first-line indent marker (shown in Figure 8.5) the desired distance on the ruler.

3. To indent both sides of a paragraph, drag the first-line indent marker until it is directly over the left indent marker. Next, drag both the left and right indent markers the desired distance inward.

**FIG. 8.5**
Look at the figure to locate the various indent markers.

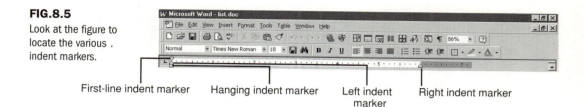

First-line indent marker        Hanging indent marker        Left indent marker        Right indent marker

4. To create a hanging indent, move the hanging indent marker to the right the desired distance.

# Adding Page Numbers, Titles, and Other Information Using Headers and Footers

Headers and footers allow you to print page numbers, document titles, and other repeating information at the top or bottom of the page. Using headers and footers can add an air of professionalism to documents, and applying page numbers can help keep documents in order.

Headers and footers can be interesting elements to work with, however, because you can't edit them in any of Word's traditional document views. To begin working with headers and footers, choose View, Header and Footer to bring up the Header and Footer toolbar (see Figure 8.6).

Add Time —
Add Date —                 Page Setup —
                            Show/Hide Document Text —

**FIG. 8.6**
Header and Footer toolbar items make creating headers and footers a breeze.

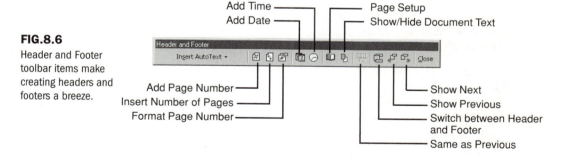

Add Page Number —
Insert Number of Pages —
Format Page Number —

Show Next —
Show Previous —
Switch between Header and Footer —
Same as Previous —

The following list describes each button on the Header and Footer toolbar:

■ *Insert AutoText.* Select a predefined header or footer from the AutoText list. For instance, you can select the Author, Page #, Date option to have Word automatically insert your name flush left, a centered page number, and the date flush right.

**N O T E**    If you want to edit the name that appears in the Author field, choose Tools, Options, and then select the User Information tab. Enter the name as desired in the Name text box.

■ *Add Page Number.* Set the insertion point in the desired location in the header, and then click this button to add the page number to your document header or footer.

- *Insert Number of Pages*. Create a "Page ? of ?" format in the desired location.
- *Format Page Number*. You can include chapter titles by defining the element's style code, you can select the format of the page numbers, you can even tell Word what page number to begin numbering with—an invaluable tool when you want to omit page numbering on the first page of a document.
- *Add Date*. Set the insertion point, and then click this button to add the current date to the document's header or footer.
- *Add Time*. Works the same way as adding a date.
- *Page Setup*. Define page margins and instruct Word to use a different header/footer for the document's first page. It's identical to the File, Page Setup menu command.
- *Show/Hide Document Text*. You can show/hide the document's text as you work on the header or footer.
- *Same as Previous*. Make the current header/footer the same as the previous one.
- *Switch between Header and Footer*. Move between the header and footer on a given page.
- *Show Previous*. Show the previous page's header/footer.
- *Show Next*. Show the next page's header/footer.
- *Close*. Exit the header/footer view.

# Setting Spelling Check Options

Word's spelling check feature can go crazy when it encounters acronyms, Internet addresses, and other unfamiliar text. The good news is that you can save time dealing with these elements by telling Word to ignore them.

Choose Tools, Options, and then select the Spelling & Grammar tab. From here, you can enable or disable the spelling checker as seen in Chapter 2. You can also tell Word to ignore words in uppercase, words with numbers in them, or file names and Internet addresses. This will save you time when running through your document to correct potential errors.

▷ **See** "Spell Checking," **p. 36**
▷ **See** "Running a Spell Check," **p. 36**
▷ **See** "Dealing with Misspelled Words," **p. 36**

# Get It Right the First Time with Grammar Checking

Avoid embarrassing errors in grammar by using Word's advanced grammar-checking features. To set grammar-checking options, follow these steps:

1. From within any Word document, choose Tools, Options, and then select the Spelling & Grammar tab (see Figure 8.7).

   In the Grammar section of the tab, you can specify whether Word should check grammar as you type, or whether you want any grammatical errors to be hidden. You may also check grammar at the same time you check spelling by placing a check mark next to that option.

**FIG. 8.7**

The grammar options selected in this figure tell Word to hide grammatical errors in the current document, but to check grammar at the same time spelling is checked.

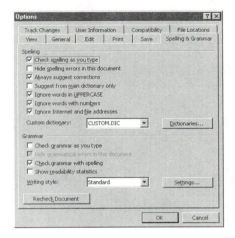

2. To have Word check for more specific errors, click the Settings button to bring up the Grammar Settings dialog box (see Figure 8.8).

**FIG. 8.8**

Select the elements you want Word to check in the Grammar and Style Options box, or request Word to double-check up to three usage requirements in the Require section of the Grammar Settings dialog box.

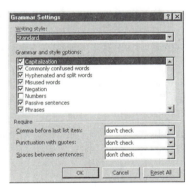

3. Scroll down the Grammar and Style Options box to select the elements you want Word to check for. Options include checking for improper capitalization, use of double negatives, and passive voice.

4. In the Require section, choose any of the three usage requirements—comma placement, use of quotation marks, and the number of spaces between sentences—and define their usage in the drop-down lists next to each one. For example, you can specify that sentences must have one space between them, and Word will tell you if it finds one that doesn't follow this rule.

5. Click OK to return to the Spelling & Grammar tab, and then click OK to apply your newly defined options.

# Printing a Word 97 Document from Within Word 97

Perhaps the most common way to print a document involves the following steps:

1. Open the document to be printed, and then choose File, Print or press Ctrl+P. This brings up the Print dialog box (see Figure 8.9).

**FIG. 8.9**

The Print dialog box gives users full control of their output.

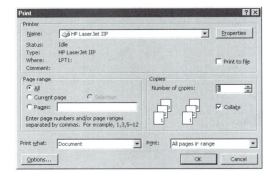

2. Confirm that the correct printer is defined. If it isn't, select the drop-down arrow next to the Name box to see the list of available choices. Click the desired printer. Specify the pages to be printed in the Page Range window (use 1-5 to print pages one through five, and 1,5 for pages one and five, for example) followed by the number of copies to be printed in the Copies window.

3. Select the Collate check box if you want multiple copies of a document to be printed in order.

   In a majority of cases, the Print What and Print boxes will be left on their default settings. It should be noted, however, that Word 97 gives its users the flexibility to print just about any part of a document, including its document properties and styles.

4. After you have all of the correct options selected, click OK to print.

   ▶ **See** "Preview Before You Print," **p. 38**

# Printing a Word 97 Document Without Launching Word 97

If you're in a hurry to print a copy of a Word file and don't have Word 97 up and running, you now have an alternative:

1. From the Windows 95 Taskbar, click Start and choose Open Office Document. The Open Office Document dialog box appears.

2. Locate the Word document you want to print and click the Commands and Settings button at the upper-right of the box.

3. Choose Print from the pop-up menu (see Figure 8.10), and you're all set without even having to run Word 97.

**FIG. 8.10**

From this Commands and Settings menu, you can perform a number of operations on a chosen file, including printing it or opening it as read-only where no edits are allowed.

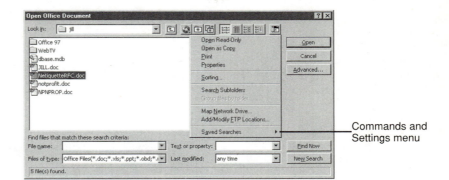

Commands and Settings menu

# Tables, Columns, and Advanced Formatting

**W**ant your documents to have that extra something that shows the reader you're a professional? Want your work on the computer to be faster and more efficient? Word 97 can help you accomplish all these things and more. It's now easier than ever to create professional-looking documents to share with and be revised by others. You can even conserve disk space by storing versions of a document in a single file. No more naming drafts of your annual report, such as annualreport1.doc, annualreport2.doc, and so on. But more importantly, you now have an accurate way to track how documents evolve over time in one convenient file.

**Advanced formatting**
Learn how to work with tables and columns in Word.

**Working with shading and borders**
Use these advanced techniques to offset or emphasize data.

**Tracking versions**
Avoid having to come up with creative file names for multiple versions of a document by storing them all in one file.

# Building a Simple Table

Simple tables are defined as tables having a maximum of five columns. The number of rows can easily be expanded, as you'll see later. To build a simple table in Word, follow these steps:

1. Place the insertion point in the location you want to begin the table.

2. Click the Insert Table button on the Standard toolbar to bring up the screen shown in Figure 9.1.

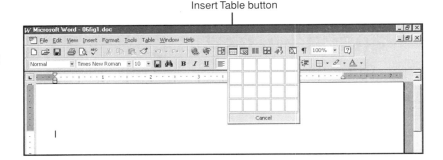

**FIG. 9.1**

Click the Insert Table button to begin creating your table in Word.

3. Select the range of cells that equals the number of rows and columns you want to include in your table. To do this, simply move your mouse pointer down to the drop-down box and select the desired number of cells.

4. Select the desired cell and then type text as usual. If the text you enter is wider than the cell allows, a second line will be created within the cell to accommodate the excess.

5. To move to the next cell, press Tab. To return to the previous cell, press Shift+Tab.

# Using AutoFormat to Improve Your Table's Appearance

Word makes it easy to polish your table's appearance. Just follow these steps:

1. Place the insertion point inside the table.

2. Choose Table, Table AutoFormat to bring up the Table AutoFormat dialog box (see Figure 9.2).

3. Select the format you want to use in the Formats list. You can preview it in the Preview box before applying it.

4. Click OK to confirm your choice and return to the main document.

**FIG. 9.2**

From the Table AutoFormat dialog box, you can select from dozens of table formats including multicolor tables, which are perfect for publishing on the Web.

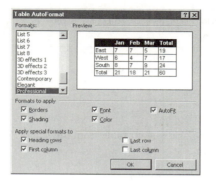

**T I P**   If you don't see a format you like in the Table AutoFormat dialog box or would simply like to change the appearance of your table text, you may do so manually by selecting the cells to be changed, and applying font and formatting changes as you would with any other text in Word. See the section "Emphasizing Content with Borders and Shading" later in this chapter to learn how to use those elements.

# Building More Complex Tables in Word

By choosing T<u>a</u>ble, <u>I</u>nsert Table, you can build a table with up to 63 columns and an infinite number of rows. What's more, this bigger table can be formatted with Table Auto<u>F</u>ormat exactly like its smaller counterpart to give it a professional appearance. To build this bigger table, do the following:

1. Position the insertion point in the desired location.

2. Choose T<u>a</u>ble, <u>I</u>nsert Table from the Standard toolbar to open the Insert Table dialog box pictured in Figure 9.3.

**FIG. 9.3**

Use the Insert Table dialog box to create tables up to 63 columns wide.

3. Select the desired number of columns and rows either by inserting the number directly or by using the arrows next to each box.

4. In the Column <u>W</u>idth box, select the desired cell size by using the arrows or by selecting AutoFit to have Word determine the size.

5. You may apply <u>A</u>utoFormat at this point by clicking the AutoFormat button, or you may make your decision after you see the table's contents in its final form by following the steps in the preceding section, "Using AutoFormat to Improve Your Table's Appearance."

**T I P**   If you have a complicated table to build or already have data in Excel, you may want to use Excel to
create the table and then put it in Word.

▶ **See** "Embedding an Excel Worksheet in Word," **p. 275**

# Drawing Tables

Want to have more control over the size of your table from the start? Perhaps drawing what
you need is the best option for you.

To draw a table from scratch, do the following:

1. Be sure there's space to work with in the document you want to add the drawn table to.
   You can always delete extra space at the end, so it's probably best at this point to give
   yourself plenty of room to work with.

2. Choose Table, Draw Table, which turns your mouse pointer into a pencil.

3. Click at the upper-left corner of your table's location, and then drag the outlined box out
   (see Figure 9.4) until you have the outline of the desired table at the appropriate size.

**FIG. 9.4**

Click at the upper-left
corner of your table, and
then drag the box out
until your table reaches
the desired size.

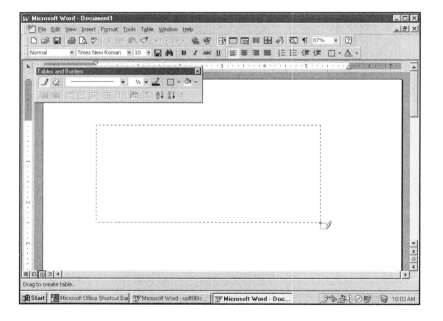

4. Use the pencil to draw the necessary rows and columns. If you can't draw, don't worry;
   Word makes it foolproof to draw straight lines both vertically and horizontally.

5. You can change drawing tools and colors at any point by making a new selection from
   the Tables and Borders Bar. Here, you can change a border's color for online presentations, or thickness for added emphasis.

6. To resize rows or columns, place the mouse pointer over the line you want to resize until it turns into a double-headed arrow. Click and drag the line in the direction you want to resize the element, and then release the mouse button to set it in place.

# Adding and Deleting Columns and Rows

Tables never come out right the first time; it seems like you always need more room. With Word 97, you can easily add the additional columns or rows you need. To do so, follow any of the procedures listed below:

- *Insert a row.* Click inside the row above which you want the new row to appear. Choose Ta̲ble, I̲nsert Rows to have Word insert the new row. You may also move to the last cell in the table (the bottom-right corner), and then press Tab to add a single row.

- *Insert multiple rows.* Select the same number of rows in the existing table as the number of rows you want to add. For example if you want to add four rows, select four rows. Choose Ta̲ble, I̲nsert Rows to have Word insert the desired number of rows.

- *Insert column(s).* Select the number of columns you want to add. For instance, to add three columns, highlight three of the columns in your table. Choose Ta̲ble, I̲nsert Columns to have Word insert the specified number of columns to the left of the column(s) you selected in your table.

In the majority of cases, you'll need to insert a row at the end of the table or a column at the far right of your table. Unfortunately, the Insert command places new rows above the bottom row and new columns to the left of the last column on the right. Because you can't drag the new rows or columns into place, consider dragging the bottom row up or the rightmost column to the left to rectify the problem.

To delete rows or columns, select the rows or columns you want to delete, and then choose Ta̲ble, D̲elete Rows, or D̲elete Columns as appropriate.

 **T I P** If you press the Delete button in this situation, Word merely deletes the contents of the rows or columns, not the rows or columns themselves.

# Adjusting Column Width

One size doesn't always fit all, which is why you may find yourself needing to adjust column widths in your table. The easiest way to do this is to move the mouse pointer over the line of the cell you want to resize until it turns into a double-headed arrow. Click the line and drag it to the desired position, and then release the mouse button to set the new size in place.

 **T I P** Pressing Alt while performing this operation displays a ruler containing each of the columns' measurements so that you can accurately compare their size.

You may also click the column markers inside the ruler to resize the desired column.

# Joining Cells to Create Column Headings

It's possible to create a column or row header by joining multiple cells. To merge cells, select the cells you want to join, and then choose Table, Merge Cells. This allows you to place a nice column or row header over more than one cell (see Figure 9.5).

**FIG. 9.5**

This table shows how joining cells can create effective table headers for both columns and rows.

| 1996-97 Fundraising | | | |
|---|---|---|---|
| | | Mrs. Petr | Mrs. Gardner | Mrs. Stowell |

Table (with "Amount" vertical header):

| | Mrs. Petr | Mrs. Gardner | Mrs. Stowell |
|---|---|---|---|
| Cookie Dough | $22.50 | $18.72 | $20.45 |
| Gift Wrap | $15.95 | $13.26 | $16.92 |
| Seeds | $8.95 | $12.65 | $7.85 |
| Photo Mugs | $10.96 | $19.25 | $14.89 |

# Emphasizing Content with Borders and Shading

When used judiciously, borders and shading can be extremely effective at drawing attention to selected text. To take advantage of these options, do the following:

1. Right-click any visible toolbar to open a shortcut menu. Select the Tables and Borders toolbar (shown in Figure 9.6) from the list.

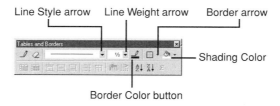

Line Style arrow    Line Weight arrow    Border arrow

Shading Color

Border Color button

**FIG. 9.6**

Use the Tables and Borders toolbar to create dynamic borders and shading effects.

2. Select the text around which you'd like to place a border (or the section of text you want to shade) by using the text selection techniques described in Chapter 5 "Selecting a Block of Text."

**N O T E**    If no text has been selected, Word will find the insertion point and apply the formatting to that paragraph.

3. Click the arrow next to the Line Style box to select a line style for the border.
4. Click the Line Weight arrow to select the thickness of your border.

5. The Border Color button may be used to add color to online documents or color printer output.
6. Click the arrow next to the Border button to open a palette of available border styles. Although the desired option is most frequently Outside Border, you have a number of options to choose from.

7. Click the Shading Color arrow to see a pop-up shading palette from which you can make your selection.

8. To close the toolbar to maximize your workspace, click the X at the top-right corner of the box.

 **TIP** Want more border and shading options than the toolbar gives you? Select the text you want to change and choose Format, Borders and Shading to bring up the Borders and Shading dialog box.

# Working with Columns in Word

You'll want to know how to work with columns in Word. To set up columns, follow these steps:

1. Set the insertion point where you'd like the columns to begin or select the text you'd like to format in columns.

 **TIP** If you want a large headline to span the width of multiple columns, put the headline in place before formatting the columns.

2. Choose Format, Columns to open the Columns dialog box pictured in Figure 9.7.

**FIG. 9.7**
The Columns dialog box gives you incredible flexibility for formatting multicolumn documents.

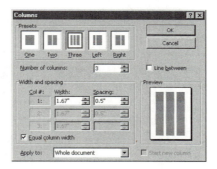

3. Select the desired format of your columns in the Presets area. You can also specify a number of columns in the Number of Columns box or select the equal column widths box.

4. To place lines between columns, check the Lines Between box.

5. You can preview the options you choose in the Preview window.

6. Column layouts can apply to selected text, the entire document, or from a designated point within a document. You can set this option in the Apply To drop-down box.

7. Click OK to confirm your selections.

# Changing the Formatting of Your Columns

Tweaking the appearance of newspaper columns can be a bit tricky. Although you can easily adjust text alignment or attributes by selecting all of the text and applying the desired font size, style, color, or alignment as you can with any Word document, working with columns brings new ways of doing things as well as new challenges.

 **TIP** While many people like the balanced, clean look of completely justified columns like those shown in Figure 9.8, it can sometimes cause text to be spaced out so much that it reduces the readability of your document. To avoid this problem, consider resizing the columns just slightly, reducing the font size, decreasing the number of columns, or eliminating justification all together.

If you have lines between your columns and feel the text looks too unbalanced in nonjustified columns, simply tweak the margins as described in the following paragraph to achieve the desired look.

To change the size of a column or the space between them, confirm that you're in Page Layout view of Word, and then drag the column markers in Word's ruler to resize the desired area (see Figure 9.8).

**FIG. 9.8**

To resize a column or adjust the space between them, click one of the column markers and drag it in the desired direction as shown.

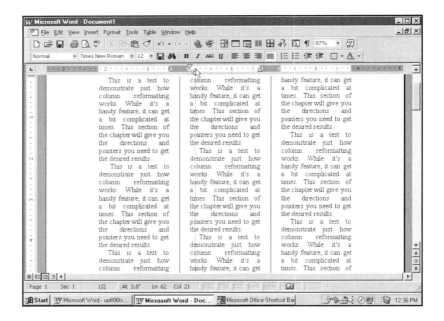

Alternatively, you can select the entire block of text and choose Format, Columns to use the Column dialog box, as described in the preceding paragraph.

You may also have, for instance, two columns on the top half of your page and three on the bottom half by selecting the text you want to include in that section, and then using the Columns dialog box to specify the desired number of columns. You can do the same for the remaining text to achieve a different look on the bottom half of the page.

Finally, the one thing that's bound to drive most people working with columns crazy is what do you do if the right column comes out longer than the left one? You can spend hours formatting and reformatting text with the same frustrating results. Most likely the culprit is Word's Widow/Orphan control which is designed to eliminate bits of text spilling over onto the next page.

To eliminate the column imbalance, follow these steps:

1. Select the offending text.
2. Choose F_ormat, _Paragraph to open the Paragraph dialog box.
3. Select the Line and Page Breaks tab.
4. In the Pagination section of the tab, deselect the Widow/Orphan control to remove the check mark.
5. Click OK to confirm the change.

Upon returning to your document, you should find that either all the columns will be even, or the left side(s) should be one line longer than the final column.

## Fit Documents in Less Space by Using Shrink to Fit

Nothing is more frustrating when typing a letter than to have two lines of it spill over onto the second page. Word has a feature to save paper (and your sanity) called Shrink to Fit. Using this feature, Word 97 attempts to fit a document of any length onto one less page, provided only a few lines of text spill over onto the final page. To access this feature, follow these steps:

1. Click the Print Preview button on the Standard toolbar. This displays your document as it would appear on paper (see Figure 9.9).

   ▶ **See** "Preview Before You Print," **p. 38**

2. Click the Multiple Pages button so that you can see just how much text hangs over onto the final page.

3. To squeeze stray lines onto the previous page, click the Shrink to Fit button. The results will be shown on the same Print Preview screen (see Figure 9.10).

   ▶ **See** "Adding Bold, Italic, Color, Underline, and Other Text Attributes," **p. 29**

Part
II

Ch
9

**FIG. 9.9**
The closing of this letter is a perfect example of something you would want to fit onto the previous page with Shrink to Fit.

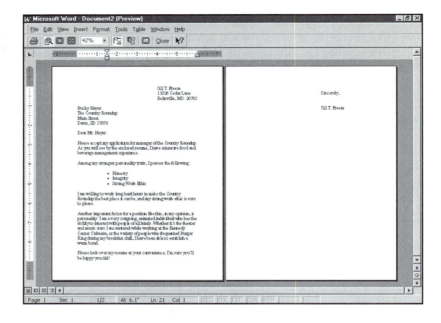

**FIG. 9.10**
Now the whole letter prints on one page.

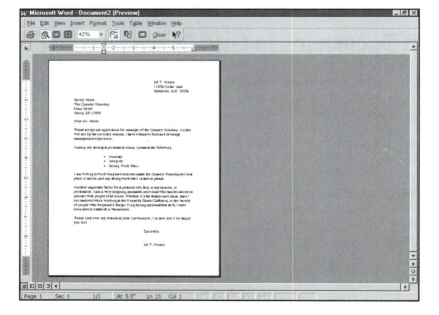

# Building an Outline

 Building an outline for a document in Word allows you to organize your document in a hierarchy. You can then use the Outline view in Word to more easily rearrange the document, navigate it, or view its structure. To start building your outline, enter Word's Outline View by choosing View, Outline, or by clicking the Outline View button. From this view, you can assign varying levels of importance to your topics or heading titles.

Part
II
Ch
9

Table 9.1 describes everything you need to use the Outline toolbar at a glance.

**Table 9.1  Outline Toolbar Buttons and Functions**

| Button | Button Name | Function |
| --- | --- | --- |
| | Promote | Increases the level of a heading. |
| | Demote | Decreases the level of a heading. |
| | Demote to Body Text | Enters body text while in Outline View. |
| | Move Up | Moves the selected heading(s) up one heading in the outline. |
| | Move Down | Moves the selected heading(s) down one heading in the outline. |
| | Expand | Shows all subheadings and body text under the selected heading. |
| | Collapse | Hides subheadings and body text under the selected heading. |
| | Show Headings | Expands or collapses the outline to show the specified heading level. For example, clicking 2 shows only levels 1 and 2. |
| | All | Toggles to expand or collapse the entire outline or hides all body text. |
| | Show First Line Only | Toggles to show all body text or only the first line of the body of text. |
| | Show Formatting | Toggles to show or hide character formatting. |

To continue creating your outline, simply enter text as you would normally do in Word. Use the arrow buttons illustrated in Table 9.1 to assign the appropriate level of importance to your headings. The resulting outline format is illustrated in Figure 9.11.

**TIP** You may also use the Tab key to decrease the heading's level of importance or Shift+Tab to increase its level of importance.

**FIG. 9.11**
Word's Outline view lets you see the organization of your document at a glance.

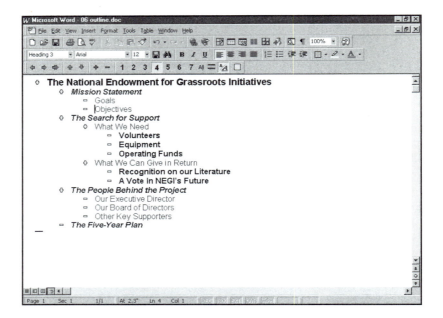

# Editing an Outline

Don't like the placement of a particular topic? Moving it in Word's Outline view is a snap. Just follow these steps:

1. Place the document in Outline view by choosing View, Outline, or by clicking the Outline View button.

2. Collapse the outline using the Show All Headings button on the Outline toolbar so that only headings are showing.

**CAUTION**

Failing to collapse the outline before moving headings could result in inadvertently leaving text fragments behind. Because body text moves with its parent header, selecting it while fully collapsed is the best way to ensure that everything gets moved safely.

3. Set the insertion point to the location you want to move text.
4. To select outline text to be moved, click on the + or – at the beginning of the heading you want to move. Note that clicking + takes with it all subheadings and body text down to the next heading at the same level as the heading to be moved.

5. Confirm that the highlighted text is the text you want to move.

6. Click the highlighted text, hold down the left mouse button (you'll see a box appear at the base of the mouse pointer's arrow), and drag the text to its new location.

7. Release the button to place the text in its new position.

 **T I P** Text end up in the wrong location? Never fear; just press Ctrl+Z or the Undo button and start the process again from the beginning.

# Viewing the Outline While You Write

Sure you can switch into Outline view within seconds, but Word has another option for letting you see the outline of your document as you write. Called Document Map, this feature displays a map of your document's headings on the left side of your screen (see Figure 9.12). Word uses heading style codes to build this map and creates hyperlinks of sorts to the respective locations in the document. Word also builds maps by honing in on specially formatted text (for example, text in bold or a larger font than the body text), so it's still possible to see a map of a non-style coded document and use it to navigate through your document.

**FIG. 9.12**
Word's Document Map feature allows you to see your outline as you write.

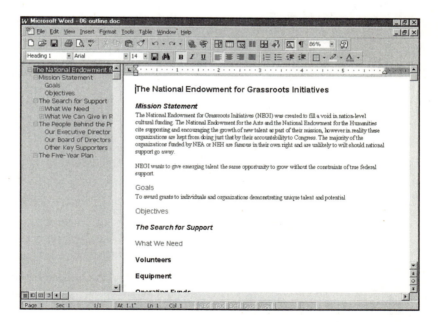

 To enable the Document Map option, choose View, Document Map, or click the Document Map button on the Standard toolbar. You can exit the document map view by repeating the commands you used to enable it, thus making it easy to toggle on and off.

This view is also very handy for jumping around the document. To move to any section in the document, click its heading in the outline at the left and Word will jump to that point in the document at the right.

# Formatting Headings with Style Codes

Using Word's style codes to format the headings that you have created in the document, you can easily generate an outline and a table of contents.

As you type the titles to your sections, apply the Heading style codes from the Style Box on the Formatting toolbar. Use Heading 1 for broad topics and increase the number for each level down that you want a heading. The Style Code box shows samples of the various styles to help guide you in your selection.

To confirm that the style code meets your needs, use the Outline View or Document Map feature to visualize the placement of your headers. Even if the style codes were inserted as you wrote the document, you can still move sections of text as described above.

# Building a Table of Contents from Style Codes

With a few clicks of the mouse, Word can automatically create a Table of Contents like the one pictured in Figure 9.13.

**FIG. 9.13**
Choose from a number of Table of Contents formats including this one.

To generate a Table of Contents from a style-coded document (one based on an outline created in Word or one with heading style codes inserted manually), follow these steps:

1. Set the insertion point at the location you want the Table of Contents to appear.

 **TIP** If you want the Table of Contents to appear on its own page at the front of the document, press Ctrl+Home (to move to the top of the page), Ctrl+Enter (to add a page break), and Page Up (to move to the top of the new page).

2. Choose Insert, Index and Tables to open the Index and Tables dialog box.
3. Choose the Table of Contents tab.

4. Click the arrows next to the Show Levels box to indicate how many heading levels you want to include in your table of contents.

5. Choose the style for your table of contents in the Formats list box. You can see the style you chose before applying it in the Preview box.

6. Click OK to generate the table of contents.

If you edit your document, you may want to update your table of contents. To do this, choose Insert, Index and Tables. When you see the dialog box, indicate that you want to overwrite the previous table of contents.

 **T I P** To save the original formatting of your table of contents, select it before overwriting it.

# Tracking Changes in a Document

Word's Track Changes feature allows you to monitor changes made to a document. The revisions are indicated with colored text. In fact, Word can accommodate multiple reviewers of a document by simply adding more text colors.

To use this feature:

1. Choose Tools, Track Changes, and Highlight Changes to bring up the Highlight Changes dialog box.

2. If you want changes to be tracked while editing, select the Track Changes While Editing box. By default, all added text will be underlined, and all deleted text will have strikethrough formatting.

By tracking changes, you can then review the changes that you and other people working on the document have made. You can go change by change through the document and accept or reject each by doing the following:

1. To accept or reject changes, choose Tools, Track Changes, Accept or Reject Changes to open the Accept or Reject Changes dialog box in Figure 9.14.

**FIG. 9.14**

The Accept or Reject Changes dialog box lets you accept or reject all changes in a document at once or address them one at a time.

2. To accept or reject all changes made to the document, click Accept All or Reject All. Accepting the changes adds any text marked to be added into the document and deletes anything that was marked to be deleted. Rejecting the changes returns the document to the condition it was in before the changes are made. Accepting or rejecting removes all of the strikethrough and underlining indicating the change.

**CAUTION**

Accepting or rejecting all changes may seem like a great time-saver on the surface, but selecting All anything can have potentially disastrous results because all data related to the change or requested change disappears permanently. To save yourself headaches (and maybe even embarrassment down the road), consider saving a version of the document with the changes still embedded, and then selecting all under a new version of the document. (See the following section in this chapter, "Saving Versions of a Document" to see how to do this.) That way you still have the changes on hand if you need them or decide to reconsider some of the suggestions.

3.  To accept or reject changes one-by-one, click the Find button with the arrow pointing to the right. You may also click Find with the left-pointing arrow to process changes made earlier in the document. Information about the change will be displayed and highlighted, and you will have the option of accepting or rejecting that change only.

4.  Click Close to return to the document.

# Saving Versions of a Document

In earlier versions of Word, you had to rename files in order to save multiple revisions of a document. With Word 97's new Save Version option, the days of conjuring up creative file names are over. To take advantage of this new feature, follow these steps:

1.  Choose File, Versions to open the Versions dialog box (see Figure 9.15).

**FIG. 9.15**

Click the Save Now button in the upper-left corner to continue the Save Version process.

2.  Click the Save Now button.

3.  Enter any applicable comments for the version to be saved in the Comments on Version text box.

4.  Click OK to save this version of the document.

**TIP** By saving versions of a document, you are archiving them. This means that a saved version of a document cannot be modified without being saved as a new version.

# CHAPTER 10

# Mail Merges, Envelopes, and AutoText

**O**n many occasions, you'll need to quickly generate and send the same information to a large group of people. Using Word's powerful consolidation features, instead of entering the same information over and over, you can draw on specific tools to help streamline your work.

With mail merge, you can prepare a carefully designed Word document that can be personalized in an instant. You can print envelopes and labels quickly and painlessly. With Word's multiple Auto options, a document is produced faster and with more accuracy than ever before. In short, these features of Word can handle much of your busy work, thus giving you more time to be productive (and maybe allowing you to leave the office a few minutes early as well!). ◼

**Using Mail Merge to create individualized documents**

With Word's powerful mail merge capabilities, you can personalize just about anything.

**Hassle-free printing on envelopes and labels**

You won't have to drag out the typewriter if you take advantage of Word's capability to neatly and easily print envelopes and labels.

**Letting Word do your work for you**

With Word 97's multiple Auto features, you can improve your grammar and spelling, and even have Word do your typing for you.

# Using Mail Merge to Get Personalized Results

Three parts make up the entire mail merge process—creating a form letter, building a data file, and merging the two for the final product. Using mail merge also introduces some new concepts in addition to the standard word processing functions. To use mail merge effectively, you have to understand the following terms and how they relate to performing a mail merge:

- *Field.* People who have worked with databases already know this term, but for those who don't, a field is a block of information (for example, first name, street address, or phone number) that acts as a placeholder in Word for information that may change in a document. These fields also make up the parts of a record in a data source.

- *Record.* All the fields pertaining to one object (in the case of the example above, each field would make up part of one person's record) come together to form a single record. A record stores all the fields pertaining to each object (or person) in a single container so that you can choose whether or not to include them in your mail merge.

- *Data Source.* It's a specially formatted document (an Excel database, an Access database, an Outlook address book, or, as described later in this chapter, a form letter in Word) used to create the individualized results of a mail merge.

The process doesn't follow the exact order of the parts listed above, however, so be sure to follow the next few sections closely and in order.

**N O T E**   Although form letters created in Word can be merged with a variety of data sources residing in other Office 97 applications, this chapter focuses on using Word for the entire process. ▦

▶ **See** "Using Alternate Data Sources for Mail Merges in Word," **p. 270**

## Creating the Form Letter

The form letter is the primary document that will be personalized with specific information about each recipient. To begin creating the form letter, do the following:

1. Create a new document or retrieve one you'd like to turn into a form letter.
2. Choose Tools, Mail Merge to open the Mail Merge Helper dialog box.
3. To create a main document with the Mail Merger Helper, click the Create button shown in Figure 10.1 to choose a main document type from the drop-down list.
4. You will be asked whether you want to use the current open document or create a new one. Choose Active Window because in step 1 of this process you opened the document you wanted to use for this.

The Mail Merge Helper dialog box remains open, and you are ready to specify a data source.

**FIG. 10.1**
Click the Create button to choose the desired main document type.

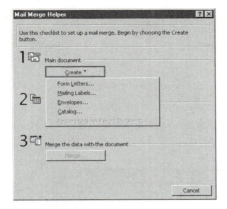

# Building the Data Source

Because you'll need to use fields from the data file in the form letter, you'll want to create your data file before preparing your form letter. Follow these steps to create the new data file:

1. After you have a document selected, the Get Data button becomes active. Click Get Data and choose Create Data Source from the drop-down list. The Create Data Source dialog box appears (see Figure 10.2).

**FIG. 10.2**
Use the Create Data Source dialog box to add and delete fields in your data source.

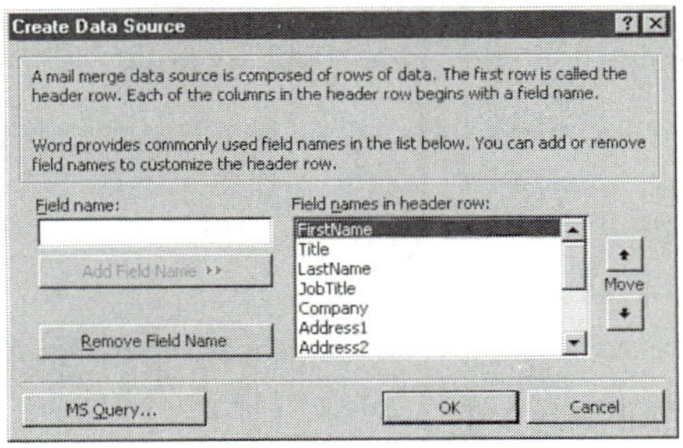

2. All the fields listed in the right side of the box are the default fields for the type of merge you are creating. To delete any field, scroll through the Field Names in Header Row list and select the field you want to remove. To confirm the field's removal, select Remove Field Name.

3. Add new fields by entering them in the Field Name text box and selecting Add Field Name.

4. To change the order of the fields in the source, select a field to move and click the up or down Move button.

5. Click OK when you've finished to bring up the Save As dialog box. Name your data source and click Save to save it.

The Mail Merge Helper will then ask you whether you want to edit the data source or main document. We will look at these operations in the next sections.

## Editing the Data Source

To enter information into your data source file, follow these steps:

1. When the Mail Merge Helper asks you whether you want to edit the data source or main document, choose Edit Data Source to bring up the Data Form dialog box shown in Figure 10.3.

**FIG. 10.3**

Enter the appropriate field data for each record in the Data Form boxes.

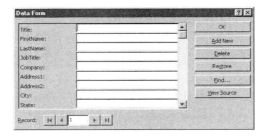

2. Fill in the fields for the first record and press Tab to move to the next field.
3. When you've finished entering data for the current record, click Add New to save the record and move to the next.
4. Click OK when you've finished entering all your records.

Word will then take you to the form letter where you can use the now visible Mail Merge toolbar to help you prepare your document for the merge.

## Editing the Main Document

Now that the data source is ready to go, it's time to prepare the main document.

1. Write the body text of the letter.
2. Set the insertion point in the location you want the first field to appear and click the Insert Merge Field button. Select the desired field from the list displayed (see Figure 10.4).
3. Click the field name to insert it.
4. Continue writing the form letter and inserting merge fields until you've completed it, as shown in Figure 10.5.
5. Save the document.

**FIG. 10.4**
Click the Insert Merge Field button on the Mail Merge toolbar to select the field you'd like to add to your document.

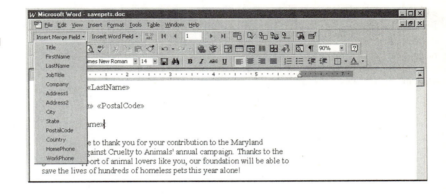

**FIG. 10.5**
Include the necessary spaces and punctuation between and surrounding the field codes to achieve the desired effect.

Field codes

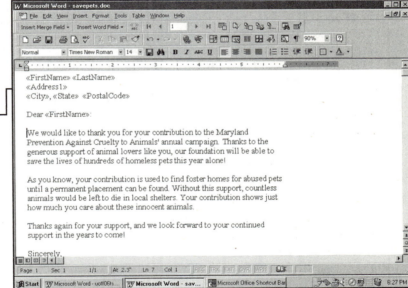

# Merging the Main Document and Data Source

To merge the two files, follow these steps:

1. From the main document, click the Mail Merge Helper button to call up the Mail Merge Helper dialog box.

2. Choose Merge to bring up the Merge dialog box pictured in Figure 10.6.

Part

II

Ch

10

**FIG. 10.6**

In the Merge dialog box
you can select which
records will be merged,
and you can instruct
Word to skip any blank
lines in the data file.

3. Choose from the following merge options:

   - In the Merge To box, select the destination of the merge. You can select from New
     Document, Printer, E-Mail, and Electronic Fax. If you select e-mail or fax, choose
     Setup. The Merge To Setup dialog box will ask for the field containing the e-mail
     or fax address. You can also enter a subject line for the message.

 Think twice before choosing the New Document option because this basically creates a new, potentially huge document containing a copy of each document you created in the merge. For instance, if
you merge 125 records from your data source with a simple one-page letter, you end up with a huge
125-page document stored on your system. The other options merely send the personalized output to
the printer, recipient's e-mail, and so on.

   - If the records are stored in order, specify which records are to be merged by
     number.
   - You can instruct Word to print or delete blank lines for empty fields. (For a more
     professional appearance, it's almost always best not to insert blanks.)
   - Click the Query Options button to set criteria for including a record in the merge.
     (For more information on how to set query options, see the following section,
     "Setting Data Query Options in a Word Data Source.")

4. When you've finished selecting your options, click Merge to send the output to the
   specified destination.

5. If you've selected New Document as your output option, you will be asked to name and
   save the newly created document.

# Setting Data Query Options in a Word Data Source

Word gives you immense flexibility when it comes to selecting desired records for a mail
merge. Just follow these steps from the Mail Merge Helper menu to select records to include
in your mail merge:

1. After you have selected your main document and data source, choose Query Options.

2. Choose the Filter Records tab to select specific records based on criteria you define (see
   Figure 10.7).

3. Use the drop-down arrow next to the first Field text box to select the field by which you
   want to filter records (the State field, for example).

**FIG. 10.7**
The Filter Records tab of the Query options dialog box lets you eliminate records from a mail merge based on criteria you specify.

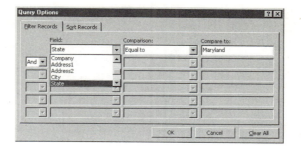

4. The Comparison box lets you set how the records must compare to the specified criteria (Equal To retrieves all records from within a given state, as in the example).

5. The Compare To box lets you specify the exact criteria the records will be compared to (for example, Maryland will return only records from the state of Maryland in this case).

6. If you need to filter records further, you can move to the second line of the Query Options form and specify additional criteria as you did in the steps above. Records must either meet both criteria (use And) or one or the other (use Or).

# Printing Labels from a Word Data File

To print labels in Word 97, grab the product number from your box of labels and follow these steps:

1. Create a new document and then choose Tools, Mail Merge to open the Mail Merge Helper dialog box.

2. Click Create and choose Mailing Labels from the drop-down list.

3. The Mail Merge Helper asks if you want to create the labels in the active window or a new window. Choose Active Window.

4. Before creating the mailing labels, you need to select a data file or create a new one from which to build the labels. To do so, click Get Data and make the appropriate selection.

5. If you choose Create Data Source, refer, if necessary, to the section titled "Building Your Data Source" earlier in this chapter.

 6. From the Mail Merge toolbar, click the Mail Merge Helper button and click Setup to open the Label Options dialog box shown in Figure 10.8.

7. Define the labels you want to create by selecting the applicable Label Products from the drop-down list. Then select the Product Number for the labels you're using.

 **TIP** Need more templates for your favorite Avery products? Make sure you have an active Internet connection and choose Help, Microsoft on the Web, Free Stuff and look for the Avery Wizard link to download a set of Avery product templates. Or, if you own the Small Business Edition of Office 97, you may already have these templates in the ValuPack that came with your software.

Part
**II**

Ch
**10**

**FIG. 10.8**
Click the arrows next to the Label Products box in the Label Options dialog box to select from a variety of popular label products.

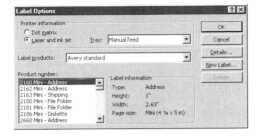

8. Click OK to bring up the Create Labels dialog box (see Figure 10.9).

**FIG. 10.9**
Insert the fields you want to include on your labels by clicking the Insert Merge Field button and selecting from the available fields.

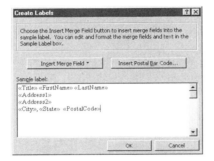

9. Click Insert Merge Field to place the fields on your label, adding necessary lines, spaces, and punctuation as you go.

10. Click OK when you've finished formatting the labels. This returns you to the Mail Merge Helper dialog box.

11. Click Merge to conduct the merge. This opens the Merge dialog box.

12. Select the desired merge options and click Merge to send the newly created labels to the output specified.

# Printing Envelopes from Your Data Source

To print envelopes instead of labels from an address list, do the following:

1. Click the New button to start a new document.

2. Choose Tools, Mail Merge to open the Mail Merge Helper dialog box.

3. Click Create, select Envelopes, and then click Active Window. The active document becomes the mail merge main document.

4. Click Get Data to select an existing data file or to begin creating a new one.

5. After the data source is selected or created, the Mail Merge Helper will return. From here, click Setup to format the main document. This will bring up the Envelope Options dialog box shown in Figure 10.10.

**FIG. 10.10**

The Envelope Options tab of the Envelope Options dialog box allows you to select envelope size as well as address placement.

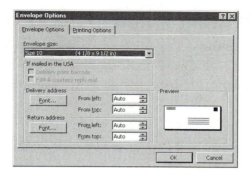

6. On the Envelope Options tab, select the envelope size you want and adjust the address format and position on the envelope.

7. Select the Printing Options tab to confirm that the selected envelope feed options are correct for your printer, and then click OK.

8. Insert the merge fields for the address information in the Envelope Address dialog box (see Figure 10.11).

**FIG. 10.11**

Click the Insert Merge Field button to add the desired fields to the envelope.

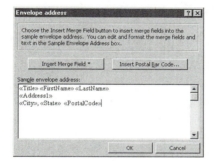

9. In the Mail Merge Helper dialog box, choose Edit in the Main Document section of the dialog box, and then choose the envelope main document. (The Edit option becomes available after you've created or selected a data source.) Insert or verify the return address, or delete it if the envelopes have a preprinted return address.

10. Click Merge in the Mail Merge Helper dialog box.

11. In the Merge To box, choose Printer.

12. To print envelopes for selected addressees only, click Query Options and specify criteria for selecting the data records. Use the Filter Data tab to select the recipients of your mailing and the Sort Data tab to print envelopes in ZIP Code order.

13. Click Merge to send the output to the printer.

# Addressing and Printing a Single Envelope

Because personal computers have virtually eliminated typewriters, you'll want to know how to print a single envelope in Word, too. To do so, just follow these steps:

1. Choose Tools, Envelopes and Labels, and then select the Envelopes tab (see Figure 10.12).

2. Enter the Delivery Address and Return Address information.

 **T I P**   To select a more distinctive font for your envelope copy or to change its size, select the text you want to change, and then right-click it to open the shortcut menu. Choose Font and make your selections from the Font dialog box. Click OK to apply them.

**FIG. 10.12**
Enter the Delivery Address and the Return Address in their respective boxes, or click Omit next to the Return address if using preprinted stationery.

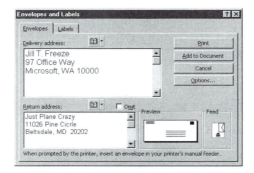

1. To select an envelope size, the type of paper feed, and other options, click Options.

2. To print the envelope, insert the envelope in the printer as shown in the Feed box, and then click Print.

# Creating a Default Return Address for Envelopes

You can avoid having to re-key your return address each time you print envelopes by creating a default return address. Follow these steps to build a default return address:

1. Choose Tools, Options, and then click the User Information tab.

2. In the Mailing address box, type the return address.

3. Click OK to confirm your entry.

# Auto Features at a Glance

If you've spent any time wandering through Word 97's menus, you've undoubtedly noticed the overabundance of AutoWhatever options. Although these features are designed to make your work hours easier and more productive, they can be downright confusing.

The list below defines some of these features, what they do, and when to use them. Pay extra attention to AutoComplete, AutoCorrect, and AutoText because their similarities and interrelationships can be particularly confusing.

■ *AutoFormat.* (When the As You Type option is activated) Automatically formats headings, bulleted and numbered lists, borders, numbers, symbols, and so on as you type in a document. To automatically format selected text or an entire document all at once, choose Format, AutoFormat and select your options in the AutoFormat dialog box.

**N O T E**  With the exception of AutoFormat and AutoSummarize, all of the "Auto" features are on by default in Word. ■

■ *AutoCorrect.* Automatically corrects many common typing, spelling, and grammatical errors as you type, and it can automatically insert text, graphics, and symbols. To enable AutoCorrect, choose Tools, AutoCorrect, and choose the AutoCorrect tab. Select (or deselect to disable the feature) Replace Text as You Type. This option corrects or replaces programmed text as you type without prompting you.

■ *AutoComplete.* Lets you insert entire items such as dates and AutoText entries when you type a few identifying characters. Unlike AutoCorrect, AutoComplete prompts you with a little yellow ScreenTip box to accept or reject the programmed text. Accepting it is as simple as clicking Return. To enable AutoComplete, choose Tools, AutoCorrect, and select the AutoText tab. Select (or deselect to disable the feature) Show AutoComplete tip for AutoText or date and click OK to confirm your request.

■ *AutoText.* A storage location for text or graphics you want to reuse. Good candidates for an AutoText entry include a company logo, an organization's mission statement, your business's return address, and so on. AutoComplete uses the programmed AutoText entries to generate its ScreenTips.

■ *AutoSummarize.* Automatically generates a summary of your long documents to be saved in a specified location. You can also choose summary attributes to make sure the summary contains needed data. To use AutoSummarize, choose Tools, AutoSummarize. Word will search the document to generate a summary and offer you various options for placing the summary.

■ *AutoSave.* Allows you to automatically save your work at specified intervals.

  ▶ **See** "Selecting Advanced Save Options," **p. 49**

■ *AutoRecover.* Nearly synonymous with AutoSave because it offers multiple ways to protect you work.

# Programming AutoText Entries

Word 97's AutoText feature allows you to store frequently used phrases, sentences, and even paragraphs so that they can be entered effortlessly. Follow these steps to program an AutoText entry:

1. Select the text or graphic you want to store as an AutoText entry.
2. Choose Insert, AutoText, New; or press Alt+F3 to save the entry.
3. Word proposes a name for the AutoText entry that you can accept, or you can type a new one.

**TIP** If you plan to create, insert, or modify a number of AutoText entries, you may want to use the AutoText toolbar rather than following the steps above. To display the AutoText toolbar, right-click on any visible toolbar and select AutoText.

# Inserting AutoText Entries in a Document

You have multiple options when it comes to inserting an AutoText entry. These include:

- Enable AutoComplete as described in "Auto Features at a Glance."
- Choose Insert, AutoText, and select the desired entry from one of the categories listed.
- From the AutoText toolbar (see Figure 10.13), click the All Entries button and make your selection.

**FIG. 10.13**

From the AutoText toolbar, click All Entries to select from the variety of AutoText options available.

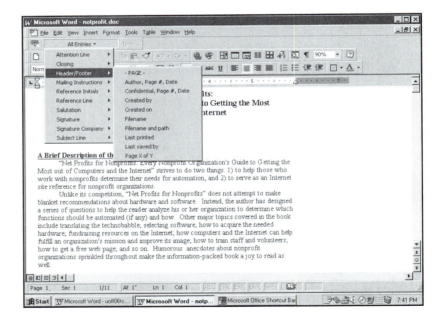

# Editing an AutoText Entry

Should the content of an AutoText entry change, you can edit the entry by doing the following:

1. Insert the AutoText entry into the document as described above.
2. Edit the entry as desired.
3. Select the revised AutoText entry text.
4. Choose Insert, AutoText, New, and type the original name of the entry.

Part

II

Ch

10

# CHAPTER 11

# Excel Essentials

**E**xcel 97 is perhaps the best spreadsheet program on the market today. Its versatility and ease of use make its powerful features within reach of virtually any computer user. Whether you need to create a household budget, produce a fancy chart illustrating your work team's achievements, or graph your company's market share, Excel is the program of choice. This chapter will quickly get you up to speed on all of the Excel essentials. In Chapters 12, 13, and 14, we'll experiment with many of Excel's more advanced features. ■

### Learning the environment

Get acquainted with Excel's workspace and spreadsheet terminology so that you can take full advantage of Excel's advanced features.

### Navigating around an Excel workbook

Use a variety of mouse and keyboard commands to make your way through an Excel workbook.

### Formatting cells

From formatting numbers to creating borders, Excel has a number of alternatives.

# Learning the Spreadsheet Lingo

Knowing the proper terms for what you want to accomplish in Excel makes learning to use the program that much easier. The general Excel definitions you want to know include those in the following bulleted list. Obviously dozens more are sprinkled throughout the chapter as we explore each function.

- *Spreadsheet.* A matrix of data cells arranged in columns and rows.
- *Worksheet.* Excel's term for an electronic spreadsheet.
- *Cell Address.* As you'll see in Figure 11.1 in the next section, Excel cells are "containers" capable of holding data. They are arranged in a series of lettered and numbered columns and rows. For example, the active cell in Figure 11.1 is A1 because the cell in the first column, A, and first row, 1, is highlighted. The Cell Address is also displayed in the Name box at the left end of the Formula bar.
- *Workbook.* Because you may want to create multiple related worksheets, Excel lets you store them all together in a workbook.
- *Range.* In Excel, you're often asked to select or perform an operation on a range. A range is simply Excel's counterpart to Word's block of text—it's a group of cells chosen at one time, which can be manipulated in any number of ways as you'll see throughout the next couple of chapters.

# Anatomy of the Excel 97 Workspace

To get the most out of Excel, you want to be familiar with its critical screen elements because these elements often hold the key to time-saving shortcuts. Figure 11.1 presents all these elements, which are explained in detail later in this chapter.

Although many of these elements are the same as those found in Word, there are also some new ones:

- *Active cell.* A cell with a dark border (called a cell selector) around it. The active cell is the one you've selected to enter or edit data.
- *Column heading.* The lettered boxes across the top of Excel's workspace. Clicking one selects an entire column of cells, which you can format or move as a whole.
- *Row heading.* The numbered boxes down the side of Excel's workspace. Clicking one selects an entire row of cells, which you can format or move as a whole.
- *Sheet tabs.* Click these to move from one worksheet in a workbook to another.
- *Tab Scroll buttons.* If you can't see all of the sheet tabs in your workbook, use these buttons to scroll to the ones that are hidden off-screen.
- *Formula bar.* This bar has two parts: a name box that displays the name given to the selected cell (or the cell's address if no name has been given) and a box displaying the selected cell's contents.

Name box        Standard toolbar        Formatting toolbar

Active cell      Menu bar        Formula bar        Column headings

**FIG. 11.1**
Many Excel screen
elements are similar to
other Office applica-
tions.

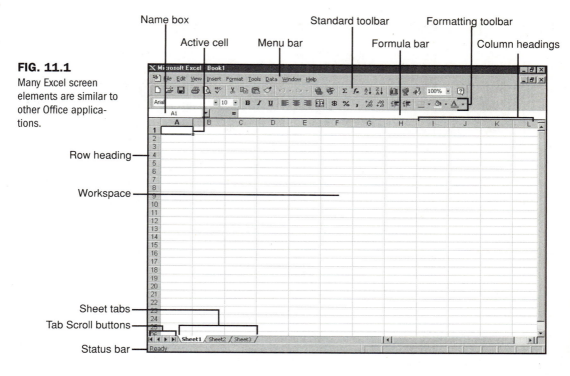

Row heading

Workspace

Sheet tabs

Tab Scroll buttons

Status bar

- *Formatting toolbar.* Excel's Formatting toolbar is nearly identical to Word's except it includes five useful buttons for formatting numbers—Currency Style, Percent Style, Comma Style, Increase Decimal, and Decrease Decimal.

- *Standard toolbar.* Excel's Standard toolbar replaces a few Word-specific buttons with AutoSum, Paste Formula, Sort Ascending, and Sort Descending buttons. This toolbar also gives you instant access to Excel's powerful ChartWizard and mapping function.

- *Name box.* This box at the far left end of the Formula bar holds the address of the cell or cell range currently selected in Excel.

- *Menu bar.* In Excel, a Data pull-down menu replaces Word's Table menu.

- *Status bar.* The left side of Excel's status bar tells you what mode Excel is in (Ready, Enter, or Edit). The other parts contain information about commands being executed, whether Caps Lock is on, and so on.

# Using the Mouse to Move Around in Excel

To make a cell active, place the mouse pointer in the desired location and click. The cell selector (a thick dark border) appears around the cell you choose. If the cell is off-screen, you may
need to use the vertical and horizontal scroll bars to find it. Click the arrows for small moves,
or drag the box in the appropriate direction for larger moves.

Part
II

Ch
**11**

# Using the Keyboard to Move Around in Excel

There are a number of shortcut keys you will find invaluable for working with larger worksheets and workbooks. Table 11.1 lists the most common ones.

| Table 11.1 Keystrokes for Navigating Through Excel | |
|---|---|
| **Press This/These** | **To Move Like This** |
| In the Name box, enter the cell address, then press Enter | Jumps to the cell specified. |
| F5 | Brings up the Go To box pictured in Figure 11.2. Simply enter the desired cell address and click OK to move directly to that cell. |
| Arrow keys | One cell in the direction of the arrow. |
| Tab | One cell to the right. |
| Shift+Tab | One cell to the left. |
| Enter | One row down. |
| Page Up/Down | One full screen up or down. |
| Ctrl+Home | To the beginning of the worksheet (usually cell A1). |
| Ctrl+End | To the last cell of the worksheet. |

**FIG. 11.2**
By entering a cell address into the Go To box, you can be instantly transported to the desired location in a worksheet.

# Moving Between Sheets

The fastest way to get to another sheet is to click the appropriate sheet tab at the bottom of Excel's workspace. If the desired tab is out of view, use the tab scroll buttons next to the sheet tabs to find it. From left to right, these buttons do the following: move to the first sheet in the workbook, move to the previous sheet (using the current sheet as a guide), move to the next sheet (also using the current sheet as a guide), and move to the last sheet in the workbook.

# Entering Worksheet Labels

One of the first things you want to do in creating a worksheet is to enter labels for the various columns and rows. These title labels show you (or anyone else entering data into your worksheet) where the various data types and calculations go. To enter these labels, do the following:

1. To begin labeling the columns across the top of the screen, select the first cell you want to enter a label in.
2. Enter the title you want to give to the first column of your worksheet.
3. Press Tab to label another column, or press Enter to move to the next line and begin labeling the rows.
4. Press Enter after each row title is typed.

**N O T E**  If some of your labels extend beyond the edge of a cell, see the section "Resizing Cells with AutoFit" in Chapter 13, "Using Excel's Automatic Features and Charting Facility," to see how to rectify the problem. ▦

# Entering Numbers into Excel

The next step in creating a worksheet is to fill in your labeled columns and rows with appropriate numbers. Simply activate the cell into which you want to place data by clicking it and enter the appropriate number. You can use the keystrokes presented earlier in Table 7.1 to move from one cell to another.

> **CAUTION**
>
> What you see in Excel is not always what you get. Watch the formatting of your number cells.

▶ **See** "Formatting Numbers," **p. 144**

# Selecting Cells

You select a cell by clicking it. To select a range of Excel cells, choose from these options:

▦ To select a large range of on-screen cells, click the first cell, hold the mouse button down, and drag it until all desired cells are highlighted (see Figure 11.3). This is perhaps the fastest way to select a large range of on-screen cells.

▦ To select a large range of cells that extend off the screen, click the first cell, use the scroll bars to find the last cell in the range, and press and hold the Shift key while you click the last cell.

▦ You may also use the keyboard to select cell ranges. Click the first cell to activate it, press and hold the Shift key, and use the arrow keys to highlight the desired area.

**FIG. 11.3**
Click the first cell you want to select and drag it until the entire range you want to select is highlighted as shown.

Select All button ┘

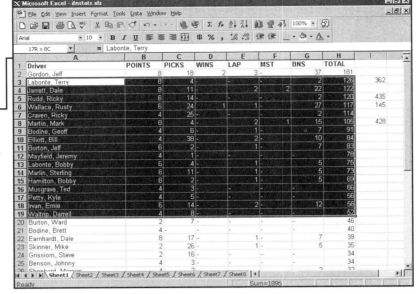

- Selecting nonadjacent cells involves clicking the first cell, holding down the Ctrl key, and then clicking additional cells.

- Select all the cells in a worksheet by clicking the Select All button, which is a blank button located above the row numbers and to the left of the column letter headers (refer to Figure 11.3).

- To select an entire row or column of cells, click the heading for the desired row or column.

# Editing Cell Contents

To edit the contents of an Excel cell, follow these steps:

1. Select the cell you want to edit.

2. Enter Edit mode by double-clicking the cell, pressing F2, or clicking the formula box.

3. If you use one of the first two methods, the insertion point appears at the beginning of the cell. If you use the formula bar, the insertion point appears there instead.

4. The keys work differently in Edit mode. For example, the left- and right-arrow keys move through the cell one character at a time instead of shifting you over an entire cell. Likewise, Home and End take you to the beginning and end of the cell, respectively.

5. Insert or delete characters as you would in any other Office 97 application.

 6. When finished editing, select the Enter button (check mark) next to the formula bar, or press the Enter key.

7. To abort the edit, press Esc or click the Cancel (x) button next to the formula bar.
8. Finally Excel returns to Ready mode, enabling you to continue with data entry or formatting.

# Copying, Cutting, and Pasting Excel Data

Excel's Copy, Cut, and Paste functions are very similar to those found in other Office 97 applications. To copy or move a range of cells, do the following:

1. Select the cell or range of cells you want to copy or move.

> **CAUTION**
>
> For now, these techniques should be used to move data only, not formulas. Although you can use these methods with formulas, there can be significant consequences. Read the section "Moving and Copying Cells Containing Formulas," later in this chapter, before trying these steps on formulas.

2. To copy the data, choose Edit, Copy. To move the cell(s), choose Edit, Cut.

   A moving dashed line, called a marquee, appears around the selected range.
3. Click the destination cell.
4. Press Enter to copy or paste the cell(s) in the new location. This returns Excel to the Ready mode.

5. If you want to copy the range of cells repeatedly, simply click the destination cell and choose Edit, Paste instead of pressing Enter. This keeps you in Move Data mode until you press Esc after the last copy or move.

Part<br>**II**<br>Ch<br>**11**

# Moving or Copying Cells Using Drag and Drop

Drag and drop is perhaps the fastest and easiest way to manipulate data within a screen view. You can drag and drop data to a new location in Excel by doing the following:

1. Select the cell or cell range you want to move or copy.

N O T E  Because Excel's drag-and-drop feature does not use the Clipboard, you should consider using AutoFill (see Chapter 13, "Using Excel's Automatic Features and Charting Facility") or the method in the preceding section if you want to repeatedly copy a block of data.

2. Place the mouse pointer on the thick border of the selected data. This turns the pointer's cross into an arrow.
3. To move the highlighted cells, click the border and drag the cell or selection to the new destination.
4. To copy the selected cell(s), press and hold the Ctrl key while dragging the selection to its new destination.

# Moving and Copying Cells Containing Formulas

There are some special considerations to keep in mind when copying or moving cells with formulas. Two of the most important are presented here:

■ When you copy a formula cell, Excel has a feature that enables a formula to change relative to the location to which the formula is copied. For instance, if you copy the cell containing the formula for adding the numbers in your first column to the bottom of the second column, it totals the new numbers in the second column.

■ If you move a cell containing a formula, however, the cell references do not change. Therefore, if you move the formula cell for adding the numbers in your first column to the second column, the cell still displays the sum of the first column no matter what changes you make to the numbers above it.

# Inserting and Deleting Rows and Columns

If you need to insert or delete a row or column in your worksheet, do the following:

1. Select an entire row (Excel will add the new row above the selected row) or column (the new column will be inserted to the left of the one you selected) by selecting the appropriate number or letter. You may also select multiple rows or columns to add the same number of rows or columns to your worksheet. For example, if you select three rows, three rows will be inserted on top of the first row in the selected range.

2. Right-click the selection to open the shortcut menu pictured in Figure 11.4.

**FIG. 11.4**

Use Excel's shortcut menu to insert or delete elements of your worksheet.

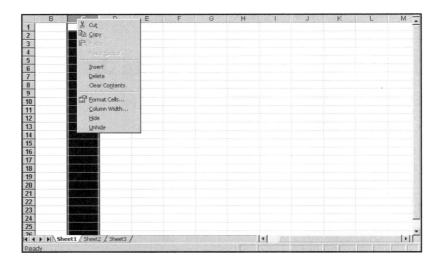

3. Choose Insert or Delete as desired.

# Inserting a Single Cell

You may find that you need to add a single cell to a worksheet without adding an entire row or column. Excel will add the new cell or cells above or to the left of the cell you selected for the insert function. To do this, follow these steps:

1. Select the cell location where you want to insert the new blank cells. You can add multiple blank cells by selecting the same number of cells as you want to insert.
2. Choose Insert, Cells.
3. Click Shift cells right or Shift cells down.

# Adding and Deleting Worksheets

You can add a single worksheet by choosing Insert, Worksheet. The new worksheet will be inserted after the current worksheet. If you want to add multiple worksheets, hold down the Shift key, and then click the number of worksheet tabs you want to add in the open workbook. When you've made your selection, choose Insert, Worksheet.

Deleting a worksheet from your workbook is also a simple task. To select the worksheets to be deleted, see Table 11.2.

Part
II

Ch
11

### Table 11.2   Selecting a Worksheet in Excel

| To Select This | Do This |
|---|---|
| A single sheet | Click the sheet tab. |
| Two or more adjacent sheets | Click the tab for the first sheet, hold down the Shift key, and then click the tab for the last sheet. |
| Two or more nonadjacent sheets | Click the tab for the first sheet, and then hold down the Ctrl key and click the tabs for the other sheets. |
| All sheets in a workbook | Right-click a sheet tab, and then click Select All Sheets on the shortcut menu. |

After the sheets have been selected, you can delete them by choosing Edit, Delete Sheet.

# Copying and Moving Worksheets

To move or copy worksheets between workbooks, follow these steps:

1. To move or copy sheets to another existing workbook, open the workbook that will receive the sheets.

2. Move to the workbook that contains the sheets you want to move or copy, and then select the sheets as shown earlier in Table 11.2 in the previous section.

3. Choose Edit, Move or Copy Sheet.

4. In the To Book box, choose the workbook into which you want to move or copy the sheets. You can move or copy the selected sheets to a new workbook by clicking New Book.

5. In the Before Sheet box, choose the sheet before which you want to insert the moved or copied sheets.

6. To copy rather than move the sheets, choose the Create a Copy check box.

> **CAUTION**
>
> Use extreme caution when you move or copy sheets. Calculations or charts based on data on a worksheet might become inaccurate if you move the worksheet.

To rearrange the order of the worksheets in your current workbook, you can drag the selected sheets along the row of sheet tabs. To copy the sheets, hold down the Ctrl key, and then drag the sheets; release the mouse button before you release the Ctrl key.

# Freezing Column and Row Labels

More commonly referred to as *freezing panes* by Excel users, this technique enables you to freeze the cells containing row or column names. This can be extremely useful when entering large amounts of data that would otherwise force these labels to scroll off the screen.

To freeze the pane at the top of the screen, select the row below the row you want to freeze. To freeze the left vertical pane, select the column to the right of the column you want to freeze. Or you can freeze both the upper and left panes by clicking the cell below and to the right of the area you want to freeze. After you've selected the desired parameters, choose Window, Freeze Panes.

# Calculating Simple Statistics on a Cell Range

Excel makes it easy to perform a simple analysis on a selection of cells. You can apply any of the following functions to a group of selected cells:

- SUM(range) gives you the total of the selected range.
- AVERAGE(range) calculates the numerical average for the selected range.

■ MAX(range) or MIN(range) returns the maximum or minimum value in a range.

■ COUNT(range) tells you how many nonzero cells are in the range.

To apply these functions to a range of cells, follow these steps:

1. Select the cell in which you want to place the result of the calculation.

2. Enter an equal sign (=), followed by one of the function names in the preceding bulleted list, and then enter an open parenthesis ((). The result should look like Figure 11.5. Notice that the formula box now carries the function name.

**FIG. 11.5**

In addition to the format of the function being shown in the active cell (the A16 you see in the figure is the address of the active cell), you will see it in the formula box at the top of the worksheet.

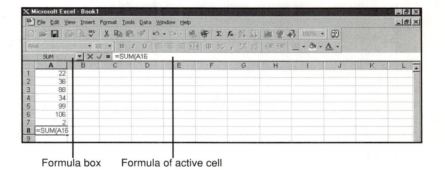

Formula box          Formula of active cell

3. Click the mouse on the first cell in the desired range. A moving dashed line appears around the cell.

4. While holding the mouse button down, drag it along to cover the desired range of cells, and then release the button. The cell range should now appear in the active cell and on the formula bar.

> **CAUTION**
>
> If you're placing the result of the calculation right below the selected range, be certain you haven't accidentally selected the formula destination cell as well. Doing so will give you a circular reference error, which will result in you having to go back and reselect the cell range.

5. Place a closing parenthesis ()) at the end of the range to complete the formula.

6. Press Enter to see the result.

# Applying More Complex Functions

In addition to enabling you to perform basic calculations on a selected range of data, Excel guides you through a number of complex functions using the Formula Palette.

To apply a complex formula, do the following:

1. Select the formula's destination cell.

2. Choose Insert, Function or press the Function button on the Standard toolbar to bring up the Paste Function dialog box (see Figure 11.6).

**FIG. 11.6**

The Paste Function box gives you quick access to the numerous function categories and function names available in Excel.

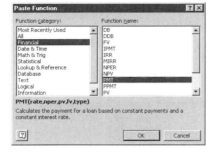

**N O T E**  You can access the Function Palette by pressing the Edit Function button on the Formula Bar and then clicking the Formula box's drop-down list arrow to see a list of functions. If the function you're looking for doesn't appear on that initial drop-down list, you need to choose More Functions to get to the Paste Function box shown in Figure 11.6. The preceding steps are merely a shortcut. The alternate method for accessing the Formula Palette described here is best used to quickly access the palette for the most recently used function. This eliminates the need to pick through the various categories and function names in the Paste Function box. ▓

3. Select a category from the Function Category list.

4. In the Function Name box, choose the desired function. If you're not sure which one you really want, click one and view its description in the gray area below the windows.

5. After you've made your selection, click OK.

6. The Formula Palette displays the arguments you need to enter for the function (see Figure 11.7) and an explanation of the active argument box.

7. Enter the appropriate number or cell address for each argument.

 Do not use formatted numbers as part of your arguments; instead use arithmetic expressions. For instance, to select 8 percent as the Rate in the PMT Formula Palette, enter **.08**. If 8 percent is the annual percentage rate, enter **.08/12**. Likewise, commas should be omitted in large numbers because commas are used as separators in a formula.

8. After all the arguments have been entered, click OK to see the result displayed in the selected cell.

**FIG. 11.7**
The PMT Formula Palette helps you calculate loan payments even if you can't remember all the formula elements needed to do so.

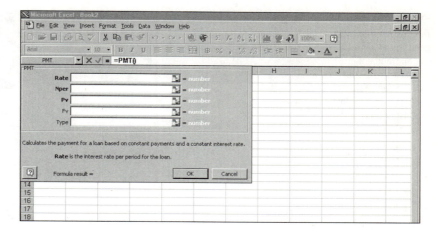

# Supplying Headers or Footers for Your Worksheets

Excel 97 comes with a number of preset headers and footers. To apply one of these, do the following:

1. Click the worksheet you want to apply the headers or footers to.

2. Choose View, Header and Footer.

3. Choose the Header/Footer tab.

4. In the Header or Footer box, click the drop-down arrow and select the header or footer you want (see Figure 11.8).

5. Click the Customized Header or Customized Footer button to build your own header or footer (see Figure 11.9).

6. Click OK to apply the header or footer.

**FIG. 11.8**
Click the drop-down arrow next to the header or footer box to choose a header or footer that most adequately meets your needs.

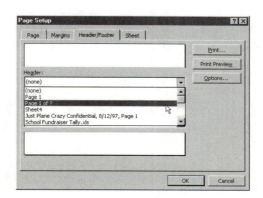

**FIG. 11.9**

The Custom Header box gives you an easy-to-use environment in which to create your own headers. A similar workspace is available for Customize Footers.

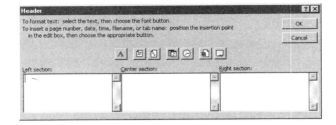

# CHAPTER 12

# Excel Formatting and Presentation

**N**ow that you are acquainted with the essential tasks and functions of Excel 97, it's time to take a look at spreadsheet formatting and presentation issues. These are the things that will make your work more readable and will project an image of professionalism. You learn how to make Excel text appear in a variety of styles and alter its placement on the page; you see how borders can help emphasize key elements of your spreadsheets; and you become familiar with one of the most important presentation elements—printing. ■

**Formatting cells**

From formatting numbers to creating borders, Excel has a number of alternatives.

**Text alignment**

Use Excel's multiple text alignment options to place text on the page in virtually any direction.

**Applying borders**

Make blocks of text stand out by applying stylistic borders.

**Printing worksheets**

Learn how to print exactly what you want the first time around.

# Formatting Numbers

Formatting numbers dictates how the selected numbers are displayed. For instance, Excel can display numbers as currency or percentages with the appropriate symbols. You can also program Excel to display numbers as integers (for example, 3.9 would appear as 4), but in all cases the raw numbers (not the formatted numbers which may be rounded) are used for formula calculations.

To format numbers in your worksheet, follow these steps:

1. Select the cell or range you want to format.
2. Choose Format, Cells to open the Format Cells dialog box pictured in Figure 12.1.

**FIG. 12.1**

The Format Cells dialog box presents a selection of formatting options. You can even view a sample of how the selected data will look in the Sample window.

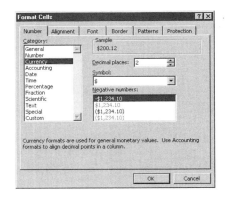

3. Select the Number tab if necessary.
4. Select the desired number format from the Category list.
5. Options for the selected category appear in the center of the dialog box. For example, Figure 12.1 shows some of the currency options available.
6. Select the desired option and then click OK to apply it to the selected range.

The quickest way to format numbers is to select them and press one of the buttons shown in Table 12.1.

**Table 12.1  Excel Number Formatting Icons**

| Button | Button Name | Function |
|---|---|---|
| **$** | Currency Style | Formats numbers in standard currency format. |
| **%** | Percent Style | Expresses cell contents as a percentage rather than a whole number. |

| Button | Button Name | Function |
|---|---|---|
| ![,] | Comma Style | Adds commas as needed to large numbers. |
| ![+.0 .00] | Increase Decimal | Take a range displayed with one decimal point and increase it to two decimal points. |
| ![.00 +.0] | Decrease Decimal | Take a range displayed with two decimal points and decrease it to one decimal point. |

# Copying Formats

There are times you'll want to copy a cell or range's formatting to another range of text. To do so, follow these steps:

1. Select a cell or range that has the formatting you want to copy.

2. Click the Format Painter button.
3. Select the cell or range you want to copy the formatting to.
4. To copy the same formatting to several locations, double-click the Format Painter button. When you finish copying the formatting, click the button again.

# Setting Cell Alignment

The Cell Alignment feature allows you to set the orientation of your cells' data. You can select cells and click the Align Left, Center, or Align Right button on the Formatting toolbar; or you can access more sophisticated options by following these steps:

1. Select the cell or range you want to align.
2. Choose Format, Cells to open the Format Cells dialog box.
3. Click the Alignment tab, which is shown in Figure 12.2.
4. Select from the following alignment options and click OK to apply them:

   - *Horizontal*. Allows you to determine how text is arranged from side to side within a cell. One option is Center Across Selection, which is perfect for centering worksheet titles.
   - *Vertical*. Use this option for multiline cells. You can specify how cells are aligned from top to bottom.
   - *Wrap Text*. This option is great for formatting long cell title data. Rather than create a wide cell, the Wrap Text option helps break the text into multiple lines.
   - *Orientation*. Another alternative for long text cells, Orientation allows you to rotate text to tighten a worksheet. See Figure 12.3 for an example of altered text orientation.

**FIG. 12.2**
From the Alignment tab you can select from a number of vertical and horizontal text alignment options.

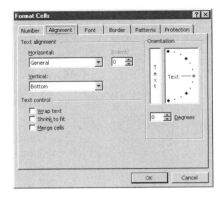

**FIG. 12.3**
This worksheet makes use of the Orientation text alignment option for its column labels. Note that cells can now overlap onto others where needed without being cut off.

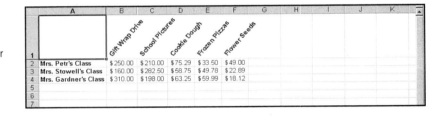

# Working with Fonts in Excel

You can change fonts, type style, and size in Excel just as you can in Word.

**TIP** To quickly change text attributes, use the Font and Size boxes on the Formatting toolbar to alter the text's font and size. In the case of fonts, use the drop-down list next to the Font box to make your selection. Selecting a size can be done via the drop-down list, or you can simply click the Size box and enter a type size even if it doesn't appear on the list.

To change the appearance of your Excel text, follow these steps:

1.  Select the range of cells you want to format.
2.  Choose Format, Cells to open the Format Cells dialog box.
3.  Select the Font tab as shown in Figure 12.4.
4.  Select your options in the various sections of the tab.
5.  Click OK to apply them.

**TIP** If you plan to convert your worksheet to a Web page, you may want to use colored fonts in selected locations to emphasize important information.

**FIG. 12.4**
Use the Font tab in the Format Cells dialog box to choose the font, type style, and size for your text.

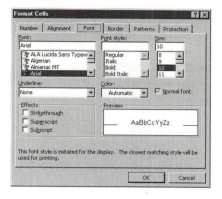

# Creating Borders in Excel

One way to dress up a worksheet for printing or to emphasize certain data is to apply borders to the desired range or cell. To apply a border in Excel, follow these steps:

1. Select the cell or range you want to place a border around.
2. Choose Format, Cells to open the Format Cells dialog box.
3. Click the Border tab to access the Border options shown in Figure 12.5.

**FIG. 12.5**
The Border tab lets you choose from a variety of border line styles and colors.

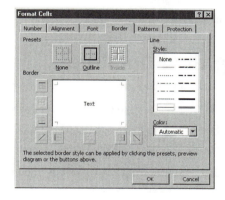

4. Choose from the options available, and then preview them in the Border box.
5. When you like what you see, click OK to apply the options.

# Printing Excel Worksheets

To print an Excel worksheet, do the following:

1. Select the range of cells you want to print.

2.  Choose File, Print to open the Print dialog box shown in Figure 12.6.

3.  Select the printer you want to send the output to.

**FIG. 12.6**

The Print dialog box allows you to specify which parts of the worksheet you want to print—the selected text, the entire workbook, or the active sheet.

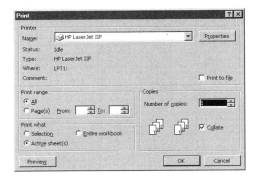

4.  Select which part of the workbook you want to print. The active worksheet means that only the tab currently displayed will be printed whereas the entire workbook means everything on each tab of the file.

5.  Select the number of copies to be printed.

6.  Click OK to send the output to the printer.

# Setting and Clearing the Print Area

To print a specific section of a worksheet, follow these steps for the best results:

1.  Select the area of the worksheet you want to print.

2.  Choose File, Print Area, Set Print Area to save the chosen range.

3.  Choose File, Print, then click OK; press the Print button, or press Ctrl+P.

Excel will remember the specified print area until you clear it by choosing File, Print Area, Clear Print Area. To confirm that Excel will print what you expect it to, enter Print Preview mode.

# Getting the Output You Want by Setting Page Setup Options

Because printing worksheets that actually look good can be a daunting task, you may want to use the Page Setup and Print Preview options in cases where making a good impression is of primary importance.

To work with Excel's Page Setup options, follow these steps:

1. Choose File, Page Setup to open the Page Setup dialog box shown in Figure 12.7.

**FIG. 12.7**

Use the Sheet tab of the Page Setup dialog box to select the print quality of your output, and if needed when the worksheet is printed, gridlines and row and column headers as well.

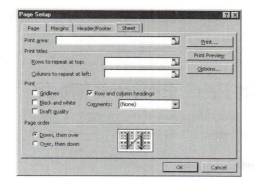

2. Select the Page tab (see Figure 12.8) to begin setting the options and work your way through all the other tabs.

**FIG. 12.8**

Be sure to set the page orientation of your document in the Orientation section since many worksheets look better in landscape than in portrait orientation.

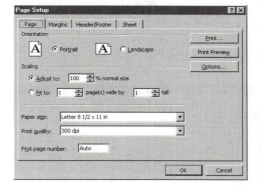

3. Some of the Page Setup options you want to be sure to address are described in the following list:

- On the Page tab, select Portrait or Landscape for your document's orientation. Many worksheets look best in landscape mode.

- Select Fit To on the Page tab to squeeze your worksheet into as little space as possible. It's similar in concept to Word's Shrink to Fit feature, which tries to fit a few lines of stray text onto one less page of paper.

- Use the Margins tab to place your worksheet in an appealing position. The easiest way to do this is to specify that the worksheet be centered both Horizontally and Vertically.

- Use the Header/Footer tab to apply a header or footer to your output. You can select from a variety of predefined headers and footers or create your own.

▶ **See** "Supplying Headers or Footers for Your Worksheets," **p. 141**

- To have the column headings printed on each page of a worksheet, go to the Sheet tab and specify that columns be repeated on each page. This is a must-have feature for long worksheets.

4. From the Sheet tab, you can Print the worksheet, enter Print Preview mode, tell Excel to print repeating title rows or columns, turn gridlines on and off, turn column and row headings on or off, and add headers or footers.

# Setting Margins in Print Preview Mode

One of the most common adjustments people want to make to their worksheets before sending them to the printer is to reposition the margins. You can save time by doing this in Print Preview mode:

▶ **See** "Preview Before You Print," **p. 38**

1. Choose File, Print Preview or click the Print Preview button on the Standard toolbar. The Print Preview window appears.
2. Click the Print Preview screen.
3. Click the Margins button to see indicators of where your margins fall (see Figure 12.9).
4. Click the margin and column indicators and drag them to reposition the worksheet on the page.
5. Click Print to send your creation to the printer.

**FIG. 12.9**
Click one of the margin lines to drag the worksheet to the position you want.

Margin indicators ——

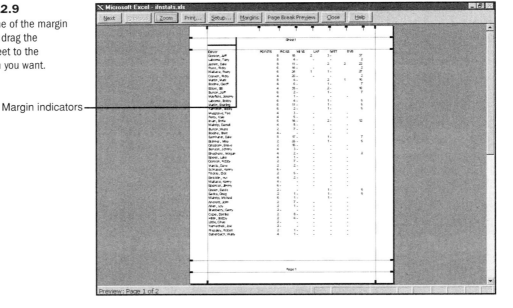

# Using Excel's Automatic Features and Charting Facility

In this chapter, you learn how to add columns and rows quickly by using the AutoSum feature, and you can make your worksheets look good by using AutoFormat. You see how you can visualize your data through the use of Excel's powerful Chart Wizard. You can even map your data with an easy-to-use mapping feature. Now you can clearly visualize your company's success in each state or country.

**Using AutoSum to add columns in your worksheet**

By pressing the AutoSum button, you can accurately add columns or rows within seconds in Excel.

**Filling cells with data automatically**

With Excel's AutoFill feature, you can have Excel copy cell formulas and their relative cell references to multiple columns in seconds, and you can even make Excel type certain row and column headers for you.

**Using AutoFormat**

Use AutoFormat to create professional-looking worksheets within seconds.

**Visualizing data with Chart Wizard**

Use Excel's powerful Chart Wizard to produce just about any kind of graph or chart to illustrate your data.

**Map your data**

Use Excel's mapping feature to track sales and other information in each state.

# Adding Your Data with AutoSum

Adding numbers is one of the most common things people want to do with their spreadsheet data. This section shows you how to get quick results with Excel's AutoSum feature.

To apply AutoSum to a range of cells, follow these steps:

1. Activate the cell in which you want to place the sum of the information added together.

2. Click the AutoSum button on the Standard toolbar. Excel tries to guess which data you want to add (see Figure 13.1).

**FIG. 13.1**

Excel has "guessed" here that the cells above the AutoSum entry are what to add.

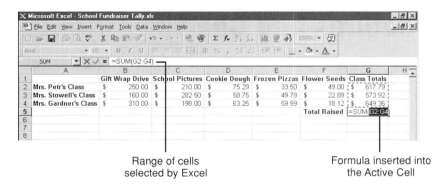

Range of cells selected by Excel

Formula inserted into the Active Cell

3. If Excel has selected the correct range of data, press Enter to apply the formula to the active cell.

4. To select a different range, simply select the first cell in the row or column of the desired numbers and drag the mouse to select the rest of the cells you want to add.

5. When the hash marks appear around the desired data range, click the AutoSum button to apply the formula. The total of the numbers you selected appears in the active cell.

**NOTE** You may want to label your sum by inserting a title in an adjacent cell. This will clarify the number to people seeing your worksheet for the first time.

# Resizing Cells with AutoFit

Although you have a variety of formatting options available to you in Excel, AutoFit is great for quick cell resizing. AutoFit makes the column width fit perfectly to the contents of the selected cell. Or if you select the whole column, it adjusts to fit the longest cell in the column.

## Using AutoFit One Column at a Time

Because rows automatically resize themselves as needed, you'll find that you use AutoFit most frequently to resize columns. To resize a column, do the following:

1. Move the mouse pointer to the border between the column header and the next column header to the right. The mouse pointer turns into a vertical line with a double arrow running crossways through it.

2. Double-click this location to resize the column on the left to fit the longest entry.

If using a keyboard is more comfortable to you, try clicking the letter head of the column you want to adjust, and then choose Format, Column, AutoFit Selection. Excel adjusts the column width of the selected text to fit the longest line exactly.

## Resizing a Range of Cells with AutoFit

Using AutoFit on a group of columns is almost as easy as applying it to a single column. Just follow these steps:

1. Click the first column header and drag the mouse pointer through the last column you want to resize.

2. Confirm that the desired range of columns is highlighted.

3. Double-click the border between any two of the selected column headers to resize the entire selected area.

# AutoFilling in a Number Series

In addition to numbering columns or rows, Excel's AutoFill feature can create a series of cells containing numbers that are incremented by virtually any specified amount. To do so, follow these steps:

1. Select the first cell in your range and enter the desired number.

2. If only one number is specified, AutoFill will number the adjacent columns or rows by increments of one.

3. If you want to have columns labeled 2, 4, 6, 8 for instance, place a 2 in the first cell and a 4 in the next cell (or a 5 and 10—Excel will pick up the pattern).

4. Select the two cells containing the numbers.

5. Click the AutoFill handle to the right to number column headers by the designated increment, or down to number the rows.

6. Release the mouse button; the desired numbers have been entered for you.

Part

**II**

Ch

**13**

# Filling a Text Series with AutoFill

AutoFill does much more than accurately copy cell formulas and their relative cell references. It can recognize a number of text patterns, including:

- Months of the year
- Abbreviated months of the year

- Days of the week
- Abbreviated days of the week
- Quarter names (notated as Qtr 1, Qtr 2, and so on)

Using AutoFill means potentially faster, more consistent column and row labeling because Excel can literally type for you. To instruct AutoFill to fill out a text series, follow these steps:

1. Select the cell in which you'd like to begin the text series.
2. Enter the first member of the text series (for example January, Monday, Qtr 1, and so on).
3. Click the AutoFill handle and drag it across the number of cells you want Excel to fill in for you.
4. Release the mouse button to have Excel fill in the selected fields (see Figure 13.2).

**FIG. 13.2**

By simply typing January and dragging the AutoFill handle eleven cells to the right, each month of the year is automatically inserted by Excel.

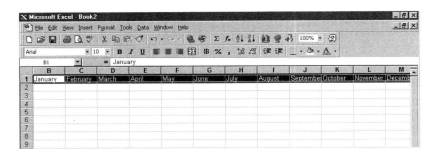

The following table gives examples of formats in which Excel will recognize patterns.

| If You Type | AutoFill Completes |
|---|---|
| **Numbers** | |
| 1,2 | 3,4,5 |
| 2.1, 2.2 | 2.3, 2.4, 2.5 |
| **Text Entries** | |
| Feb, Jun | Oct, Feb, Jun |
| Q1, Q3 | Q1, Q3, Q1 |
| a, b, c | a, b, c, a, b, c |
| **Calendar Entries** | |
| 1-Jul, 15-Jul | 29-Jul, 12-Aug |

# Incrementing Dates with AutoFill

To increment dates with AutoFill, do the following:

1. Select the first cell in the range.
2. Enter the desired date or dates as needed.
3. If only one cell is used, Excel increments the dates by one.
4. If you want to move by weeks, for instance, place one date (1/1/98) in the first cell, and another one week later (1/8/98) in the second cell.
5. Select the cell or cells, and drag the AutoFill handle the desired distance and direction.
6. Release the mouse button, and the incremented dates appear.

## AutoFill as a Formula Cell Copying Shortcut

AutoFill is a great way to copy cell formulas while appropriately modifying cell references. It accomplishes the same thing as copying the formula cell, only the process is shortened with AutoFill.

To copy a cell formula to adjacent locations, do the following:

1. Select the cell you want to copy (for example, the cell containing the AutoSum formula).
2. Look for the little black box at the bottom right corner of the highlighted box (see Figure 13.3). This is called the AutoFill Handle.

AutoSum formula

**FIG. 13.3**
Click the AutoFill handle and drag it in the desired direction to copy the selected cell formula.

AutoFill handle —

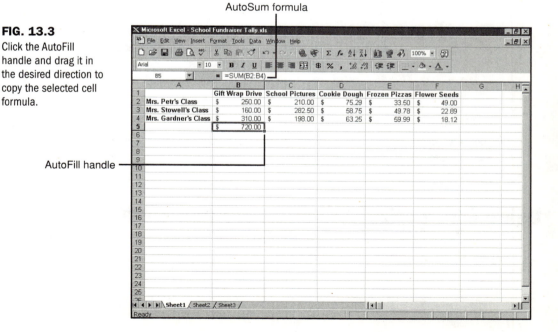

Part
II

Ch
13

3. Click the AutoFill handle and drag it down or to the right to the desired direction.

4. Release the mouse button to copy the formula into the desired cell(s).

Notice that the copied formula cells now base their calculations on the numbers above them.

▶ **See** "Copying, Cutting, and Pasting Excel Data" **p. 135**

# Make Your Worksheets Look Good Using AutoFormat

If you're in a hurry but still need to make a good impression, consider using AutoFormat to make your worksheets look their best.

To apply AutoFormat, do the following:

1. Select the range of cells you want to format.

2. Choose Format, AutoFormat to bring up the AutoFormat dialog box pictured in Figure 13.4.

**FIG. 13.4**
Use the AutoFormat dialog box to choose a format for your table, and then preview it in the Sample box.

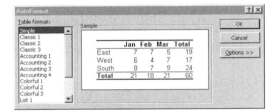

3. Click the Options button to bring up a list of formatting elements. Insert and delete the check mark next to each element to toggle the various formatting options on and off. You can preview these in the Sample window.

4. When you see a result you like, click OK to apply it.

**CAUTION**

Before applying AutoFormat to a range of cells containing formulas and cell references, be sure to save your worksheet so you can verify that AutoFormatting has maintained the integrity of your data.

# Using Chart Wizard to Visualize Your Data

Creating a dynamic, professional-looking chart can speak volumes for your data because it shows, not tells, the reader what's going on.

To create a chart of your data on the current worksheet, do the following:

1. Select the range of data you want to chart.

2. Press the ChartWizard button on the Standard toolbar to guide you through the process.

3. The first step in using the Chart Wizard is to select a chart type. Start with the Standard Types tab. Select a chart type and subtype of interest; preview the result by choosing the Press and Hold to View Sample button.

4. If you don't see anything you like there, try the Custom Types tab shown in Figure 13.5. The selected chart type automatically appears based on your data.

**FIG. 13.5**
The Custom Types tab in ChartWizard lets you preview your data in the selected chart's format on-the-fly.

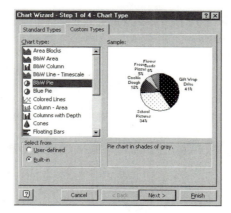

5. Accept the data range to be used by clicking Next.

6. Step 3 of Chart Wizard enables you to set a number of options:

   - *Titles tab*. Allows you to assign a title to your chart and various parts of it where applicable.

   - *Legend tab*. Enables you to place a legend by your chart. You can even select the legend's position based on your page's layout.

   - *Data Labels tab*. Lets you choose how your data is labeled—by value, by percent, by name, or a combination thereof.

7. Step 4 asks where you'd like to place your chart—in its own sheet or embedded in the current sheet.

8. Click Finish to place the chart.

# Mapping Your Data in Excel

Want to track your company's sales in each state? Want to show your board of directors the distribution of your membership graphically? Excel 97's mapping feature can help.

Part

II

Ch

13

To map your data, do the following:

1. Make sure you have data the mapping feature can use. It needs a list of states spelled out or abbreviated, and a number assigned to each where appropriate. For instance, you may have used Excel to group and count your members in each state. Place the states in one column, and their respective numbers next to them in the adjacent column.

2. Select the range of cells that meet the criteria in step 1.

3. Click the Map button on the Standard toolbar.

4. The mouse pointer changes to a crosshair. Drag the mouse across a rectangular range to select a spot for the map.

5. If Excel can't determine which map should be used based on the values of your data, the Multiple Maps Available dialog box appears asking you to select a map for Excel to build. Make the appropriate choice.

6. Your customized map will appear, along with the Microsoft Map Control dialog box (see Figure 13.6) for fine-tuning its appearance.

**FIG. 13.6**
Double-click the map to open the Map Control dialog box.

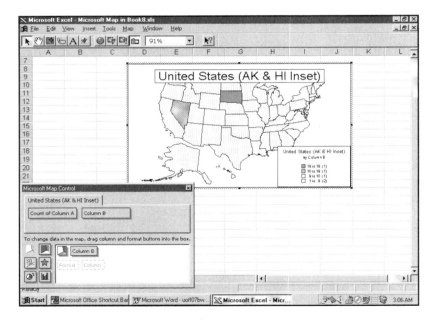

**N O T E**   Should you decide to edit any of the data used for the map, change the table as usual, and then right-click the map and select Refresh Data. The map will be updated instantly.

# Moving and Sizing the Chart or Map

If you need to move or resize your chart or map, follow these steps:

1. Select the chart or map by clicking it. Small black selection handles appear around the object's parameter.

2. Position the mouse pointer over a handle, at which point it will turn into a double-headed arrow.

3. Click and drag the handle in the desired direction to make the object larger or smaller.

4. To move the object, click inside its boundaries and drag it to a new location.

Part

II

Ch

13

# CHAPTER 14

# Excel Databases and the Small Business Edition's Financial Manager

If you own Office 97's Standard or Small Business Edition, you may want to use Excel as your database program. Even if you have Access, you may find Excel's database capabilities quicker and easier to work with. This chapter shows you how to get the most out of Excel as a database.

**Excel as a database**

Standard and Small Business Edition owners can learn how to use Excel as a database instead of investing additional funds in a special database program.

**Using AutoFilter**

Use AutoFilter and Excel's data consolidation features to quickly and powerfully manipulate data

**Working with pivot tables**

Learn how to use Excel's Pivot-Table Wizard to analyze your data.

**Import live data from the Web to your Excel workbooks**

Get stock quotes and other information directly from the Web.

**Further manipulate your data with the Small Business Financial Manager**

If you use Excel as part of the Small Business Edition (SBE), use SBE's reporting tools to create balance sheets and other business reports, as well as run small business-specific what-if scenarios.

# Creating an Excel Database

If you have the Standard or Small Business Edition of Office 97, you won't have Access to use as a database program. That certainly doesn't mean you're without database capabilities. Excel has the capability to create and manipulate simple databases of its own.

The first thing you'll need to do before creating a database is to decide what types of information (or fields) you want to maintain for each record or entry. After you've determined that, you can begin creating your database as follows:

1.  Click the New button on the Standard toolbar to open a fresh workbook if necessary.

2.  Enter the field names in row 1, one per cell.

3.  If you want these field headers to be visible no matter where you are in the worksheet, select the row below the field header row and choose Window, Freeze Panes. Now the field headers will always be visible to simplify accurate data entry.

4.  Save your database by clicking the Save button on the Standard toolbar.

# Using a Data Form to Enter Excel Database Records

Excel's Data Form feature helps you enter, edit, and find Excel database data. The Data Form is a dialog box that holds text boxes for up to 33 database fields (see Figure 14.1)

**FIG. 14.1**
Use the vertical scroll bar to the right of the text boxes to move from one record to another.

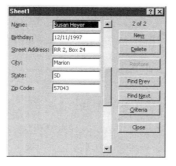

To use a Data Form, follow these steps:

1.  Select any cell within the database. If there is no data yet, enter the column headers from which Excel can build the data form.

2.  Click Data, Form to bring up the data form shown in Figure 14.1.

3.  To add records, click the New button, and then enter the data in the appropriate field. Press Tab to move to the next field, or simply click inside the desired text box.

4.  Choose one of two ways to save the new record:

    *   Click the New button to automatically save the current record and enter a new one.

    *   Click Close to save your work and close the data form.

# Editing Data with the Data Form

Use the Data Form to find and edit records by doing the following:

1. Select a cell inside the database.

2. Choose Data, Form to open the data form (refer to Figure 14.1).

3. Click the Criteria button to bring up an empty data form (notice that the word Criteria appears above the column of buttons).

4. Type in the criteria you want to search for in one or more of the text boxes.

5. Click the Find Prev or Find Next buttons until you locate the desired record.

6. Edit the record by changing the desired text box.

7. If you decide to return to the original record after changing some of the fields, simply choose Remove before saving the record.

8. To delete the record permanently, choose Delete.

9. When you've finished, choose Close.

10. Save your workbook.

# Sorting Excel Database Records

Knowing how to sort your database can help you take advantage of even more advanced Excel functions, like subtotaling a group of records or counting entries that meet a specific criteria. You don't have to have a true Excel database to use these functions; any spreadsheet formatted as a series of rows can be sorted.

Sort your database by following these steps:

1. Select any cell in the database you want to sort.

2. Choose Data, Sort to open the Sort dialog box (see Figure 14.2).

**FIG. 14.2**
The Sort dialog box allows you to sort up to three of your database fields in ascending or descending order.

Part
II

Ch
14

3. Click the Sort By drop-down list box to choose the field you want to sort by. If you haven't given the columns field names, you can select the column by the column label.

4. Select Ascending or Descending to specify the sort order for that field.

5. Repeat the process if necessary by using the Then By boxes.

6. Click OK to sort the database as specified.

You may also perform a simpler sort if your database meets any of these criteria:

▪ The database contains only two column headers/fields.

▪ The column you want to sort by comes either first or last in order.

To perform one of these sorts, do the following:

1. Select the column header you want to sort your data by.

2. Highlight the remainder of the database table.

> **CAUTION**
>
> If you can't highlight the entire data table after selecting the desired sort column, you should abort the sort and perform it using a Sort box. Continuing at this point would jumble your records—some of the fields would be sorted, while others would remain in their original positions.

3. Click the Sort Ascending or Sort Descending button on the Standard toolbar.

4. Be sure to save your newly sorted table before closing or exiting.

# Using AutoFilter to Find Specific Data

There are times you may want to extract records that meet specific criteria. For instance, maybe you want to send checkup notices to families whose pet is due for vaccinations during a specified month.

To select records in an Excel database, follow these steps:

1. Select a cell within the database.

2. Choose Data, Filter, AutoFilter. A drop-down arrow appears to the right of each column header (see Figure 14.3).

3. Click the drop-down arrow next to the column you want to filter, and then select the desired filter option. You can choose from the following:

   • You can select only records containing one of the field's listings. For example, you can extract all the records of people who live in South Dakota.

   • You may also choose only records left blank in the chosen field.

   • By selecting Top 10, you can filter the most common values in the selected field.

- Choose All to remove any filters from the selected field.
- By choosing Custom, you can use the Custom AutoFilter dialog box shown in Figure 14.4 to specify multiple criteria for advanced filtering.

**FIG. 14.3**

To the right of each cell is a drop-down arrow to a list box containing an entry for each different element in that column. Select the filter option you want to use from this list.

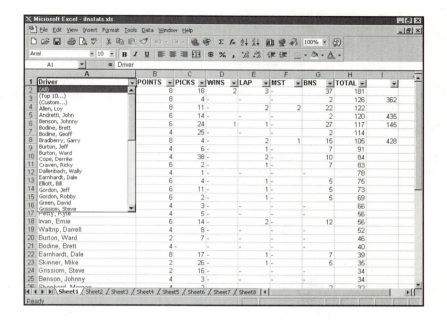

**FIG. 14.4**

Use the Custom AutoFilter to select multiple filtering criteria. For instance, you could view customers from a particular ZIP Code, or search for people expressing an interest in your products from a particular state.

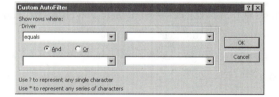

4. You will see only the selected records in the database, which you can edit or print.
5. To remove the filter, choose Data, Filter, AutoFilter to remove the check mark next to AutoFilter.

# Grouping and Subtotaling Your Database

Excel will also group and count data in your database. This allows you to count the number of people from each state, for example.

To group and then count selected data in your database, do the following:

1.  Select a cell within the database.
2.  Sort the database as directed earlier in "Sorting Excel Database Records" so that all the records are grouped according to the field you want to group and subtotal.
3.  Choose Data, Subtotals to bring up the Subtotals dialog box (see Figure 14.5).

**FIG. 14.5**

Use the Subtotals dialog box to count or average like data, among other functions.

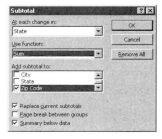

4.  In the At Each Change In drop-down list, choose the field you want Excel to group your records by.
5.  In the Use Function drop-down list, specify which function you want to perform on the data.
6.  In the Add Subtotal To list, select the same field you chose to group your data by.
7.  Choose OK to subtotal your database.
8.  To remove the grouping, choose Data, Subtotals, Remove All. Your database will return to normal.

# Working with Natural Language Formulas and Ranges

With Excel 97, working with formulas and ranges is more intuitive than ever before. Excel can now take the existing labels for both rows and columns and use them to reference the values they label. This is referred to as *Natural Language*.

Let's take the mock budget presented in Figure 14.6 as an example. The active cell represents January's Student Loan payment, which carries with it a cell address of B6. With Excel's new Natural Language capabilities, you can get the same result by typing **=January student loan** into a cell.

**FIG. 14.6**
The active cell above can be referenced by using B6 or January student loan.

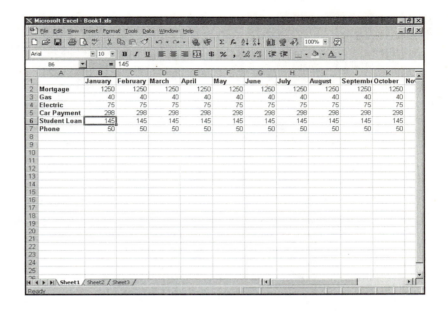

**N O T E**  Natural Language references are not case sensitive, so *student loan*, *Student Loan*, or even *Student loan* would work in the preceding example.

You can also apply a function to this capability. For instance, entering **=SUM(January)** in a cell will produce the total of the January bills in the example. Or use **=SUM(April)/2** to calculate a partner's share of the bills. There are definitely times when using this Natural Language will speed up your calculations, and for those of us who can remember column names better than cell addresses, it's a dream come true.

# Creating Pivot Tables to Summarize Data

Excel 97 gives you a simple way to summarize and compare data found in a spreadsheet or list. You can use a wizard to create a pivot table, which allows you to manipulate your data in all kinds of interactive relationships. Moreover, pivot tables can quickly be modified without altering the original formatting of your data.

To create a pivot table using Excel's PivotTable Wizard, follow these steps:

1. Choose Data, PivotTable Report to bring up Step 1 of the PivotTable Wizard.

2. Specify the type of data you want to analyze with your pivot table. Choose Microsoft Excel List or Database, and then click the Next button. Step 2 of the Wizard appears.

3. Specify the location of the list to be analyzed in the Range text box. You can either type the range address, or click the Cell Reference button to manually select the data with the mouse. Step 3 of the Wizard appears (see Figure 14.7).

**FIG. 14.7**

The field labels of your list will appear in boxes on the right side of the dialog box. You can drag them into various positions to analyze data in a variety of ways.

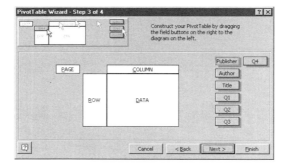

4. Set the layout of your pivot table by dragging the field names to the desired position.

   Fields moved to the Row area appear in each row of the pivot table. Fields dragged into the Column section appear across the top of the table. Fields in the Page area filter the data using a drop-down list box from which you can select various parameters. Finally, a Field placed in the Data section is totaled, averaged, or whatever function you define by grouping the elements in the Row, Column, or Page areas.

**T I P**   To change the function performed on the fields in the Data section, double-click the field's box, and choose the desired function from the list box. You may also hide specific values by accessing field information in this fashion.

5. Click Next to display the final step in the PivotTable Wizard.

6. Choose whether you want the pivot table to be included in a New worksheet or an Existing worksheet.

7. To apply formatting parameters or other options to your pivot table, click the Options button at the bottom of Step 4. After you've made your selections, click OK to return to the wizard.

8. Choose Finish to see the results (see Figures 14.8 and 14.9).

**T I P**   Is the Pivot Table menu in your way? Click its title bar (the blue bar at the top of its box) and drag it out of your way.

# Capturing Live Data from the Web

With Excel's Web Query feature, you can actually pull down data from the Web and analyze and manipulate it on your desktop.

The following steps show you how to capture stock quote data from the Internet, which you can use to monitor and track your own investment portfolio. You can find other queries by checking Microsoft's Web site at **http://www.microsoft.com/excel/webquery/ samples.htm**.

**FIG. 14.8**
Take a simple list like this....

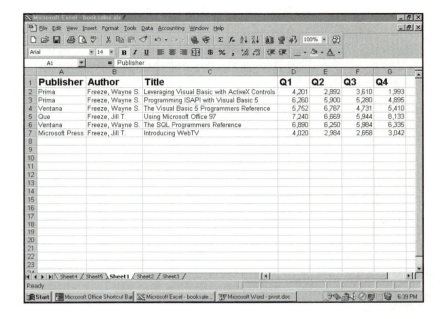

**FIG. 14.9**
...and turn it into a data analysis tool like this! Click the drop-down list box as shown here to instantly filter your data without modifying the original document.

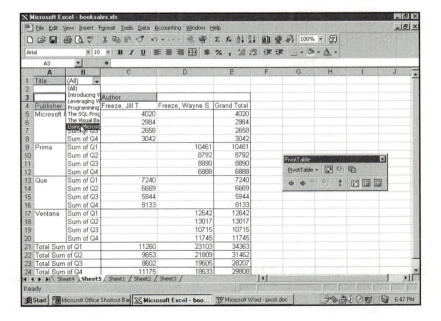

1. Make sure you have an active Internet connection.
2. Create a new Excel workbook.
3. Enter the stock quote symbols for the stocks you want to capture data for in column A.

4. Choose <u>D</u>ata, Get External <u>D</u>ata, Run <u>W</u>eb Query to bring up the Run Query dialog box (see Figure 14.10).

**FIG. 14.10**

Choose Multiple Stock Quotes by PC Quotes, Inc.

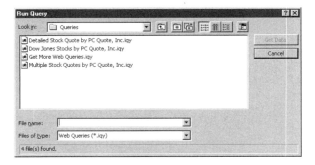

5. Double-click Multiple Stock Quotes by PC Quotes, Inc.iqy to load the necessary Web query.

 **T I P** If you're very proficient in HTML, you can customize or build your own Web queries. (See Que's *Special Edition Using HTML, Third Edition*.)

6. You'll see a Returning External Data to Microsoft Excel dialog box, which will ask you where you want to place the new data. Click the <u>E</u>xisting Worksheet option button, and then choose the Para<u>m</u>eters button.

7. In the Parameters dialog box, click the option button next to <u>G</u>et Data from the Following Cell.

8. Click on the worksheet and select the stock quotes listed in column A.

9. Click OK.

10. Click OK on the Returning External Data to Microsoft Excel dialog box. The program will pause for a few seconds while Excel retrieves the data.

11. The output in Figure 14.11 will appear.

12. Manipulate the data as you desire whether you chart it, add up the value of your holdings, or speculate on what you could earn if you invested more in a certain company.

13. Save the worksheet if desired.

# What Is Small Business Financial Manager 97?

If you or your business purchased Office 97's Small Business Edition, or if your new computer came with Office 97 Small Business Edition preinstalled, then chances are you've seen this program's icon floating around your desktop.

**FIG. 14.11**
Within seconds, Excel 97 will retrieve current quotes for the stocks you specified, and they'll be formatted for quick sorting, analysis, and filtering.

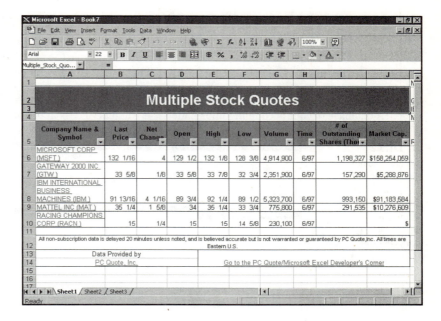

Microsoft's Small Business Financial Manager 97 (see Figure 14.12) is a companion Excel application designed especially for the needs of small businesses. It can take data from a variety of popular accounting packages and import it into Excel for complex analysis and charting; it can help businesses run What-If scenarios using Small Business Financial Manager's powerful wizards; and it can generate balance sheets, income statements, and several other reports using its Report wizard.

Here is a look at some of the basics of the financial manager—converting your accounting data and working with the program's Report and What-If wizards.

# Importing Accounting Data

To import accounting data, follow these steps:

1. Launch the Small Business Financial Manager.

**T I P**
Be sure to import your data *before* closing out a fiscal period.

2. Choose Accounting, Import Wizard from the menu bar to bring up the Import Wizard.
3. The first step asks whether you want to Import or Update your data. Make your selection, and then click Next.
4. Step two of the Import Wizard asks you where to look for the accounting files. You can specify a folder for it to search, or you can have it look through your entire system.

Part
**II**

Ch
**14**

5. The third step prompts you to select the data you want to import. Make your selection, and then click Next.

6. The final step in the Import Wizard asks you to choose the next action. You can Remap your accounting data, create a Financial Report, or run a What-If scenario.

7. Choose Remap Data to confirm that your accounts were imported properly.

A database of your accounting information is created in Access .mdb format.

**FIG. 14.12**
The Small Business Financial Manager's start-up screen enables you to access its features quickly and easily by clicking the Import, What-If Analysis, and Report buttons.

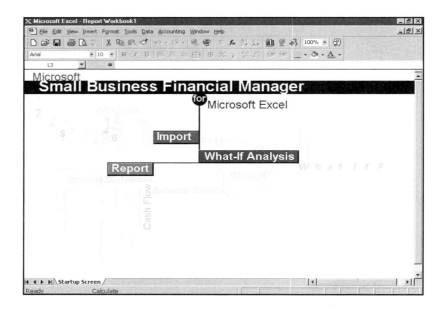

# Creating a Financial Report with Report Wizard

The Report wizard gives you enormous flexibility when it comes to generating reports based on your data. To create a report using the wizard, follow these steps:

1. Choose Accounting, Report Wizard from the menu bar to open the Report wizard.

**N O T E**  It's always tempting to try out a new toy (software programs included), but before going to all the work of importing your data to generate a financial report, you may want to review your accounting program's specifications to make sure it can't generate the same report internally.

2. The wizard asks you to select a Report and Company to work with. Click Next to move to Step 2.

3. In Step 2, you are asked to select a report type from the Report Types box. Make your selection, and then click Next to continue.

4. Select the End Date for the report in Step 3, and then click Next.

5. Click Finish. Small Business Financial Manager builds the selected report (see Figure 14.13).

**FIG. 14.13**
This Income Statement based on the fictitious Volcano Coffee Company shows you the high quality of output Microsoft's Small Business Financial Manager is capable of generating.

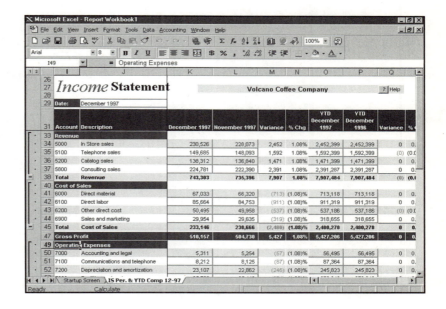

# Running What-If Scenarios Using the What-If Wizard

Strategic planning for any organization or business nearly always results in playing the What-If game. The Small Business Financial Manager makes it easy with its What-If Wizard. To use the What-If Wizard, do the following:

1. Choose Accounting, What-If Wizard to bring up the Perform a What-If Analysis dialog box.

2. The first step asks you to select a Company or database to perform the scenario on. Double-click its name, and then click Next to continue.

3. To create a new what-if scenario, click New, and in the New box type a name for the scenario. The name may be up to 50 characters long.

4. Select the starting date for the scenario in the Begin date box.

5. In the End date box, choose the ending date for the scenario.

6. Click Finish.

7. Click Save when prompted to save your workbook.

Part
II

Ch
14

**TIP**  To make sure that the Small Business Financial Manager can find your scenario again, do not change the name assigned to it by the What-If Wizard in the Save Scenario Workbook As dialog box.

# CHAPTER 15

# Creating, Editing, and Running a PowerPoint Presentation

**P**owerPoint is Office 97's tool for creating professional quality presentations to be viewed on the computer, the Internet, on paper, even on transparencies via overhead projector.

If you need to do a first-class job in record time, PowerPoint's wizards and templates are just what you're looking for. This chapter helps you get started by showing you all of your options for building a presentation to meet your needs.

**Picking the best PowerPoint design tool**

Get familiar with the various presentation design options available in PowerPoint so you can choose the best one for the job.

**Getting to know the screen elements**

Get acquainted with the location and terms used for PowerPoint's critical screen elements.

**Using the AutoContent Wizard**

PowerPoint's AutoContent Wizard is the fastest way to produce a high-quality presentation.

**Saving a PowerPoint presentation**

Learn how to save your work in PowerPoint.

**Inserting, deleting, and moving slides**

Learn the techniques needed to add, delete, and move slides within a presentation.

**Choosing a color scheme**

Use PowerPoint's features to add color and life to your presentations.

**Running your slide show**

Learn how to program your presentation's slide display times.

# Picking the Right Tool to Help You Design Your Presentation

PowerPoint gives you four ways to create a presentation based on your needs and experience with PowerPoint (see Figure 15.1):

- *AutoContent Wizard* helps you choose an appropriate presentation template based on how you plan to show your presentation (electronic slide show, paper handouts, and so on).

- *Template* creates an empty presentation based on professionally chosen backgrounds and color schemes. This is a good choice if you know what text you want to add to your presentation, but maybe don't have the time to define nice-looking color schemes.

- *Blank Presentation* allows you to start with a clean slate and apply whichever design elements you want. Although this option offers the least assistance for the beginning PowerPoint user, it offers the most flexibility for the experienced user.

- *Open an Existing Presentation* enables you to open an existing presentation for editing or showing.

**FIG. 15.1**

The startup box you see after launching PowerPoint enables you to select from PowerPoint's various design options.

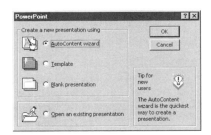

**N O T E**    The commands you use and the dialog boxes you see when you create a presentation will vary depending on whether you're already in PowerPoint or launching the application for the first time. They'll all accomplish the same things, but they may look slightly different depending on where you are in PowerPoint when you access them.

# Anatomy of the PowerPoint Workspace

The PowerPoint screen contains some elements in common with other Office 97 applications, and a few unique ones (see Figure 15.2).

▶ **See** "Common Screen Elements," **p. 20**

**FIG. 15.2**
As with other Office 97 applications, the PowerPoint workspace contains a number of familiar screen elements along with a few unique ones.

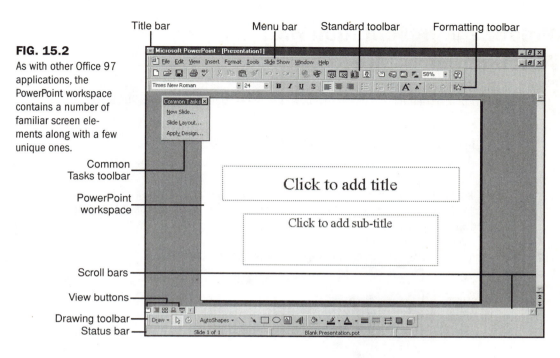

Some of the unique features in PowerPoint include:

- A Slide Show item on the Menu bar that holds the key to animation, sound effects, and other advanced features.

- Four PowerPoint-specific buttons on the far right of the Standard toolbar allow you to switch to black-and-white view, make a new slide, apply a new design, and alter a slide's layout.

- At the right end of the Formatting toolbar are buttons for increasing/decreasing font size, adding animated effects, among others.

- PowerPoint's status bar is slightly different from those in other applications. By default, the screen is in Slide View, and the status bar displays the slide number, number of slides in the presentation, and the design template used.

- The View buttons, which will be explained in detail later in this chapter, give you four different views of your presentation. There's even a fifth button for running the slide show.

- PowerPoint displays more toolbars by default than the rest of the applications. Among them are the Standard and Formatting toolbars at the top of the workspace, a Drawing toolbar at the bottom of the window, and a floating Common Tasks toolbar.

# Creating a Presentation with the AutoContent Wizard

Using the AutoContent Wizard is perhaps the easiest way to create a presentation in PowerPoint. To launch the wizard from within PowerPoint, follow these steps:

1. Start PowerPoint.
2. In the PowerPoint dialog box, select the AutoContent Wizard.
3. Press OK to see the first step of the AutoContent Wizard, as shown in Figure 15.3.

**N O T E** If PowerPoint is already running, and you then decide you'd like to access the AutoContent Wizard, choose File, New and select the Presentation tab. Double-click the AutoContent folder to open the Wizard.

**FIG. 15.3**

Click Next to begin working your way through the AutoContent Wizard.

From the AutoContent startup screen, you will be guided through the following steps:

1. Select the type of presentation you'd like to give (see Figure 15.4). Click one of the general type buttons to narrow the field of choices, or browse all the options, and then click Next.

**FIG. 15.4**

Press the button describing the type of presentation you want to give and click the desired item in the list on the right.

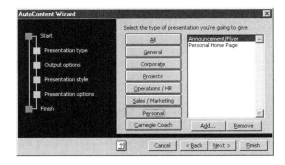

2. You are then asked how the presentation will be used. Make your selection and click Next.

3. Specify the output you will use as well as whether or not you plan to print handouts from your presentation. Click Next to continue.

4. Enter the information for your title slide, which may include the presentation's title, your name, and any additional information you want to include. Click Next.

5. Click Finish to put the AutoContent Wizard to work. Within seconds, you will see an outline view of your presentation with a tiny color preview box in the upper-right corner.

From here, you can begin creating the content of your presentation by inserting necessary text, which is discussed in the later section "Adding Text to Your Presentation."

# Creating Presentations Based on Templates, Designs, or Blank Presentations

To create a presentation without using the AutoContent Wizard, follow these steps:

1. Launch PowerPoint.

2. The next step depends on how you want to create your presentation:

   - To create a presentation based on a Presentation Design, choose Template and select the Presentation Design tab. In the New Presentation dialog box, double-click the template you want to use. The New Slide dialog box shown in Figure 15.5 appears.

 **TIP** You can preview your selection in the Preview window by clicking it; to apply it, double-click its icon or click OK.

   - To create a presentation using a Presentation Template, select the Presentations tab; then click an icon to preview your choice or double-click to apply it. The first slide of the presentation will appear.

   - You can start from scratch by choosing Blank Presentation. Click OK to see the New Slide dialog box pictured in Figure 15.5.

3. If you are creating a presentation using a Presentation Design or are starting from scratch with a Blank Presentation, choose the layout for your first slide in the New slide dialog box, and then click OK.

4. You see the first slide of the presentation on-screen and can begin to work with it.

**FIG. 15.5**
You can choose the layout of your slide by clicking the desired icon in the New Slide dialog box.

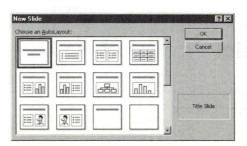

## Creating a New Presentation from Within PowerPoint

The process for creating a new presentation varies slightly when starting from within PowerPoint:

1. Choose File, New to bring up the New Presentation dialog box (see Figure 15.6). Click one of the tabs described in Table 15.1 to accomplish specific tasks.

**FIG. 15.6**
Use the New Presentation dialog box to select the desired designs or templates for your new presentation.

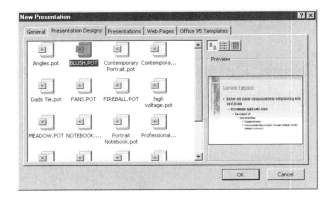

**Table 15.1   Creating a New Presentation from Within PowerPoint**

| To Do This | Choose This |
|---|---|
| Create a blank presentation | General tab, click Blank Presentation, and click OK. |
| Create a presentation based on a Presentation Design | Presentation Designs tab, double-click your chosen template. |
| Create a presentation using a template with sample text | Presentations tab, double-click the template you want. |

2. If you're creating a blank presentation or one based on a Presentation Design, the New Slide dialog box (refer to Figure 15.5) will appear, prompting you to choose your slide's layout.

▶ **See** "Creating a Word Outline to Use in Designing a PowerPoint Presentation," **p. 283**

# Saving a PowerPoint Presentation

 After you've designed the foundation of your presentation, you'll want to save it before you start making changes. To save a PowerPoint presentation, choose File, Save. You will be prompted to name the file in first-time saves. PowerPoint will automatically insert its .ppt file extension so that you can quickly retrieve your presentations when needed.

# Changing Your View of the PowerPoint Presentation

You can view your work in PowerPoint one of four ways:

 *Slide view.* This view (the first View button at the bottom of the PowerPoint workspace) shows an entire slide one at a time. Use this view to edit text, add pictures, and so on. This is the only view that allows you to select individual parts of a slide for editing. Just click a text area, or double-click a graphic to open it for editing.

 *Outline view.* A presentation's text is displayed as an outline in this view (see Figure 15.7). This view provides you a way to see the contents of your presentation at a glance. You can insert slide titles from this view, or even call in an outline from Word from which to build a presentation.

> ▶ **See** "Building an Outline," **p. 109**
> ▶ **See** "Creating a Word Outline to Use in Designing a PowerPoint Presentation," **p. 283**

 *Slide Sorter view.* The third View button gives you the Slide Sorter view. This view presents each slide in miniature and allows you to rearrange the slides and add slide transitions and animations, which you'll learn about in the next chapter.

 *Notes Page view.* The final View button places you in Notes Page view, which means each slide is presented one at a time with its speaker notes placed at the bottom of the slide.

**FIG. 15.7**
PowerPoint's Outline toolbar enables you to manipulate a presentation's contents much like you can with Word's outline function.

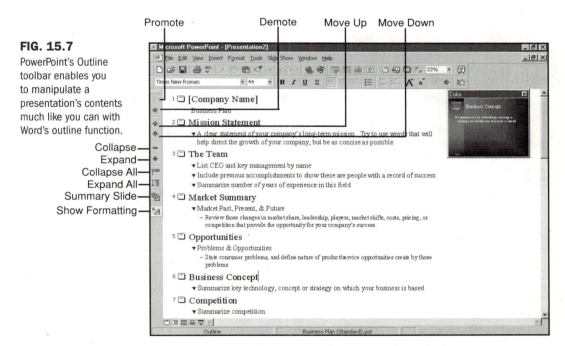

# Adding Text to Your Presentation

Adding text to a PowerPoint slide is one of the first things you'll need to do after you've chosen a template or presentation design from which to work. In cases where a template or existing design is being used, you'll have predefined text placeholders with which to work. Simply click inside the placeholder and begin typing.

If you're starting with a blank presentation, you'll have to start from scratch by creating the text box yourself. You can either adjust the slide's layout (see "Changing Slide Layouts" later in this chapter), or create your own text box.

**N O T E**  Those who have worked with Microsoft Publisher will notice PowerPoint's similar need to have everything in a frame or placeholder. These frames give you added design flexibility when it comes to laying out a slide because you can move the whole chunk of text (or the image) at once in its original formatting and size.

To create your own text box, click the Text Box button on the Drawing toolbar at the bottom of the page, click your desired location for the text box, and then begin typing. The box will grow as you type.

 **T I P**  You can also move an entire paragraph at a time. Move the mouse pointer to the left side of the slide until it turns into a four-headed arrow; left-click, and then drag it to its new position.

# Altering Slide Text Appearance

Changing the appearance of text in a PowerPoint slide can be done by selecting the text you want to change, and then choosing Format, Font from the menu bar. You can also alter text appearance and alignment by pressing the appropriate button on the Formatting bar.

# Adding Speaker Notes to Your Slides

You may not have much room to enter text on each slide, but PowerPoint's Speaker Notes feature enables you to generate a miniaturized version of a slide with room for your notes about it. This is especially great for keeping track of things you want to say as each overhead is displayed.

To add speaker notes to a slide, do the following:

1. Click the Notes Page view button to enter Notes Page view, as shown in Figure 15.8.
2. Use the Next Slide and Previous Slide buttons to select the slide you want to make notes for.
3. Click inside the text box at the bottom of the screen to begin entering your notes.
4. Repeat steps 2 and 3 as necessary to make notes for multiple slides.

**FIG. 15.8**
PowerPoint's speaker notes feature enables you to create a miniaturized view of your slides along with your notes.

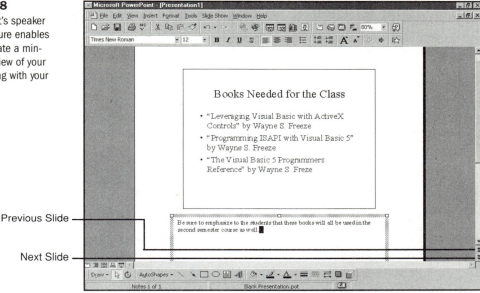

Previous Slide ——

Next Slide ——

 Is the notes text box too small for you to work with effectively? Click the Zoom drop-down combo box to choose from a variety of zoom options, or type in your own percentage. For example, Figure 15.8 is displayed with an 80 percent zoom.

# Editing Notes Using the Notes Master

After you've entered notes, you can always go back and reorganize or edit them as necessary. Just follow these steps and edit the text or graphics as you would in Word:

1. Choose View, Master, Notes Master.
2. Resize or change the location of the slide image or notes box to suit your needs.
3. Add the elements you want on the notes master—art, text, headers or footers, the date, time, or page number, or anything else that may help you give a complete presentation.
4. Click Close on the Master toolbar.

# Resizing PowerPoint Slide Elements

Whether it's a picture or a block of text, you can change its size by clicking it and then dragging one of the white boxes in the direction you want to resize the box.

# Formatting Bulleted Slides in Outline View

As is the case with any document or presentation, it's always a good idea to create it using an outline so that you're sure you hit all the necessary information.

 **TIP** One way to give a concise, organized presentation is to use Bullet Slides. Like bulleted lists in Word, these bulleted slides communicate your point in an easy-to-understand format. You'll find that bulleted slides will make up the majority of text for your slide presentations or transparencies, and they're easy to format in PowerPoint.

To format bullet slides from the Outline view, do the following:

1. Enter Outline view by pressing the Outline View button.
2. To replace default or existing slide text, select it as you would in Word by dragging the mouse over it. You can also select an entire bulleted item by clicking the bullet, or you can select a slide by pressing the Slide icon to the left of the slide title.
3. Insert and delete text as needed.
4. Use the Promote and Demote buttons to do the following:
    - Turn a bulleted point into a slide title by selecting it and then pressing Tab or the Promote button.
    - Change a slide title to a bulleted point (or a bulleted point to a sub-point) by pressing Shift+Tab or clicking the Demote button.
5. Move a slide up or down in a presentation's order by selecting it, and then clicking the Move Up or Move Down button.

# Moving from Slide to Slide

In Slide or in Notes Pages view, you can move to the next or previous slide by clicking the appropriate button at the bottom of the scroll bar at the right side of the workspace. You can also click the vertical scroll box and drag it until the desired page number appears in the ScreenTips box, and then release it to view the desired slide.

Alternatively, you can enter Slide Sorter view, select the desired slide, and then click the Slide View button to see the whole thing.

# Inserting and Deleting Slides

If you built your presentation from a Presentation template or from an entirely blank presentation, your presentation will have only one slide in it. To add more slides, do the following:

1. If you're not already in Slide view, click the Slide View button.
2. Move to the slide before the slide to be added using the Previous Slide and Next Slide buttons at the bottom of the vertical scroll bar.

**T I P**  To duplicate a slide, choose Insert, Duplicate Slide. The new slide will be instantly inserted behind the one you just copied.

3. Click the Insert New Slide button on the Standard toolbar or the New Slide button on the Common Tasks toolbar. The New Slide dialog box appears.

4. Select the desired layout for the slide, and then click OK to apply it. The new slide appears in the presentation.

 **N O T E**  To move a slide from one presentation to another, open the presentations you want to move slides to and from, and then display them in Slide Sorter view. Choose Window, Arrange All to display both presentations side by side, and then click the slide you want to move and drag it to the other presentation. You can select more than one slide by pressing the Shift key while you click.

If you chose a template with sample text, you may find that you have too many slides. To delete a slide, do the following:

1. Put your presentation in Slide View.

2. Move to the slide you want to delete.

3. Choose Edit, Delete Slide to permanently delete the slide from your presentation.

# Changing Slide Layouts

Just because you selected a slide layout doesn't mean you're stuck with it for good. You can always apply a new layout to a slide by following these steps:

1. If you aren't already in Slide view, get into it by clicking the Slide View button.

2. Bring the slide you want to change on-screen.

3. Click the Slide Layout button on the Common Tasks toolbar to see the Slide Layout dialog box similar to the New Slide dialog box pictured earlier in Figure 15.5.

4. Choose the layout you want, and then Reapply the layout over the existing one.

# Choosing a Background

Choosing a background for your slides is simple when you follow these steps:

1. Open the presentation you want to work with, and then enter Slide view by clicking the Slide View button.

2. From any slide within the presentation, choose Format, Background to bring up the Background dialog box shown in Figure 15.9.

3. Click the arrow in the Background Fill box to see a small selection of colors. If you don't see a color you like, choose More Colors.

**FIG. 15.9**
From the Background dialog box, you can apply the chosen background to all of the slides in the current presentation, or just the selected slide.

4. Choose the Standard tab to select a color from a palette or the Custom tab to mix your own, and then click OK.

  Light colors look best for overhead transparencies and paper printouts, while dark colors can have stunning results for slide shows and online content.

5. After you return to the Background dialog box, you can see what your selection looks like by clicking Preview, and then apply it by clicking Apply (to apply the background to the current slide only) or Apply to All (to apply your selection to the entire presentation).

# Creating Rich Backgrounds

PowerPoint's features enable you to create backgrounds so rich and lush that your readers (and bosses) will think you spent hours creating them. They can run the gamut from fun to classy, so don't be afraid to explore.

To create an unforgettable background, follow these steps:

1. Open the presentation you want to work with.
2. Choose Format, Background to bring up the Background dialog box.
3. Apply the desired color.
4. To access the dozens of fill effects available in PowerPoint, click the list box arrow below the preview picture, and select Fill Effects. The Fill Effects dialog box pictured in Figure 15.10 appears.
5. Select one of the following tabs to begin working with the fill effects:
   - *Gradient*. Allows you to shift the background from its starting color to a deeper shade of the same color, or to a different color entirely. The effect offers six shading styles with four variants for each. As you tweak the options, you can see a tiny preview in the lower-right portion of the dialog box.
   - *Texture*. Allows you to choose from a variety of textures, including water, concrete, marble, and wood.

- *Pattern.* Enables you to choose a background and foreground color to which you can apply a number of patterns from polka dots to grids, among others. Even though one of the colors is called a foreground color, it defines the foreground color of the background, not the text.
- *Picture.* Lets you take a .jpeg, .bmp, .pcx, or other popular picture formats file and convert it to a background image for your slide(s).

6. Preview your work in the lower-right corner of the Fill Effects dialog box.

7. Click OK when you find a background you like.

8. When you return to the Background dialog box, you can apply your background to the selected slides only, to the entire presentation, or cancel your work altogether.

**FIG. 15.10**
The Fill Effects dialog box holds the key to literally thousands of special effects, which you can easily mix and match. Choose a tab to browse the options available in each category.

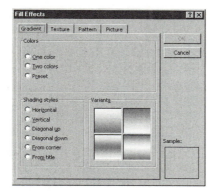

# Selecting a Color Scheme

Sure you can change font and background color as you go, but you may also want to consider applying a predefined color scheme to your slides. To do this, follow these steps:

1. Open the presentation you want to work with.

2. From within any slide, choose Format, Slide Color Scheme to open the Color Scheme dialog box.

3. Choose the Standard tab to apply one of seven predesigned color schemes or the Custom tab to design your own.

4. If designing your own color scheme using the Custom tab, just double-click an element's color box to access a large palette from which to choose a color. Your selections will automatically be reflected in the preview window at the bottom-right corner of the box.

5. After you've completed your selections, select Apply or Apply to All to apply the scheme to the current slide or entire presentation respectively.

# Running Your PowerPoint Slide Show

Before you can run a slide show, you'll want to set it up by following these steps:

1. Choose Slide Show, Set Up Show from the menu bar to open the Set Up Show dialog box pictured in Figure 15.11.

**FIG. 15.11**

Use the Set Up Show dialog box to select the type of presentation, which slides you want included in the presentation, and whether you want to switch the slides manually or by preset timer.

2. Specify whether you want to show the slides in full screen (Presented by a Speaker), in a window (Browsed by an Individual), or in a continuous loop (Browsed at a Kiosk).

3. Choose the slides to be displayed by selecting All or by specifying a range of slide numbers.

4. Check whether you want to present the slide show manually or automatically based on timings you inserted into the slides.

5. Click OK to exit the setup screen.

# Setting the Timer to Advance Slides Automatically

You can program your slides to advance from one to another automatically by setting a timer for each slide. Follow these steps to set the timer for each of your slides:

1. In Slide or Slide Sorter view, select the slide or slides for which you want to set the timing.

2. Choose Slide Show, Slide Transition to open the Slide Transition dialog box.

3. In the Advance window, click Automatically After, and then enter the number of seconds you want the slide to appear on-screen.

4. Click Apply to set the timing on the selected slides or Apply to All to apply it to the entire presentation.

5. Repeat the process for each slide or range of slides you want to set the timing for unless you've selected Apply to All.

6. To view the timings, click the Slide Show button at the end of the row of View buttons.

# Printing Your PowerPoint Slides

To print your PowerPoint slides, follow these steps:

1. Choose File, Print to bring up the PowerPoint Print dialog box shown in Figure 15.12.

**FIG. 15.12**
PowerPoint's Print dialog box allows you to print your slides in a variety of ways.

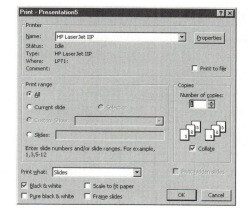

2. Select the range of slides you want to print—All, Current Slide, or Slides. If you check Slides, enter the range of slides you want to print (for example, 1-3 to get 1, 2, and 3, or 1,3 to get slides 1 and 3).

3. In the Print What list, choose Slides.

4. Place a check mark next to Black & White unless you have a color printer and desire multicolor output.

5. Enter the number of Copies you want to print (1 is the default number).

6. Click OK to send the slides to the printer.

# Printing Handouts and Notes from Your Presentation

Presentation attendees often appreciate having copies of the material covered to help them recall the event or to give them space on which to write their own notes and impressions. PowerPoint gives you numerous ways to produce handouts, some of which can significantly reduce paper use.

To create handouts or to print your own presentation notes, follow these steps:

1. Choose File, Print to open the Print dialog box (refer to Figure 15.12).
2. To print handouts, select Handouts (2 Slides per Page), Handouts (3 Slides per Page), or Handouts (6 Slides per Page) from the Print What list box.
3. To print your speaker notes, select Notes Pages from the Print What list box.
4. Refer to the previous steps for any additional options.
5. Click OK to send your slides to the printer.

# Troubleshooting Printing Problems

Sometimes an attractive on-screen background can produce disastrous results on paper. To print clean handouts or transparencies, you'll want to suppress the slide's background while you print. To do this, do the following:

1. Choose Tools, Options, and then click the Print tab.
2. Under Printing options, deselect the Background printing check box, then print as usual.

# CHAPTER 16

# Incorporating Pictures, Multimedia, and Advanced Presentation Techniques

**P**owerPoint gives you much more than visual appeal. With the information in this chapter, you can animate your text, you can record a voiceover for your presentation, you can use an audio CD for background music, along with several other techniques.

Use this chapter as your guide for breathing life into ordinary presentations, and make your work memorable.

**Designing impressive slide transitions**

Creative slide transitions can turn an ordinary presentation into an extraordinary one.

**Animating objects to grab attention**

Adding animation to presentations will quickly grab the reader's eye.

**Using sound and video**

Learn how to incorporate these elements into your presentation.

**Hiding slides**

When you give a presentation, you never know what additional information your audience will want to know, so be prepared by hiding some key slides to pull out if you need them.

**Rehearsing your slide show**

Learn how to control the presentation from one computer while your audience views it from another.

**Building an organization chart**

Use Microsoft Organization Chart to add an organization chart to a PowerPoint presentation, or embed the chart as an object in any other Office 97 application.

# Adding an Imported Picture to Your Slide

Adding your company's logo or another image file to your presentation is a simple process; just follow these steps:

1. Open the presentation in which you want to insert the picture.

2. Move to the slide you want to insert the picture in.

**N O T E**   To add the picture to every slide in your presentation, choose <u>V</u>iew, <u>M</u>aster, <u>S</u>lide Master to add it to the Slide Master.

3. Choose <u>I</u>nsert, <u>P</u>icture, <u>F</u>rom File to open the Insert Picture dialog box. From here, you can browse your files to select the image you want.

4. Double-click the picture file to select it.

# Animating Text

Animating text can be a unique way to give your presentation powerful impact. For instance, you can time the appearance of text so that each point makes a grand entrance as you discuss it.

To animate PowerPoint text, follow these steps:

1. In Slide view, display the slide that has the text you want to animate.

2. Choose Sli<u>d</u>e Show, Custo<u>m</u> Animation, and then click the Timing tab.

3. Under Slide Objects Without Animation, select the text you want to animate, and then click Animate.

4. To start the animation by clicking the text, click the On Mouse Click button. To start the animation automatically when the slide is accessed, click Automatically, and then enter the number of seconds you want to elapse between the previous animation and the current one.

5. Click the Effects tab.

6. Under Entry Animation And Sound, select the options you want. If you need help on an option, click the question mark button, and then click the option.

7. Repeat steps 3 through 6 for every block of text you want to animate. You can click the Preview button to see how your animations look.

A quick way to animate text from the Slide view is to select the block of text you want to animate, choose Sli<u>d</u>e Show, <u>P</u>reset Animation, and then click the option you want. You can preview animations in Slide view by choosing Sli<u>d</u>e Show, Animation Pr<u>e</u>view. The animation plays in the slide miniature that appears. Click the slide miniature again to replay the animation.

# Animating Objects to Grab Attention

Animating objects in your presentation can attract or detract a reader's attention from your content, depending on how it's implemented.

Do the following to effectively animate objects in your presentation:

1. Open the presentation you want to work with, and enter Slide view.
2. Scroll through the presentation until you locate the object you want to animate, and click to select it.
3. Choose Slide Show, Custom Animation to open the Custom Animation dialog box shown in Figure 16.1.

**FIG. 16.1**
The Effects tab on the Custom Animation dialog box allows you to select the entry effect and sound for the chosen object. You can also determine what order the objects appear in by tweaking the Animation Order rankings.

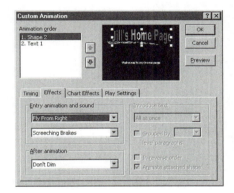

4. Use the Timing tab to determine how an animation is triggered—by mouse-click or elapsed time.
5. Access the Effects tab to choose the desired effects and rank their order of execution.
6. You may exit the screen without making a change by clicking Cancel, or you can click OK to apply the effects. To preview the effects, click Preview.

# Simplifying Navigation Through Your Presentation by Adding Action Buttons

Adding action buttons to your presentation enables your audience to find the desired information quickly without necessarily having to sit through the entire presentation. It can also direct them to "hidden" slides that augment information presented in the main slide show.

To add action buttons to your presentation, follow these steps:

1. Make sure that the first slide in the presentation is on-screen, and then choose Slide Show, Action Button from the menu bar.

2. Select the desired button (or choose the blank one if you want to create a customized button) from the drop-down menu.

3. The mouse pointer turns into a cross enabling you to click and drag a button's outline into existence.

4. When you release the mouse button, the Action Settings dialog box appears (see Figure 16.2).

**FIG. 16.2**
The Action Settings dialog box allows you to define where the button will take the reader. The drop-down list in the Hyperlink To option allows you to define the slide, URL, document, or other source to be linked to.

5. Choose the Hyperlink To option and define the resource—whether it's the next slide in the presentation or the home page of one of your organization's big supporters.

   ▶ **See** "Hyperlinks in PowerPoint," **p. 281**

7. To change the look of an Action Button, right-click it and select Format AutoShape.

8. Select the desired options in the Format AutoShape dialog box, and then click OK to save the settings.

# Adding Basic Sound Clips to Your Presentation

To add basic sound clips to your presentation, follow these steps:

1. Open the desired presentation.

2. Enter Slide view if you're not already in it.

3. Move to the slide in which you want to cue the music or sound effect.

4. Choose Insert, Movies and Sounds from the menu bar to bring up Microsoft Clip Gallery 3.0.

   Microsoft Clip Gallery 3.0 is a shared Office 97 resource. You can access it from most Office

**NOTE**  97 applications, including Publisher 97. You can even find a host of sound effects online with a single mouse click and a live Internet connection.

5.  Select the Sound tab from the Gallery, and double-click the chosen sound effect or music clip.

6.  An icon for the sound file appears. Drag it to the corner of your slide.

7.  Click the Sound icon, and then choose Slide Show, Custom Animation. The Play Setting tab of the Custom Animation dialog box appears.

8.  Choose Play Using Animation Order and Hide While Not Playing if desired.

9.  To play the sound clip over and over until the reader moves on, click the More Options button, and select Loop Until Stopped.

10. Click OK to return to the presentation.

# Using Audio CD Tracks for Background Sound

One way to get high-quality sound effects is to use an audio CD track. Follow these steps to incorporate one into your presentation:

1.  Open the presentation you want to add the CD track to.

2.  Enter Slide view, and then move to the slide you want to have trigger the music.

3.  Choose Insert, Movies and Sounds, Play CD Audio Track.

4.  The Play Options dialog box in Figure 16.3 allows you to specify which track(s) you want to use. You can even select part of the track and have it go into a continuous loop.

5.  Select OK when finished.

**FIG. 16.3**
Define the track (or partial track) you want to include in your presentation in the Play Options dialog box.

Part
II

Ch
16

# Recording a Voiceover for Your Presentation

With a sound card and a microphone, you can record a voiceover or narrative to go with your presentation. This is an excellent way to include a special message from your CEO.

To record the voiceover/narrative, do the following:

1. Verify that the microphone is properly hooked up to your computer.
2. Select the slide you want to be accompanied by the voiceover.
3. Choose Slide Show, Record Narration from the menu bar.
4. A dialog box appears showing the amount of free disk space and the number of minutes you can record. Keep in mind that if you increase sound quality, your available recording time will decrease sharply.
5. If you plan to take your presentation on the road, it may be easier to embed the narration in the presentation. This reduces the number of files you have to worry about. To do this and begin recording, click OK.
6. Linking to narratives can increase your presentation's performance by spreading out the files on your local system. To insert the narration as a linked object, place a check mark in the Link Narrations In check box, and then click OK to begin recording.
7. As the slide show is shown, add narration as desired.
8. At the end of the show, a message appears asking if you want to save the timings along with the narration. Click Yes if desired. To save only the narration, click No.
9. A sound icon appears in the lower-right corner of each slide that contains a narration.

# Designing Impressive Slide Transitions

The Slide Transition dialog box is your guide to creating professional-looking slide transitions.

To create dynamic slide transitions, do the following:

1. Open the presentation you want to work with, and then enter the Slide Sorter view.
2. Select the slides you want to apply the transition to by clicking on the first slide, pressing Ctrl, and then clicking any other slides you want to select.

**N O T E**  Remember that transitions and any other special effects will be applied to selected slides only, so you may want to double-check your selection before moving forward.

3. Choose Slide Show, Slide Transition from PowerPoint's menu bar, or click the Slide Transition button on the Slide Sorter toolbar. The Slide Transition dialog box in Figure 16.4 appears.
4. Under the picture in the Slide Transition dialog box is an Effect list box from which you can choose your slide transition.

**FIG. 16.4**
From the Slide Transition dialog box, you can select a funky slide transition, set the timer for the length of time to pass between transitions, and even apply sound effects to your slide(s).

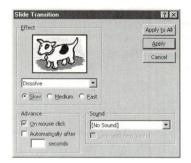

**TIP** If you have design elements in a slide's background, a transition like Dissolve will keep the background steady while dissolving the text only.

5. Select a speed for the transition from Slow, Medium, or Fast.

6. Repeat steps 4 and 5 until you get the transition that meets your needs.

7. You can specify whether one slide transitions to another based on a mouse-click, or a specified amount of time expressed in seconds.

8. Preview the animation by clicking on the sample slide.

9. Choose Apply to apply the transition to the selected slides, or Apply to All to apply the transition to all slides whether they were selected or not.

**TIP** While it's technically possible to apply more than one transition to a presentation, applying too many can distract a reader and may even look amateurish if overdone.

# Hiding Slides to Pull Out if You Need Them

Maybe you have a big presentation to make to your board of directors. You want the presentation to be short, yet you want to be prepared should they have additional questions or concerns.

One way to deal with this is to anticipate their questions and concerns, and then prepare slides based on that information. These slides can be hidden during the presentation, but can quickly be retrieved if needed.

To hide slides in a presentation, do the following:

1. Open the presentation you want to work with.

2. Move to the slide you want to hide.

3. In Slide view, choose Slide Show, Hide Slide. Or from Slide Sorter view, select the slide you want to hide, and then click Hide Slide. A "null" sign appears over the slide number.

Part
II

Ch
16

**T I P**  If there's a high degree of probability the slide will need to be displayed, you can place the slide at the rear of the presentation. You can specify that the presentation move through all the slides except the "hidden" ones tacked on to the back end of the presentation. Do this by choosing Slide Show, Set Up Show, and specify the nonhidden slide numbers in the Slide To/From boxes. You can access the hidden slides by placing Action Buttons linking to the hidden information on the pages you think will trigger a request for this backup data.

You can retrieve one of these hidden slides during a presentation in one of two ways:

- Right-click the slide that precedes the hidden slide, point to Go, and then click Hidden Slide. You can access this command only if the next slide is hidden.

- To retrieve the hidden slide from anywhere within a presentation, right-click any slide, point to Go, and then select Slide Navigator to open the Slide Navigator dialog box (see Figure 16.5). Double-click the slide you want. If a slide number is in parentheses, that means it's a hidden slide.

**FIG. 16.5**

Look for numbers in parentheses in the Slide Navigator dialog box to find hidden slides quickly.

 **T I P**  To avoid spelling errors, return to the first slide of your presentation, and then choose Tools, Spelling, or press F7. The spelling checker will then search for spelling errors. You can also have PowerPoint check your spelling as you type. To do this, choose Tools, Options, and then select the Spelling tab; there, you can choose a variety of options.

# Rehearsing a Slide Show

Instead of programming slide timing manually as shown in the last chapter, you can record them during a rehearsal. Grab your speaker notes or speech, and then follow these steps:

1. Open the presentation you want to rehearse.

2. Choose Slide Show, Rehearse Timings to launch the presentation.

3. The Rehearsal dialog box shown in Figure 16.6 appears at the bottom-right corner of the presentation.

Elapsed presentation time

**FIG. 16.6**

Make sure your slide show meets its budgeted time allotment by using the Rehearsal dialog box.

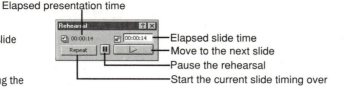

— Elapsed slide time
— Move to the next slide
— Pause the rehearsal
— Start the current slide timing over

4. Click Repeat to start the current slide's timing over again.

5. Use the Pause button to suspend the rehearsal's progress temporarily.

6. Click the right-arrow button to move to the next slide in the presentation.

7. When you've made it through the entire presentation, a message box will appear telling you how long the presentation lasted. You will then be asked whether you want to save the newly rehearsed timings, or fall back to the timings you may have set manually. Choose Yes to save the new timings or No to try again or keep the old timings.

# Monitoring Your Progress with Slide Meter

Some presentations have very rigid time constraints. To get through your entire presentation while maintaining an air of flexibility and responsiveness, use the Slide Meter to track your progress. Do this by following these steps:

1. Choose Slide Show, Set Up Show.

2. Under Advance Slides in the Set Up Show dialog box, check Manually, and then click OK.

3. Choose Slide Show, View Show to begin the presentation.

4. Right-click the first slide, and choose Slide Meter from the shortcut menu. The Slide Meter box pictured in Figure 16.7 will appear at the bottom-right corner of the slide.

**FIG. 16.7**

Stay in the green on the Slide Meter to ensure that your presentation timing is right on track.

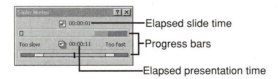

— Elapsed slide time
— Progress bars
— Elapsed presentation time

5. Green bars appear on the upper progress bar to tell you whether the length of time you're displaying the slide is within the range of time you rehearsed for that slide. If the bars turn yellow or red, you're lingering too long.

# Viewing the Presentation on One Computer While Controlling It from Another

If you're giving a presentation at a major conference or are even just taking it on the road, you may want to consider the possibility of displaying the presentation on a computer with a large-screen monitor while controlling it from your laptop.

Before you can do this, however, you'll want to confirm the following:

- Make sure you have a null-modem cable available.
- Confirm that each machine has a free COM port to link the machines together.
- Be sure PowerPoint 97 is available on both systems.

To set up the machines for the presentation on site, do the following:

1. Open the presentation you want to run on the controlling computer.
2. Choose Slide Show, View on Two Screens.
3. In the View on Two Screens dialog box shown in Figure 16.8, click the Presenter option button to define your computer as the controlling computer.

**FIG. 16.8**
You can define the computer to be used by the presenter or the audience using the View On Two Screens dialog box.

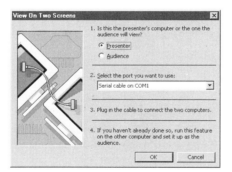

4. Select the port you want to use.
5. Hook the computers together with the null-modem cable attached to each machine's COM port.
6. Run the same setup on the attached computer, but in step 3 click the Audience option button.
7. Click OK when the setup is complete.

 **TIP** By right-clicking the slides on your screen, you can access the shortcut menu without the users knowing it. This is a great way to view your speaker notes in a dark room, or to control the speed of the presentation based on audience response.

# Using the Electronic Pen to Highlight Your Points

While running a slide show, you can right-click a slide to access a variety of slide management tools. One of these tools, a pen, allows you to draw on-screen while making your presentation.

To use this tool, do the following:

1. When showing a presentation, right-click a slide to access the shortcut menu.

2. To turn your mouse pointer into a pen, place a check mark next to Pen on this menu.

3. To write on-screen, point the mouse to the location you want to begin drawing in, and then left-click and drag the mouse to produce the desired result.

4. Is the pen's default color hard to see on your background? Change it by right-clicking the slide, and then choosing Pointer Options, Pen Color. A list of pen colors appears. Make your selection; PowerPoint will automatically return you to the full presentation screen.

Part
II

Ch
16

# Building an Organization Chart

If you're giving a presentation about your organization, odds are you'll want to include an organization chart to introduce the staff and its structure.

With Office 97 comes a small application called Microsoft Organization Chart 2.0. You can access this tool from within other applications by choosing Insert, Object; but for the sake of this chapter, we'll focus on how to use Microsoft Organization Chart in PowerPoint.

**NOTE**  If you can't access Microsoft Organization Chart, chances are it wasn't installed on your system. To rectify this, put the Office CD in your computer, and run the Office setup program again to install it.

To create an organization chart from PowerPoint, follow these steps:

1. Choose the spot for the organization chart by creating a new slide or moving to an empty one.

2. Choose Insert, Picture, Organization Chart.

3. Click Chart Title to enter the title text for your chart. You can press Enter to get additional centered lines if needed.

4. Click a box to enter text inside it.

5. Microsoft Organization Chart will prompt you to insert names, titles, and comments (see Figure 16.9), though you can enter anything you want.

6. Press Esc or click outside of a box to complete it.

7. To create a new box, select the appropriate type of box (for example, subordinate, peer, assistant, and so on) from the program's toolbar, and then click the box to which you want to attach the new box.

**FIG. 16.9**

Microsoft Organization
Chart will prompt you for
the text to include on
your organization chart.

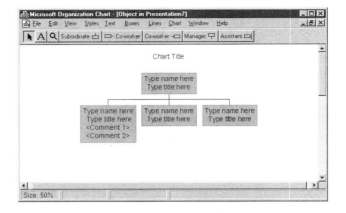

8. Keep adding boxes as needed, or use the Styles menu to add groups of boxes at one time.

9. To change text color, style, or alignment, select the text and choose the appropriate item from the Text menu.

 To select all boxes to which to apply colors and formatting, choose Edit, Select All, or press Ctrl+A.

10. Use the Boxes menu to adjust box color, border style, and so on.

11. Choose File, Update to update the current organization chart.

12. Close the Microsoft Organization Chart window by choosing File, Exit, and Return.

# CHAPTER 17

# Getting Professional Results with Publisher 97

If Word is capable of creating newsletters and Web pages, why would you want to work with Publisher 97? For starters, Publisher 97 has even more flexibility and versatility than Word when it comes to working with objects and text columns. It also comes loaded with templates to create anything from business cards to catalogs, even paper airplanes for those mid-afternoon breaks!

Publisher 97 delivers a product that makes you look like a desktop publishing professional, even if you aren't. And if you're worried that it will take forever to learn another program, rest assured that Microsoft has incorporated a lot of familiar Office 97 menus and functions into Publisher 97, so you'll be proficient in Publisher before you know it. ■

**The Publisher 97 workspace**

With a thorough knowledge of Publisher 97's workspace and screen elements, you can accomplish a lot with just a few short mouse-clicks.

**Using PageWizard to get professional results**

Let Publisher 97 do the hard work for you when creating specialized output, such as newsletters and brochures.

**Working with frames**

Everything in Publisher must fit into a box, so you'll learn how to create all the box types Publisher has to offer.

**Manipulating text and objects**

Learn how to move text and objects in Publisher, as well as how to change text attributes.

**Importing Word documents**

You can take a document written in Word and quickly import it into Publisher for use in one of many specialized documents.

# Anatomy of the Publisher 97 Workspace

Publisher 97 has many buttons and toolbars in common with other Office 97 applications, and a few unique to Publisher, as you can see Figure 17.1.

**N O T E** Need help? Unfortunately you won't find the automated Office Assistants here, so you'll have to rely on more traditional methods of seeking help. Press the question mark button at the right end of the Publisher toolbar to see a list of context-sensitive help topics from which you can choose with a single mouse-click. For more specific help topics, choose Help, Show Index (or press Ctrl+F1) to see a searchable index of topics similar to the Index help tab found in the core Office 97 applications.

**FIG. 17.1**
Many of Publisher 97's screen elements will look familiar if you've used Word reguarly.

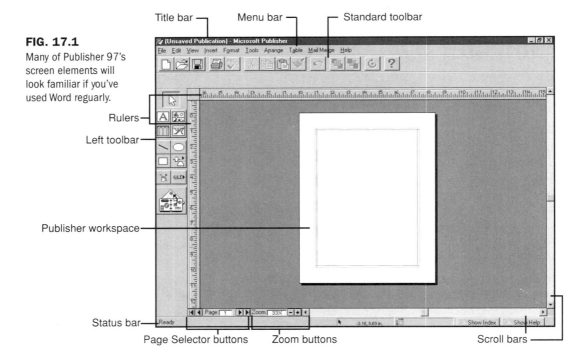

A brief description of Publisher's screen elements follows:

- *Title bar.* This bar displays the name of the application, along with the file name of the current document.
- *Menu bar.* This bar gives you access to Publisher's Arrange, Tables, and Mail Merge menus, along with more traditional menu bar items.
- *Standard toolbar.* The only new items in this toolbar are the Bring to the Front and Send to the Back buttons, which dictate how objects are layered in Publisher 97.

■ *Left toolbar.* This toolbar is the key to constructing all kinds of boxes in Publisher 97. See Table 17.1 for a detailed listing of each box type available. You can also access WordArt from this toolbar.

■ *Rulers.* Use these rulers as a guideline for measuring the size of images on a page, or for formatting a document's layout around preprinted paper or stationery.

■ *Scroll bars.* These bars function the same as scroll bars found in other Office 97 applications.

■ *Page Selector buttons.* These buttons surround the Page Number box, which displays the number of the current page. From left to right, these buttons display the first page, previous page, next page, and last page in the document. You also can click the Page Number box to jump directly to a certain page.

**N O T E** Because Publisher displays only one page at a time, by default, you need to click the Page Selector buttons to move to a new page. The Scroll buttons move you around the current page only. ■

■ *Status bar.* This bar shows you the position of an object, gives you access to the Help index, and enables you to hide Help boxes when called up.

■ *Zoom buttons.* These buttons enable you to zoom in and out of a Publisher screen, either to view an entire page or to work closely with an object by zooming in on it.

## Table 17.1  Publisher Buttons and Their Functions

| Button | Button Name | Function |
|---|---|---|
| | Pointer Button | Select an object |
| | Text Tool | Create a text frame |
| | Picture Tool | Create a picture frame |
| | Table Tool | Create a table frame |
| | WordArt | Create a WordArt frame |
| | Line Draw | Draw a line |
| | Oval Draw | Draw an oval |
| | Box Draw | Create a rectangle |

*continues*

**Table 17.1   Continued**

| Button | Button Name | Function |
|---|---|---|
|  | Custom Shapes | Create your own shapes |
|  | PageWizards | Create an area for a PageWizard |
|  | Insert Object | Insert a picture, document, chart, or some other type of object |
|  | Design Gallery | Start the Design Gallery tool |

# Frames: The Essence of Publisher

Unlike Word, everything in Publisher—every picture, every imported object, every block of text—must have a box or frame of its own. While it may seem like a major hassle, it's great for quickly moving objects or applying special effects.

So what else distinguishes a Publisher document from other documents?

- Publisher docs differ from word processing documents because they have two layers—and every element, be it a block of text or a picture, must occupy its own frame. Two layers simply means objects can overlap one another.
- A publication can be one or more pages of frames arranged in layers.
- Frames on publication pages hold either text or graphics, not just graphics or charts as is the case with other applications.

Later in the chapter, you learn how to work manually with frames. But first, you'll see how the PageWizard can automate some of these tasks.

# Designing Professional-Looking Documents Using PageWizard

The fastest way to produce a high-quality document in Publisher 97 is to use the PageWizard. It will ask you a series of questions and then tailor the output based on your responses to meet your specific needs.

To use PageWizard, follow these steps:

1. Launch Publisher 97 to bring up the start-up screen, shown in Figure 17.2, or choose File, Create New Publication if Publisher is already running.

**FIG. 17.2**
The PageWizard tab displays a large selection of document categories, ranging from business forms to calendars to paper airplanes.

2. Select the PageWizard tab if it didn't display as the default tab.

3. Double-click the category of choice to see options within that category, and to begin working with the PageWizard Design Assistant. Use the arrow buttons on the right side of the box to scroll through your options.

4. Click the desired document type or layout, then click Next.

5. Depending on the type of document you chose, the Design Assistant may or may not ask you a series of questions to help customize the output.

6. Answer each question as appropriate, then click Next to move on to the next screen.

7. After all necessary questions have been answered, the Design Assistant will ask if you want to create the document. To do so, click the Create It! button.

8. You will be asked if you'd like to have step-by-step help in working with your document. Select Yes or No, as desired.

9. Your new document will be ready for the insertion of custom text and graphics.

# Editing Text in a Publisher Document

Because PageWizard and the Design Assistant create documents with sample text already filled in, you need to learn how to manipulate existing text and images. Creating a document from scratch will be covered later in this chapter.

To edit text in Publisher, follow these steps:

1. In your newly created document, choose Tools, Options, and select the Editing and User Assistance tab.

2. In the Text Editing box, place a check mark next to the Typing Replaces Selection box. From that point on, Publisher 97 will replace the text you select with any newly entered text.

3. Click OK to apply the option.

4. To select a block of text, you have three options:

- Place the mouse pointer right in front of the first text character you want to select, click your mouse button and drag it over the text until the area you want to highlight is covered.
- With the insertion point inside the desired text frame, click it. In many cases, the entire box will become highlighted.
- Click inside a text frame and then click Ctrl+A to select the entire box.

5. Either click Delete and enter the text or, if the Typing Replaces Selection option is enabled, simply type the text into the highlighted box.

6. To change the appearance of selected text, select it and then choose the desired option(s) from the Formatting toolbar.

# Formatting Text in Publisher

Here is where Publisher's similarities to Word begin to appear. Text size, font selection, and even creating bulleted and numbered lists are done the same way in Publisher as it's done in Word. Simply select the text, and then press the desired button to apply the change. See Table 17.2 for a look at the icons you'll need most. The same method can be used to align text within its frame.

**Table 17.2  Publisher Text Formatting Icons**

| Icon | Button Name | Function |
|------|-------------|----------|
| **B** | Bold | Makes selected text appear in bold. |
| *I* | Italic | Makes selected text appear in italic. |
| ABC | Small Capitals | Makes words appear all in capital letters. Letters you have capitalized will appear in normal size, but all the other letters will be short capital letters. |
| ⊤ | Font Color | Adds color to online content or publica tions being printed with a color printer. |
| ≡ | Left Align | Aligns all the text to the left side of its frame. |
| ≡ | Center | Centers the text within the frame's sides. |
| ≡ | Right Align | Aligns all the text to the right side of its frame. |

| Icon | Button Name | Function |
|------|-------------|----------|
| 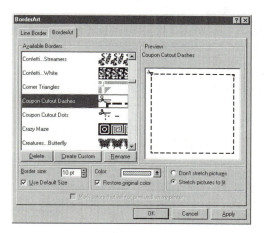 | Justified | Flushes all text up to both edges of its frame. |
| | Bulleted or Numbered List | Press to choose a style for your list. |

# Changing a Picture

Replacing a picture is even simpler than replacing text. Just double-click inside the picture frame to open Clip Gallery 3.0, click the chosen image to select it, and then click the Insert button to place it in the active picture frame. You may be asked if you want to adjust the frame to fit the image, or adjust the image to fit the frame. Answer as desired to insert the new image.

# Applying Borders to Publisher Objects

In Publisher, an object refers to any kind of Publisher 97 box or frame, be it a text or a picture frame. To apply a border to one of these objects, do the following:

1. Select a frame by clicking inside its boundaries. It will be outlined with several tiny black boxes.

2. Choose Format, Border to bring up the BorderArt dialog box, pictured in Figure 17.3.

**FIG. 17.3**
Choose the Line Border tab to apply a simple border, or the BorderArt tab to choose from a variety of borders, ranging from baby rattles to Halloween cats.

3. Choose the Line Border tab to apply a simple border, or the BorderArt tab for something more fancy or fun.

4. Define the border's size, color, and placement and then click Apply to apply it to the selected box or frame.

Part
II

Ch
17

# Adding Text and Picture Frames

To add a text or picture frame to your Publisher 97 document, follow these steps:

1. Open or create the document in which you want to insert a frame.
2. From the Left toolbar, select either the Text or Picture tool icon.
3. Position your mouse pointer over the area in which you want to place the frame.
4. Click the mouse and drag it diagonally until the frame reaches its desired size, and then release the mouse button.

 **TIP** Don't worry if the frame isn't positioned or sized perfectly the first time; you can always click inside the frame and pull one of the tiny black handles to tweak it later on.

5. Enter the text if you've created a Text frame; choose Insert and one of the following options for a Picture frame:

   - Picture File to insert a picture file stored on your hard disk. Because Publisher supports a number of file formats, you can choose from .gif, .tiff, and .jpeg among others
   - Clip Art to choose an image from Clip Gallery 3.0 or to download an image from the Web
   - Object to insert an Excel chart, a PowerPoint slide, or WordArt, among others

# Manipulating Frames

As you refine your Publisher document, you'll undoubtedly need to tweak frame placement and size. To do so, follow the directions in Table 17.3.

**Table 17.3  Manipulating Frames in Publisher**

| To Do This | Do This |
| --- | --- |
| Copy a frame | Right-click the desired frame and choose Copy (type of frame) Frame from the shortcut menu (see Figure 17.4). Right-click the location you want to place the copied frame, then select Paste (type of frame) Frame. The frame will appear, ready for you to move or resize it as needed. |
| Resize a frame | Click on a frame, then drag one of the resizing boxes in the desired direction. |
| Deleting a frame Frame | Right-click a frame, and then choose Delete (type of frame) from the shortcut menu. |
| Moving a frame pointer | Click the frame you want to move, and then place the mouse inside it until it becomes a moving van (see Figure 17.5). Click and drag the frame to the desired location. |

**FIG. 17.4**
Publisher's shortcut menu helps you manipulate frames in no time.

**FIG. 17.5**
When you see Publisher's moving van, you're in the position to move a frame.

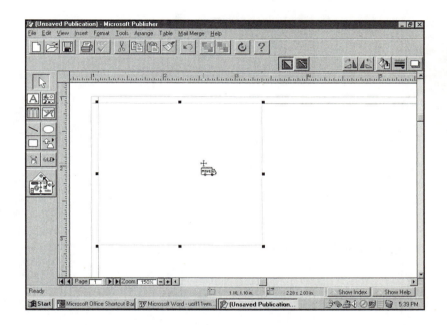

# Insert Graphics on Text Frames

After the text and picture frames have been created, you can move the picture frame onto the text frame as described in the preceding section, "Manipulating Frames." When you do so, Publisher will generally wrap the text around the image. If it doesn't, don't worry. You can click the Bring to Front or Send to Back buttons on the Standard toolbar until you get the desired results.

Of course, this will only work if the frames are large enough to accommodate the result. For example, you can move a small image into a large frame of text, but you may need to increase the size of the text frame to allow for wrap-around text.

 Making an object transparent or opaque is as easy as selecting it and then clicking Ctrl+T.

# Converting a Single Text Frame to Columns

Sometimes it's easier to edit text in a more conventional text block than it is to work with it in columns. To convert a larger text frame into columns, follow these steps:

1. Click inside the text frame you want to format to select it.

2. Choose Format, Text Frame Properties to open the Text Frame Properties dialog box, shown in Figure 17.6.

**FIG. 17.6**
The Text Frame Properties box enables you to define the number of columns in a frame, as well as the spacing of those columns.

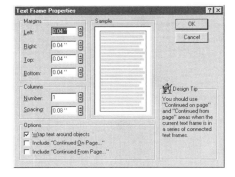

3. Set the desired margins for your frame in the Margins box.

4. Select the number of columns to be included in the frame and their spacing in the Columns box.

5. In the Options box, tell Publisher whether you want the text to wrap around objects, or whether you want a "Continued On" or "Continued From" tag line appended to the appropriate location in the frame.

6. Preview the settings in the Preview box.

7. Click OK to apply the columns as defined.

# Continuing Columns in Another Location

If you find that you are running short of space in a column, you can continue the column elsewhere by doing the following:

1. If a text frame for continuing the story or article doesn't already exist, create one as described above.

2. Select the text frame that holds the first part of the story.

3. Click the Connect button at the bottom of the frame. If the frame is not full, the box will be gray with a white diamond in the middle. If the frame has overflow text, the white diamond will be replaced by three black squares. At this point, the mouse pointer will turn into a pitcher.

4. If you created the text frame to continue the text on another page, go to that page by using the Page Selector keys at the bottom-left side of the workspace.

5. Click inside the text frame in which you want to place the overflow text.

6. If the second frame's Connect button still shows three black squares, repeat the process until all the text is shown as desired.

# Adding a Table

Tables can be a great way to display items for sale in a brochure or to present statistics in your newsletter.

To create a table in Publisher 97, follow these steps:

1. Click the Table tool button on the left toolbar.

2. Position the mouse pointer where you want the upper-left corner of the table to appear, and then click and drag the mouse diagonally.

3. In the Create Table dialog box, shown in Figure 17.7, select the number of rows and columns you want your table to have; choose from the wide variety of table formats; approve your selections in the Sample box; and then click OK to complete the request.

**FIG. 17.7**
In the Create Table dialog box, you can select a basic format for your table, as shown here, or you can apply something a little fancier depending on your needs.

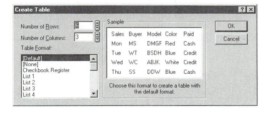

4. Type in the desired text by pressing the Tab key to move to the next cell, or Shift+Tab to back up a cell.

5. The table will expand automatically to accommodate larger amounts of text, but you'll need to follow a different procedure to add rows or columns after you've applied the format.

# Adding Rows and Columns to a Table

As you enter the text for your table, you may discover that you need more space than you first thought. To add a row or column to the table, do the following:

1. Select a cell in the table to which the new row or column will be attached.

2. Right-click to bring up the shortcut menu from which you can choose Insert Rows Or Columns.

3. In the Insert dialog box, shown in Figure 17.8, specify whether you want to add rows or columns, select the number of rows or columns, then determine whether those rows or columns will be inserted before or after the selected cell.

**FIG. 17.8**

The Insert dialog box lets you insert multiple rows or columns at one time simply by entering the desired number.

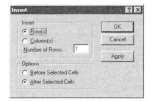

4. Click OK to add the specified rows or columns.

 To add another row to your table on-the-fly, select the bottom-right cell of the table, and then click Tab. A new row appears, ready for you to enter the necessary text.

## Separating Columns with Lines

Many of Publisher 97's templates use lines to separate columns and to enhance a publication's appearance. You can draw lines anywhere in your document by following these steps:

1. Select the Line tool from the Left toolbar.
2. Position the mouse-pointer over the starting point of the line.
3. Click the left mouse button and drag the mouse in the desired direction to draw the line.

 Depress the Shift key while executing step 3 to draw a straight, horizontal line.

## Importing Word Files for Use in Publisher

Perhaps you've asked a colleague to write an article for your newsletter, or maybe the artist for one of the products you have for sale has written a product description you'd like to use in your brochure. If the author used Word, there's no need to re-key the text.

To import a Word file into Publisher 97, follow these steps:

1. Click the text frame into which you want to insert the file, or create a new frame if needed.
2. On the menu bar, choose Insert, Text File to open the Insert Text File dialog box.
3. Locate the file you want to import, then click OK to insert it into the selected text frame.
4. If the text doesn't fit into the frame, Publisher 97 will ask you if you want to Autoflow the text into other boxes in your publication. Select Yes to send it on its way, or No to specify that the box flow as described in the previous sections.

## Adding a Fancy First Letter

You've seen the fancy, oversized first letters that are used to begin an article or chapter in magazines and books—now you can give your publications that same professional look. Just follow these steps to add a fancy first letter to your paragraph of choice:

1. Click the beginning of the paragraph to which you want to add the fancy first letter.
2. Choose Format, Fancy First Letter to open the Fancy First Letter dialog box.
3. Open the Fancy First Letter tab to choose from one of the designs provided, or create your own with the Custom First Letter tab.
4. Click OK to apply the fancy first letter.

## Drawing Attention to Articles by Using Pull Quotes

If you've ever skimmed through a magazine, chances are that you've been drawn into an article by an effectively used pull-quote. With Publisher 97, you can use the Design Gallery to add these stunning elements to your publication, or you can design your own.

To use a Design Gallery object in a pull-quote, do the following:

1. On the Left toolbar, choose the Design Gallery tool.
2. Click Pull-Quotes to see a sample of formats available. If you don't see one that appeals to you, click More Designs to see other available options.
3. Select the design you want by clicking it.
4. Click Insert Object to apply it to your publication.
5. Click Close to return to your document.

Follow these steps to design pull-quotes for your publications:

1. Create a text frame to house the pull-quote.
2. Enter the desired text.
3. Adjust the font and type size as necessary.
4. Choose Format, Border to add a fancy border to the top and bottom of the pull-quote box, if desired.

## Creating an Address List and Merging It with Your Publication

As you may have noticed while using PageWizard, Publisher 97 provides a way to print addresses on your publications so you can mail them directly.

Using the address list is great for small businesses who want to produce their brochures on a laser printer and mail them as they get requests. This can be a great money-saving technique. But, for the larger corporation or for bulk mailings, you may want to consider having the brochures photocopied commercially and then applying mailing labels from your data source of choice.

To create a Publisher address list, do the following:

1. Click inside a text frame on the location you want the address list information to appear, or create a new text frame if necessary.

2. On the menu bar, choose Mail Merge, Open Data Source. A box will appear offering you an overview of mail merge or step-by-step instructions, or you can click Continue to go on without them.

3. In the Open Data Source dialog box, select Create an address list in Publisher.

4. The New Address List dialog box, shown in Figure 17.9, will appear, prompting you to insert specific information.

**FIG. 17.9**

Enter the desired text, then click New Entry to save the current record and move to the next one.

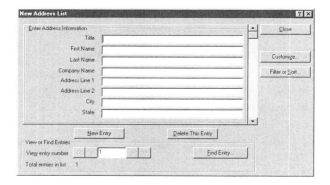

 If the field you want doesn't exist, click the Customize button to add it. You can also rearrange field order by using the Customize options.

5. Click New Entry to save the current record and clear the fields for a new record.

6. Repeat steps 4 and 5 until all the desired records have been added.

7. Click Close.

8. The File Name dialog box appears, prompting you to choose a name for the current address list.

9. Click Save.

10. Choose Yes to connect the address list to your open publication.

11. Under Fields, click the first field you want to insert into your publication, and then click Insert. Publisher will insert a field code to hold the field's place.

12. Add any spaces, punctuation, or carriage returns needed to format your fields, as desired.

13. Repeat steps 11 and 12 until all the necessary fields have been entered.

14. When all the field codes have been inserted, click Close.

**N O T E**  After you click Close, the field codes can be manipulated just like any other text. ■

15. Choose <u>M</u>ail Merge, <u>M</u>erge to have Publisher insert the address into your document.

16. The Preview Data dialog box appears. Use this to take a look at how any record appears in your publication.

17. The document is ready to be printed. For details on printing your publication, see the next section about printing.

Part
II

Ch
17

# Printing Publisher Documents

Before you print Publisher documents, you may want to confirm that the Print Setup is correct by following these steps:

1. Open the document you want to print.

2. Choose <u>F</u>ile, <u>P</u>rint Setup to bring up the Print Setup dialog box.

3. Confirm that the desired printer is selected.

4. In the Paper box, specify the Si<u>z</u>e and <u>S</u>ource of the paper to be used.

**T I P**  Because the types of publications you can create with Publisher are so diverse, you may want to use a nonstandard paper stock, depending on your printer's capabilities. To do this, you'll need to be sure the Manual Feed option is set. To access this option, open the Print dialog box as described in the preceding steps, and then click the <u>P</u>roperties button in the Printer section. Select the Paper tab and click the drop-down arrow next to the Paper <u>s</u>ource box. Choose Envelope manual feed, or simply manual feed as appropriate.

5. Select the proper orientation for the printout, if necessary.

6. Click OK to apply the settings.

With the proper Print Setup, you're ready to send your work to the printer. Follow these steps for the best results:

1. Open the document you want to print.

2. Choose <u>F</u>ile, <u>P</u>rint to access the Print dialog box shown in Figure 17.10.

**FIG. 17.10**

Publisher 97's Print dialog box helps you get the output you want with minimal hassle. For instance, you can select virtually any combination or range of pages in the Page Range box.

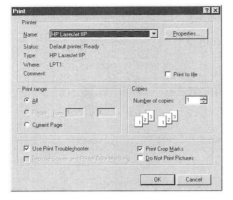

3. Choose the desired printer to which you want to send the output.

4. In the Print Range box, specify which pages you want to print.

5. Select the desired number of copies in the Copies box.

6. Click OK to send the output to the specified printer.

# CHAPTER 18

# Access 97 Essentials

**D**o you need an easy method to enter data into a database? Is your boss looking for professional reports? Have you outgrown your Excel database? Does a programming language like Visual Basic intimidate you?

Access 97 is the key to solving your problems. With Access you can build a database to hold all of your information, use forms to view and update the information, search and sort the information, and finally, generate professional reports to present the information. ■

**Databases and switchboards**

Use the Database Wizard to create any of 22 predefined databases. Learn to open and close your own databases. Take advantage of Switchboards to select database functions like Forms and Reports.

**Forms**

View and edit database information with Forms. Scroll through the database using scroll buttons, and search the database using filters and the Find button.

**Previewing and printing reports**

Preview reports before sending them to the printer.

# The Access Workspace

Access keeps your data and other related objects in a database. An Access database can contain tables, queries, forms, reports, macros, and modules (see Figure 18.1). A table is similar to a spreadsheet. It has a collection of fields that can contain such information as a name and an e-mail address. A table also has a series of rows that contain a set of related information such as Christopher Freeze and CFreeze@JustPC.com.

**N O T E**   Access 97 is based on the relational database model and SQL (Structured Query Language). This allows someone using Access a great deal of flexibility when building applications. If you are familiar with SQL, you can take advantage of some really advanced features that I'm not going to cover in this book. If you are interested in more detailed information about Access 97, Que publishes a number of good books, including *Using Microsoft Access 97* and *Special Edition Microsoft Access 97* that can help you better use this powerful tool. ■

**FIG. 18.1**

An Access database contains tables, queries, forms, reports, macros, and modules.

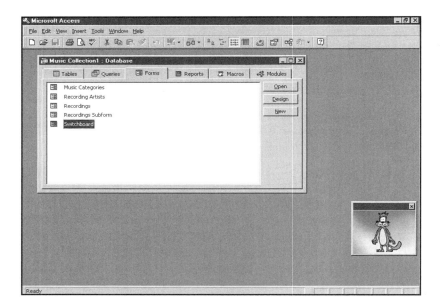

A *query* is a way to retrieve selected information from one or more database tables. It can be used with forms and reports to display information to the user. Although all queries can be used to read data from a database, some queries can also be used to update the information in a database.

A *form* is a window associated with the application. Typically a window contains information from a single row that may be edited. You can also scroll through the database one row at a time. Another type of form presents the data using a spreadsheet-like format. A third type of form is special because it does not display any data. It is called a switchboard, and it is used to provide menus that can run the various forms and reports that make up the application.

*Reports* are used to create a printed view of the database. A preview facility is used to see what the actual output would look like before it is sent to the printer.

# Using the Database Wizard to Create a New Database

The easiest way to create a new database is to use Access's Database Wizard. The Database Wizard provides 22 predefined databases ranging from Asset Tracking and Inventory Control, which help you run your business, to Recipes and Music Collection, which allows you to sort your ABBA CDs by release date. Through a series of questions, the wizard customizes the database to help you meet your specific requirements.

To create a database using the Database Wizard, do the following:

 1. Start Access, select the Database Wizard option button (see Figure 18.2), and then click OK. If Access is already running, choose File, New to display the new database window, and then click the Databases tab to display a list of predefined databases.

**FIG. 18.2**
Use the Database Wizard to create a new database.

2. Select a predefined database from the icon list as shown in Figure 18.3 and click OK.

**FIG. 18.3**
You can select a predefined database.

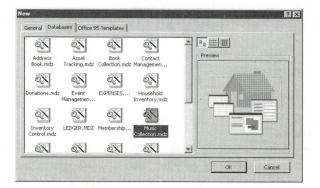

3. By default, Access saves the new database in the My Documents folder, using the database name as the default name. If you want, you can change the directory and database file name. After you decide on the directory and database name, click OK.

4. Access creates an empty database and then starts the Database Wizard. The wizard begins by describing the information that is to be kept in the database. To continue running the wizard, click Next.

 If you don't want to create this database, click Cancel. You can accept the default values for the database at any time and create the database by clicking Finish or pressing Alt+F. To return to the previous step of the wizard, click Back or press Alt+B.

5. The wizard next shows a list of tables in the database and the fields in each table. By clicking each table, you can review the fields. Beside each field is a check box indicating which fields are included in the database. Any field listed in italic is optional and may be included if you desire. The other fields are required and can't be removed. You also have a check box that includes sample data when checked. After you have reviewed the information, click Next to continue.

6. The next screen allows you to select the style that is to be used for screen displays, such as forms and queries. Select the display that you want and click Next.

 The Standard style gives you the most Windows-like display. This style is usually easier to use and read than the other styles.

7. The style used for printed reports is next. After selecting the desired report style, click Next.

8. The wizard now asks you to choose a name for the database. This information will appear on the printed reports and forms. It also allows you to include a picture on each report. This is an ideal way to include a company logo on the report. When finished, click Next.

9. The wizard has finished collecting customization information about the database and is ready to create it. When the wizard has finished, you may click the Start The Database and the Display Help On Using A Database check boxes to start the database and to display information about how to use a database. Click Finish to create the database.

10. The wizard shows a window containing progress information as it builds the database, then it runs the main switchboard for the application (see Figure 18.4).

# Closing a Database

There are several ways to close a database:

- If the main switchboard has an exit button, all you need to do is click that button.
- To close a database from the database window, choose File, Close from the main menu bar.
- You can click the database window's close button in the top right corner of the window.
- You can double-click the Control-menu icon in the top left corner of the window.

**FIG. 18.4**
Use the switchboard to navigate through your new application.

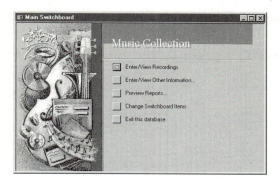

# Opening an Existing Database

To open an existing database, do the following:

1. Start Access, choose the Open an Existing Database option button, and select the name of the database from the list of existing databases. If the database doesn't appear in the list, choose More Files and click OK. You can also get to this window by choosing File, Open from the main menu.

2. If you selected More Files in the previous step, a list of files is displayed. Select the directory and file name of the database you want to open and click OK.

After selecting the database you want to open, Access loads it and displays the main switchboard or the database window.

# Using Switchboards and Database Windows

Switchboards provide an easy way for users to access the functions available in an Access database. Simply click the field to run the appropriate function. The form, report, or other function is displayed.

To use a database window, do the following:

1. Select the tab for the desired general function: Tables, Queries, Forms, Reports, Macros, or Modules, as shown in Figure 18.5.

**FIG. 18.5**
Each tab in a database window contains reports or other objects that you can modify.

Part
II
Ch
18

2. To run an existing form (or other object), select the item and double-click the icon, or you may select the icon and click the Open button.

3. To make changes to an existing form (or other object), select the item and click the Design button.

4. To create a new form (or other object), click the New button.

# Using Forms

Forms provide an easy way for a user to look at the data in your database. The data can come from either a table or a query. A form generally displays a single record at a time, and is known as the current record. The form includes controls to move forward and backward through the data and to insert new records into the table.

Each record consists of a number of fields. Each field has an associated label that contains the name of a field. These fields may contain different types of data. Text fields can contain any combination of characters, numeric fields can only contain numbers, and date fields can contain only valid dates. Some fields require you to enter a value from a list of acceptable values.

While any record is displayed, you can change the value in any field. Moving to another record saves the values. If you entered data and want to restore the original data, press the Esc key once to restore the default value for the current field. Pressing the Esc key a second time restores all of the old values. This information is illustrated in Figure 18.6.

**FIG. 18.6**

A form allows you to enter and edit information in your database.

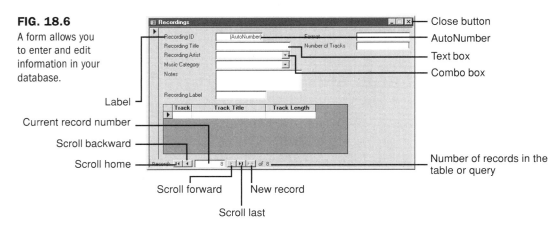

- *Label.* Displays the name of the field.
- *Text box.* Displays the contents of a field in the database.
- *Combo box.* Displays the contents of a field that must exist in another table or query. Clicking the down arrow button at the right end of the file displays a list of legal values for this field. To add a new value to this list of values, double-click the field and a new form is displayed to add the new value. After you enter the required data in the new form, you can close it by clicking the close button and continue working with the old form.

- *AutoNumber.* Displays this value only when a new record is being added to the database. You don't need to enter anything in this field. When you save the record, the next available number is placed in this field.

- *Scroll home.* Goes to the first record in the table or query.

- *Scroll backward.* Goes to the previous record. This button is not available when you are viewing the first record.

- *Current record number.* Displays the number for the current record.

- *Scroll forward.* Goes to the next record. Moving the current record beyond the last allows the form to insert a new one. While in insert mode, this button is disabled.

- *Scroll last.* Goes to the last record in the table or query.

- *New record.* Moves the current record beyond the last in order to insert a new one. To save your data after entering it into the fields, simply move to another record. If you don't want to save the record, press the Esc key until you have a blank form and move to another record. Access never saves a blank record. If Access determines there is a problem with the record when it tries to save it to the database, it displays a message box explaining the error and gives you a chance to correct the problem.

- *Number of records in the table or query.* Updates automatically whenever the database is updated.

- *Close.* Closes the current form. Any changes to the current record are then saved. If you are inserting a new record, it is saved into the database provided that it is not blank.

# Using the Access Toolbar with Forms

In addition to the functions on the form, the Access toolbar contains a number of other useful functions (see Figure 18.7).

**FIG. 18.7**
You can perform many different database operations using a database form.

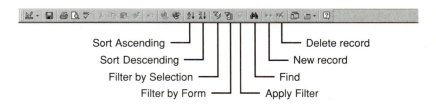

Sort Ascending
Sort Descending
Filter by Selection
Filter by Form
Delete record
New record
Find
Apply Filter

- *Sort Ascending.* Select a field and click this button to arrange the records in ascending order based on the value in the selected field.

- *Sort Descending.* Select the field that you want to sort on and click this button. The records are arranged in descending order based on the value in the selected field.

- *Filter by Selection.* Select the field with the value you want to filter and click this button. Only those records with that value are selected.

*Filter by Form.* Click this button to display a blank version of the regular form as shown in Figure 18.8. Fill in one of the fields with a value that you want to see. By using the Or tab at the bottom of the form, you can select a new blank form and specify another value. After you have finished specifying these values, click the Apply Filter button. Any record that matches any of the values specified is selected.

**FIG. 18.8**
Use the Filter window to select only the records you want from the database.

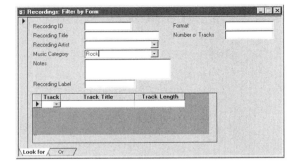

 *Apply Filter.* Click the Apply Filter button after specifying Filter by Form information. Also, clicking this button after using Filter by Selection or Filter by Form restores the original data.

 *Find.* Click this button to display a Find window (see Figure 18.9). Type in a value to be searched for in the Find What field. Specify a value for Search to determine whether to search all the records (All), from the current location to the end of the records (Down) and from the current location to the beginning of the records (Up). Buttons are available to find the first record (Find First), find the next record after the first record was found (Find Next), and to close the search. Closing the Find window leaves the last record as the current record.

**FIG. 18.9**
Use the Find window to search for specific values in your database or query.

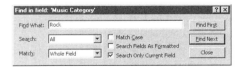

 *New record.* Click this button to add a new record. This is the same as the New record button on the form.

 *Delete record.* Click this button to delete the current record. A window appears asking you to confirm that you want to delete it. Clicking Yes deletes the record, and clicking No leaves it in the database.

# Viewing and Printing Reports

Reports can be selected from either a switchboard (by clicking the appropriate button) or from a database window (by clicking the Reports tab and then double-clicking the desired report). The Report window is shown in Figure 18.10.

**FIG. 18.10**
Use the Report window to view your report before sending it to the printer.

Print
Zoom
One Page
Two Pages
Multiple Pages
Zoom Size
Close
OfficeLinks
Last Page
Next Page
Page Number
Previous Page
First Page

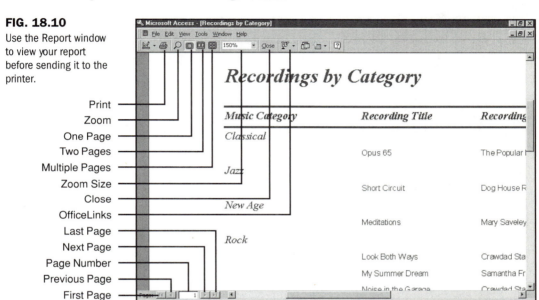

■ *Print.* Sends the report to your default printer. You can also choose File, Print from the Access menu line to see a print dialog window as shown in Figure 18.11. This dialog box allows you to select the printer you want to use, the range of pages, and the number of copies.

▶ **See** "Preview Before You Print," **p. 38**

**FIG. 18.11**
The Print dialog box allows you to change the default print options by pressing the Properties button.

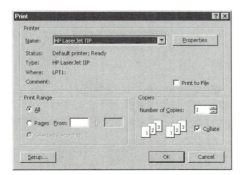

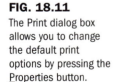

■ *Zoom.* Toggles between the best fit and the value specified in the Zoom Size window.

 ■ *One Page.* Displays one page in the print window.

 ■ *Two Pages.* Displays two pages in the print window.

 ■ *Multiple Pages.* Displays a small window showing six tiny pages. Select any combination of the pages to be shown in the same fashion in the print window.

■ *Zoom Size.* Select how large or small the page is to be displayed when zoomed. Values range from 200% (very large) to 10% (very small) and Fit (meaning that the print display is sized to fit in the entire window).

■ *Close.* Closes the print window and returns to the Switchboard or database window.

■ *OfficeLinks.* Transfers the information into Word or Excel.

■ *First Page.* Views the first page of the report.

■ *Previous Page.* Views the previous page of the report.

■ *Page Number.* Displays the current page number or the first page in the print preview window.

■ *Next Page.* Views the next page of the report.

■ *Last Page.* Views the last page of the report.

# CHAPTER 19

# Access 97 Advanced Topics

**W**hat do you do if none of the predefined databases that come with Access 97 meets your needs? Do you need a new report or form for an existing database? Is there information in your database that you do not want to include in a report?

Access 97 is a rich and powerful tool that enables you to build your own custom applications. You can create your own databases and tables and develop your own forms and reports to help you manage your information.

**Databases and tables**

Create your own custom database. Add new or change existing tables to meet your custom requirements using the Table Wizard.

**Forms**

Create your own forms with the Form Wizard.

**Reports**

Use the Report Wizard to produce a variety of reports quickly and easily.

**Queries**

Find information in the database using the Query Wizard and sort it in your forms and reports.

# Creating an Empty Database

If none of the predefined databases meets your needs, you can always create an empty database and fill it with the objects you do need. To create an empty database, follow these steps:

1. Start Access.
2. Choose the Blank Database, and click OK.
3. Select the file name you want to use for the new database and the directory you want to put it in, and click Create.

The database window is shown with the empty database.

# Creating a New Table with the Table Wizard

Tables are added to a database to hold information. Each table has a series of fields. One field is known as the primary key, which is used to uniquely identify a row in the table. The rest of the fields contain additional information you want to keep.

A database may contain multiple tables. Although the tables are usually related to each other, it isn't necessary. When the tables are related, the primary key from one is a regular field in a table. For example, consider a database containing information about customers and orders. The Customer table contains a primary key called Customer Number and a number of other fields like Customer Name and Customer Address. The Order table contains a primary key called Order Number. It also contains a field called Customer Number, which can be used to get information from the Customer table.

 Try a few different designs before actually filling a database with live data. Take a look at the sample databases that are supplied with Access. They are a good source of design ideas. And keep it simple. A single table that keeps track of all of your information is much easier to build and use than a very complicated database. For databases with less than a few hundred records, it is often the best solution.

To create an empty database, do the following:

1. From the database window, select the Tables tab.
2. A window appears with a number of ways to create a table. Click Table Wizard and then click OK.
3. Another window appears with a number of predefined tables as shown in Figure 19.1.
4. Select either the Business or Personal option button and then select one of the listed Sample Tables.
5. Review the Sample Fields for this table. To add one of the fields to your table, select it and then click the single right arrow to add a field to the Fields in your new table box. If you change your mind and want to delete a field from the fields in your new table, select it and click the single left arrow.

**FIG. 19.1**

Select sample fields for your new table.

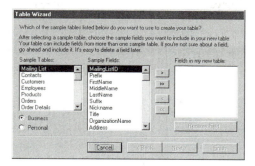

To add all the listed fields into the new table box, click the double right arrow. Click the double left arrow to remove all fields from the new table box.

 **T I P** When choosing fields for your table, it's a good idea to think about how you plan to use this information. The best way to do this is to visualize the reports you would like to see. When you figure out the column headers you need, you have a list of fields that you should add to your table.

6. After selecting all the fields you want in your new table, click Next.

7. Select a name for your new table. The wizard either picks a primary key for you or helps you pick your own primary key. Select one and click Next.

8. If you want to create your own primary key, the wizard asks you to select the field that you want to contain the primary key and the kind of data it should contain. The value of this field must always be unique. When you have chosen, click Next. If you have only one table, skip to step 12. If you have more than one table, continue with step 9.

 **T I P** The wizard offers you three choices for the type of data kept in the primary key: an automatic number supplied by Access, a number you supply, or a text string you supply. Unless you have a strong reason for using your own values, let Access supply an automatic number.

9. If you already have one or more tables in your database, the wizard asks you how they are related. Select one of the listed tables and relationships and click the Relationships button to change how they are related.

10. If you clicked relationships, a new window appears listing three options (see Figure 19.2):

   • The tables aren't related. Assume that the new table contains information about students and another table contains information about courses. These tables have no common fields and are thus unrelated.

   • One record in the new table matches many records in another table. Assume that the new table contains information about students and another table contains information about student schedules. Then for each record in the student table, there will be multiple records containing information about their schedule. These tables will probably share a common field called Student Number.

Part

II

Ch

19

- Many records match one record in another table. This relationship is similar to the previous relationship, except that the student schedules table was created first and then the students table was created.

Select the appropriate option and click OK to return to the previous window.

**FIG. 19.2**

Select how your table is related to other tables in your database.

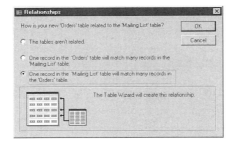

11. When finished reviewing the relationships, click Next.

12. The final screen in the wizard provides three options:

- Modify the table design
- Enter data directly into the table
- Let the wizard build a form automatically

Select an option and click Finish to build your new table.

 Let the wizard build a form for you. After all, you can use that form to enter the data.

# Building Queries with the Simple Query Wizard

Forms and reports can access data from the tables in your database, or they can access data from a query. A query is a way to ask the database for information. The data can be extracted from one table or combined from multiple tables. Selection criteria can be specified so that only selected records and fields can be returned. The data can then be summarized, sorted, and grouped together to simplify writing reports and designing forms.

**CAUTION**

Not all queries can be used for updating. If your query contains summary information or uses more than one table, it may not be updateable.

To create a query using the Simple Query Wizard, do the following:

1. From the database window, select the Queries tab and click the Underline{N}ew button.

2. A window appears with a number of ways to create a query and asks which table or query should be used to supply the data. Click Simple Query Wizard and specify the query or table. (If you want to extract information from more than one table, don't specify a table.) Then click OK.

3. Another window appears with information about the tables and fields inside your database. Select the fields you want to have available in your query by using the arrow buttons to move them to Selected Fields, and then click Next (see Figure 19.3).

**FIG. 19.3**

Select the fields you want in the query.

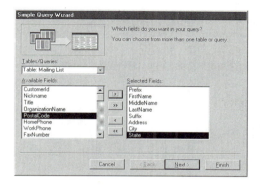

4. The wizard then asks whether you want to see the detailed records or just a summary of the records. If you would like summary information, click the Summary Options button.

5. The Summary option allows you to compute the sum, the average, the minimum, and the maximum for any numeric field you have selected. It also returns a count of the number of records retrieved. Select the options you want and click OK.

6. After choosing Summary or Detailed records, click Next.

7. If you have selected a field with a date value and requested summary information, the wizard asks you how you want to group the value. They can be grouped by day, month, quarter, or year. The default option is to group them by unique date and time. Thus, for each group, the database returns the sum, average, minimum, maximum, or count on the group rather than the entire set of data. Click Next to continue.

8. The last window displayed by the Simple Query Wizard lets you open the query to view the results or modify the query design. Select an option and click Finish to build the query.

Part

II

Ch

19

**T I P**

I suggest that you view the results unless you have a good understanding of database systems. This is a good way to verify that you get what you expect from the database.

# Building Forms with the Form Wizard

To create a form using the Form Wizard, do the following:

1. From the database window, select the Forms tab and click the <u>N</u>ew button.

2. A window appears with a number of ways to create a form and asks which table or query should be used to supply the data. Click Form Wizard and specify the query or table. If you would like to extract information from more than one table, don't specify a query or table, and then click OK.

3. Another window appears with information about the tables and fields inside your database. Select the fields you want to have on your form (see Figure 19.4) by using the arrow buttons to move them to <u>S</u>elected Fields, and then click <u>N</u>ext.

**FIG. 19.4**

Select the fields you want in the form.

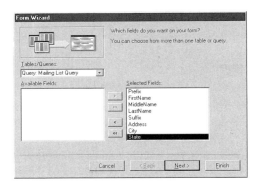

4. In the next step you are asked how the fields should be arranged on the form. There are four basic ways to arrange the fields:

   • *<u>C</u>olumnar.* Lists the fields down a column (see Figure 19.5). If more fields are selected than can fit in a single column, more columns are automatically added.

**FIG. 19.5**

A <u>C</u>olumnar form arranges the fields and field labels as a series of one or more columns on the form.

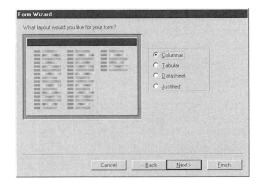

- *Tabular*. Lists the fields across in a single row (see Figure 19.6). If no data exists in the table or query, only one row is displayed. Additional rows are displayed to show additional data if it is available.

**FIG. 19.6**

A Tabular form arranges the fields and their labels as a table.

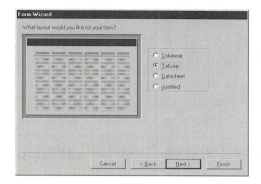

- *Datasheet*. Displays the data using a spreadsheet-like display (see Figure 19.7).

**FIG. 19.7**

A Datasheet form presents the fields using a spreadsheet-like display.

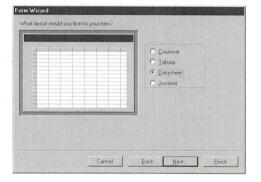

- *Justified*. Displays the fields in a row with labels above them (see Figure 19.8). If more fields are present than can fit on the form in a single line, then additional lines are displayed so that all of the fields are displayed. Select one of the options and click Next.

5. Select a background style for the form and click Next.

**TIP** The Standard style gives you the most Windows-like display. This style is usually easier to use and read than the other styles.

6. The last step in building a form is to give it a name and select an option to either open the new form or use the form editor. Select your option and click Finish to build the form.

Part

**II**

Ch

**19**

**FIG. 19.8**
A Justified form
squeezes as many fields
and field labels as
possible into each row
on the form.

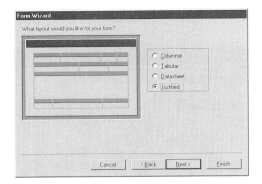

# Building Reports with the Report Wizard

To create a form using the Report Wizard, do the following:

1. From the database window, select the Reports tab and click the New button.

2. A window appears with a number of ways to create a form and asks which table or query should be used to supply the data. Click Report Wizard and specify the query or table. If you would like to extract information from more than one table, don't specify a query or table, and then click OK.

3. Another window appears with information about the tables and fields inside your database. Select the fields you want to have on your report by using the arrow buttons to move them to Selected Fields, and then click Next.

**TIP** You may be tempted to include a lot of fields in a report, but you probably shouldn't. By selecting a few key fields you build a smaller, easier-to-read report. You can always build more reports.

4. The Report Wizard displays a simplified version of the report and asks whether you want to add grouping levels. The field selected for the group uses grouping levels to sort the data, and then the value of the field is displayed on the report only when it changes.

**TIP** For really advanced users, the Report Wizard allows multiple grouping levels for a report, with one grouping level being nested inside another (see Figure 19.9). The order of the grouping levels can be changed by selecting the grouping level to be moved and clicking the priority up and down arrows. When you are finished, click Next.

5. The fields that have not been selected for a grouping level are known as detail fields. Together they are called a detail record. The Report Wizard asks you to select up to four fields for sorting the detail records.

6. The Report Wizard then asks you to select a layout for the report (see Figure 19.10). Six different layouts are available and are selected by clicking the corresponding option buttons. There are also option buttons that allow you to display the report in portrait

mode or landscape mode. In addition, there is a check box that lets Access select widths for the fields so that reports fit on a page. Make your selections and click Next.

**FIG. 19.9**
Create easy-to-read reports by grouping together common data.

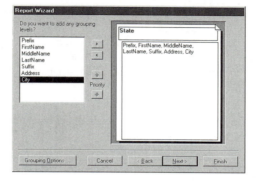

**FIG. 19.10**
Select the report layout and orientation you want to use.

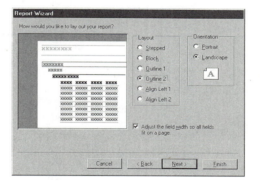

**T I P**  Select landscape mode if you have a lot of fields in the detail records. It makes the report much easier to read.

7. The next window allows you to select a style for the character fonts and how the headings and detail information are arranged. Select a style that you like and click Next.

8. Finally, the Report Wizard asks you to name the report and gives you a chance to preview it. Click Finish to save the report.

# Building a Chart with the Chart Wizard

To create a form using the Chart Wizard, do the following:

1. From the database window, select the Reports tab and click the New button.

2. A window appears with a number of ways to create a form and asks which table or query should be used to supply the data. Click Chart Wizard and specify the query or table. If

Part
II

Ch
19

you would like to extract information from more than one table, don't specify a query or table, and then click OK.

3. Another window appears asking you to select the fields you want in the chart. Select the fields you want to have on your report by using the arrow buttons to move them to <u>S</u>elected Fields, and then click <u>N</u>ext.

 **T I P** You may be tempted to include a lot of fields in a chart, but you shouldn't. A pie chart should probably have only two fields. Bar and line charts become too complex to understand if you have more than four or five fields.

4. The Chart Wizard displays a table of the available chart types (see Figure 19.11). Select a chart type and click <u>N</u>ext.

**FIG. 19.11**
Select a chart type from the Chart Wizard.

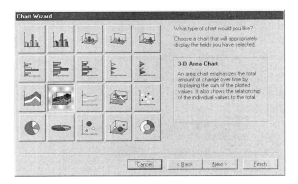

▶ **See** "Using Chart Wizard to Visualize Your Data," **p. 156**

5. Next, the Chart Wizard asks you to lay out your chart. You can drag and drop the fields selected onto different positions on the chart. There is a button in the upper-left corner called Preview Chart that you can click to see a preview of the chart. When finished, click <u>N</u>ext.

6. Finally, the Chart Wizard asks you to name the chart. It also asks whether you want to display a legend and gives you a chance to preview it. Click <u>F</u>inish to save the chart.

# CHAPTER 20

# Outlook Essentials

**M**icrosoft's new addition to the Office family, Outlook 97, is like a virtual DayTimer. With Outlook 97, you can manage your contacts, schedule group meetings, coordinate projects, and e-mail your friends and associates. Outlook is Microsoft's entry into the Personal Information Manager (PIM) market, but it goes beyond that to earn the title Desktop Information Manager, as well.

Whether you're a busy executive who needs to assemble a scrambling staff for a meeting, or an overworked single mom with four kids on the go who inherited Outlook on her new PC, Outlook has what it takes to help you get organized and stay in touch. ◼

**What is Outlook?**

Because Outlook is so new, it's worth taking a closer look at what Outlook is capable of doing.

**Getting around in Outlook**

Learn about all the toolbars and workspaces you'll run into while working with Outlook.

**E-mailing with Outlook**

See how you can use Outlook to send, receive, and manage your e-mail.

# What Is Outlook?

Microsoft refers to Outlook as a Desktop Information Manager—a new breed of application that is an enhancement of, and extension to, typical Personal Information Managers (PIM). So what does this mean from a functionality point of view?

In addition to doing all the typical PIM tasks, such as maintaining an address book, a calendar, a task list, and providing a notepad, Outlook boasts a powerful concept: the *universal inbox*. In addition to sending and receiving e-mail, this universal inbox is capable of letting you do the following:

- Exchange e-mail with people using almost any e-mail program.
- Send a fax (assuming you have a fax/modem configured, of course) the same way you send an e-mail message.
- Unsend messages sent to other Outlook users if they have not already read them.
- Attach voting buttons to a message to quickly tabulate group opinions.
- Compose your messages offline, and send them in batches.
- Organize your mail in personally defined folders.

But there are several other unique features that set Outlook apart from traditional PIMs. These include a universal address book, a journal, file management, and unparalleled integration of its components.

**N O T E**   Because there's so much ground to cover in so little time, the Outlook coverage that follows will assume that you already have Outlook configured for, and running on, your system. If you need help setting up Outlook, refer to Microsoft's help options, visit Microsoft on the Web, or ask your network administrator, if applicable.

# Anatomy of the Outlook Workspace

Upon launching Outlook, you see a screen like the one pictured in Figure 20.1.

The Outlook workspace is loaded with buttons, icons, and toolbars, many of which you've encountered in other applications. Some of these screen elements, however, are unique to Outlook. To give you a better feel for what these elements do, here is a brief description of each:

- *Outlook bar.* Click one of these icons to jump to the respective folder/function.
- *Group icons.* Surrounding the Outlook bar are three Group buttons: Outlook, Mail, and Other. Clicking the Outlook button customizes your Outlook bar to give you instant access to the Inbox, Calendar, Contacts, Tasks, Journal, Notes, and Deleted Items. The Mail button displays icons, including Inbox, Sent Items, Outbox, and Deleted Items. Finally, the Other button provides file-management options such as My Computer, My Documents, and Favorites.

**FIG. 20.1**

When Outlook is launched, you will immediately see your universal inbox. Use the Outlook bar on the left side of the screen to access other Outlook functions (also known as folders).

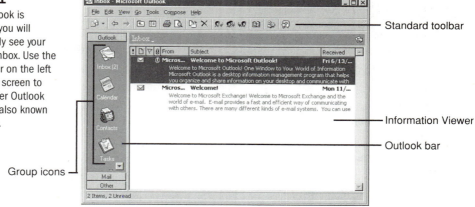

- *Information Viewer.* This window is Outlook's equivalent to a workspace. The selected item's contents are displayed in this window.

- *Standard toolbar.* Although its icons are noticeably different from those found in other Office 97 applications, Outlook's Standard toolbar functions the same way any other standard toolbar does—no matter what your view in the application, you can use these familiar buttons to complete the desired tasks. See Table 20.1 for a close-up of these icons and their functions.

### Table 20.1 Outlook's Standard Toolbar Functions

| Icon | Name | Function |
|------|------|----------|
| | New Mail Message | Creates a new mail message |
| | Back | Opens the previous item or file in a list of 10 recently accessed items |
| | Forward | Opens the next item or file in a list of 10 recently accessed items |
| | Up One Level | Opens the folder up one level from the current folder |
| | Folder List | Shows or hides the list of all your Outlook folders |
| | Print | Prints the current item |
| | Print Preview | Examines your output before sending it to the printer |

Part
II

Ch
20

*continues*

**Table 20.1   Continued**

| Icon | Name | Function |
| --- | --- | --- |
| | Undo | Undoes the last command or deletes the last entry |
| | Move to Folder | Allows you to move the selected item to another folder |
| | Delete | Deletes the current item |
| | Reply | Returns the message or file to the sender |
| | Reply to All | Returns the message to everyone on the To and CC line |
| | Forward | Sends the message or file to the person you specify |
| | Address Book | Displays a list of e-mail addresses |
| | Find Items | Searches for items meeting the criteria you specify |
| | Office Assistant | Calls up the animated Office Assistant you've selected |
| | New Appointment | Creates a new appointment |
| | Day | Shows your calendar one day at a time |
| | Month | Shows your calendar a month at a time |
| | New Contact | Allows you to enter a new contact to your list |
| | AutoDial | Automatically dials a phone number if your computer has a modem installed |
| | New Task | Enter a new task on your task list |
| | Group By Box | Shows or hides the Group By box so you can easily group related tasks |
| | AutoPreview | Shows or hides the first line in a table |

| Icon | Name | Function |
|------|------|----------|
| | New Journal | Creates a new journal entry |
| | New Note | Creates a new note |
| | Large Icons | Displays files as large icons |
| | Small Icons | Displays files as small icons |
| | New Office Document | Creates a new Office document from within Outlook |
| | Map Network Drive | Establishes a connection and assigns a drive letter to a network computer |
| | Disconnect Network Drive | Removes the connection to a network computer |

## Using Outlook's Inbox

Outlook's inbox can be used to send and receive e-mail and faxes, assign tasks, even request a meeting. This universal inbox (refer to Figure 20.1) is the clearinghouse for all your electronic messages.

Outlook can do some pretty neat things, too. For instance, you can include voting buttons in your e-mail message to tally your recipients' opinions, or you can apply rules to incoming messages. You can even delay the delivery of your e-mail messages (a must-have if you want to leave the country before firing a bunch of your employees).

But there's bad news, too. Many of Outlook's neatest features are available only if your company runs Microsoft Exchange Server, and sometimes, only if the recipient uses Outlook as well. Be sure to ask your network administrator if you use Exchange Server before trying some of Outlook's more advanced functions. Home users should consult their Internet service provider to learn whether or not Microsoft Exchange Server is in use there.

## Sending a Simple E-Mail Message with Outlook

To send an e-mail message using Outlook, follow these steps:

1. Launch Outlook.
2. To bring up the Message dialog box, shown in Figure 20.2, do one of the following:
   - From the Inbox screen, choose Compose, New Mail Message.
   - Click Ctrl+N.

Part

II

Ch

20

- From within any Office 97 application, choose <u>F</u>ile, Send To, and then choose Mail Recipient, <u>R</u>outing Recipient, or <u>F</u>ax Recipient. This attaches the current file to an e-mail message.

- Click the New Message button on the Standard toolbar.

**FIG. 20.2**

To send a message from within Outlook, click the New Message button on the Standard toolbar, click Ctrl+N, or choose Com<u>p</u>ose, <u>N</u>ew Mail Message.

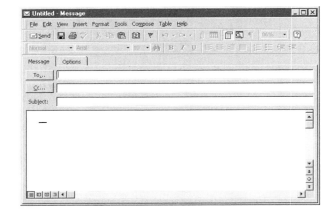

3. If you selected Send To from within another Office 97 application, a file will be attached to the Message dialog box.

4. Click inside the To text box to enter the address manually.

5. Click inside the Cc text box and enter the desired e-mail address to send a courtesy copy of a message to someone.

6. Enter a title for your message in the Subject line, and then type the contents into the large text box at the bottom of the window.

7. If desired, you can attach a file to an e-mail message by clicking the Insert File button on the message's toolbar. The Insert File dialog box will appear, enabling you to navigate through your system files until you find the file that you want to attach. Double-click its name to attach it.

8. Click the <u>S</u>end button to send the message on its way.

**CAUTION**

Attaching a large text or image file? Attaching such a file can dramatically increase the amount of time needed to send the note. And if you have a bad phone line or flaky Internet connection, the opportunities for mailing errors to occur are greatly increased. To ensure safe transport of your messages and their attachments, consider using a data compression utility like WinZip to speed up the mailing process and reduce the potential for errors.

# Reading and Processing Outlook E-Mail

Any e-mail received will show up in your universal inbox. To read it, simply double-click it, and then take any of the actions listed in Table 20.2.

**Table 20.2  Actions Taken on New E-Mail**

| To Do This | Do the Following |
| --- | --- |
| Delete it | Click the Delete button on the toolbar. |
| Close it and save it in the inbox | Click the Close button, or use the Next or Previous buttons to scroll through other items. |
| Reply to the message | Click Reply, then enter your response. |
| Reply to all recipients | Click Reply to All, then write your response. |
| Forward the note to someone else | Click Forward, then type in any additional information. |
| View an attachment | Double-click its icon, and the appropriate application will launch displaying the attached file. |
| Mark the message for later follow-up | Click the Message Flag button, choose an action in the Message Flag dialog box, then enter a date, if desired. |
| Print the message | Click the Print button on the toolbar above the message. |

# Managing E-Mail Files in Outlook

If you've worked with e-mail for any length of time, you know how quickly messages can pile up in your inbox, making them virtually impossible to find. That's where Outlook's nested folder structure comes in. With Outlook, you can create subfolders for all your major projects. You can even define subfolders within the project folder for maximum organization.

To create a subfolder, follow these steps:

1. Display the Inbox Information Viewer either by launching Outlook or by clicking the Inbox icon on the Outlook Bar.

2. Click the Folder List button to display the list of Outlook folders.
3. Right-click the folder under which you want to create the subfolder.
4. Select Create Subfolder from the shortcut menu, shown in Figure 20.3.
5. The Create New Folder dialog box, shown in Figure 20.4, appears.
6. Give the folder a descriptive name that will assist you in finding what you need quickly.

**FIG. 20.3**
Choose Create Subfolders to start building a nested filing system for your projects or contacts.

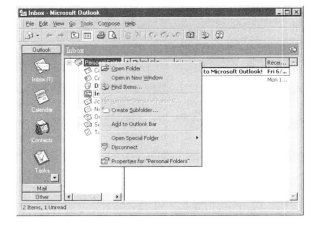

**FIG. 20.4**
Give your folder a name and specify its contents by entering the appropriate information into its respective fields.

A word about naming folders: You may want to think through your folder name choices carefully. For instance, if you're a writer, Books or Magazine Articles may seem like logical folder names, especially if you add subfolders. But if you access those subfolders often, picking through several layers can be time-consuming. You may, instead, want to give the specific project its own folder to make it quick and easy to find. In this case, your structure will be dictated more by frequency of a folder's use than anything else.

7. Select the type of item (most frequently mail messages) that will be stored in the folder.
8. Outlook automatically creates a shortcut to the new folder in the Outlook bar unless you specifically tell it not to. To keep Outlook from creating the shortcut, remove the check mark next to Create a Shortcut to This Folder In the Outlook Bar.
9. Click OK to create the subfolder and see its name displayed in the Folder List.

# Moving Outlook Items to the Desired Folder

Outlook will take care of filing most items for you. For instance, it will file your contacts in its Contact folder automatically. Unfortunately, all e-mail received stays in your Inbox until you move it, so those newly created folders and subfolders will be put to good use!

To move an Outlook object to a folder or subfolder, follow these steps:

1. Select the item you want to move from the Inbox Information Viewer.
2. Choose Edit, Move to Folder or click Ctrl+Shift+V to bring up the Move Items dialog box, shown in Figure 20.5.

**FIG. 20.5**
Select the folder to which you want to move the selected item from this list, then click OK.

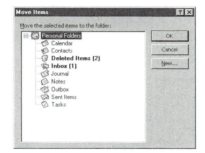

3. Choose the folder or subfolder to which you want to move the selected item.
4. Click OK to complete the move.

Another alternative is to open the File List, and then drag the desired item to the new location. ●

Part
II

Ch
20

# CHAPTER 21

# Using Outlook for Contact Management

**O**ur lives both on and off the job are getting busier each day. It's becoming increasingly more important to manage workloads, time commitments, and contacts, and to be more effective in what little time we have to do things.

Outlook provides a number of tools to help make better use of your time. These tools include an address book (contact list), a calendar, a task manager, a journal, and a note pad. In this chapter, these tools will be examined, as well as how you can get the most out of them. ■

**Managing your contacts**

Work with Outlook's Address Book to build and manage a contact list.

**Requesting a meeting with Calendar**

Use Outlook's Calendar feature to manage your time, then request a meeting with a colleague.

**Tracking tasks**

Discover how to use Outlook's Task List to monitor what's been done and what needs to be done.

**Creating virtual Post-It notes**

Create notes to remind yourself of tasks to be done.

# Using an Address Book

Creating an address book may not seem like a thrilling prospect on the surface, but Outlook's integration with e-mail and all the other Office 97 applications makes having an address book a tremendous help in doing the following tasks:

- Dial a contact's phone number automatically.
- Create an e-mail message or send a fax without having to enter the contact's e-mail address or fax number manually.
- Print a telephone or address list.
- Insert a name and address into a Word document on-the-fly.
- Schedule a meeting with other Outlook users on your company's intranet.

# Building an Address Book

To create an address book in Outlook, do the following:

1. Launch Outlook.
2. Choose File, New, Contact, or click Ctrl+Shift+C to open a Contact dialog box like the one illustrated in Figure 21.1.

**FIG. 21.1**

Add the desired information about a contact, then click Save and Close to complete the entry. Remember also to access the Details tab to collect the most complete listing.

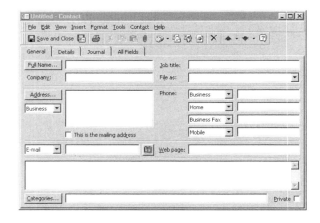

3. Enter the desired information in each box, pressing Tab to move to the next field or Shift+Tab to move back a field. You may also click inside a field's text box to enter necessary information.
4. Fill out all the information possible in the General and Details tabs to give you the most complete database.
5. Use the following shortcuts and options to make the most of your contact list:
   - If you enter a person's full name in the Full Name text box, Outlook will break out the fields for you for later use in mail merges and so on. If a name is particularly

complicated, you may want to click the F<u>u</u>ll Name button to see a breakdown of the fields (see Figure 21.2). You can fill out the desired fields in the Check Full Name dialog box manually.

**FIG. 21.2**
Enter the desired information in the Check Full Name dialog box, then click OK to apply it to the Full Name text box.

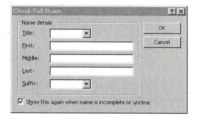

- Outlook does the same for Addresses, too. Simply click the A<u>d</u>dress box to see the Check Address dialog box, and then enter the information manually.

**N O T E**  The Check Full Name or Check Address dialog box will also appear if Outlook is unable to correctly translate an address into the proper fields.

- You can enter up to three addresses for a contact by clicking the drop-down arrow under the A<u>d</u>dress button. Make the appropriate selection from Business, Home, or Other, and then enter the address. Be sure to check the This Is The Mailing Add<u>r</u>ess box when the preferred mailing address is currently displayed. Word will use this information to import the proper address into a letter.

- Outlook will keep track of up to four phone numbers per contact. It displays boxes for Business, Home, Business Fax, and Mobile, by default, but you can easily give a phone number a new label by clicking the drop-down arrow next to the number you want to label.

- You may also enter up to three e-mail addresses by clicking the drop-down arrow and labeling each entry.

- Click the <u>C</u>ategories button to declare multiple contact categories for a person, as shown in Figure 21.3. If you don't see a category you like, create your own entry by clicking the Master Categories button from this dialog box.

6. The Journal tab tracks contact information you have recorded about that person, including exchanged e-mail messages or scheduled meetings. You must select Auto<u>m</u>atically Record Journal Entries to enable the Journal tracking feature.

7. The All Fields tab enables you to see selected fields in table form.

8. Click <u>S</u>ave and Close when you've finished editing or viewing the selected contact.

# Finding Entries in Address Book

You essentially have two ways to locate entries in Outlook's address book. If you know the person's name and its proper spelling, you can find it by following these steps:

**FIG. 21.3**

Choose the appropriate categories for your contact by placing a check mark beside the desired box. By designating this information, you give yourself maximum mail merge functionality.

1. Click the Contacts button on the Outlook Bar to see your address list.

2. Begin typing the last name of the contact you want to find.

**N O T E**   Please note that as you type, you will see nothing on-screen. The list will simply scroll with each letter you enter, much like the Help feature's Index tab does.

3. When you find the entry you're looking for, double-click it to retrieve it.

If the contact's exact name eludes you, but you can remember some other key part of the person's entry, use Outlook's Find Items feature to track it down:

1. Click the Find Items button on Outlook's Standard toolbar to see the dialog box shown in Figure 21.4.

**FIG. 21.4**

Click the drop-down arrow next to the Look For text box to choose which type of Outlook entry you'd like to search for.

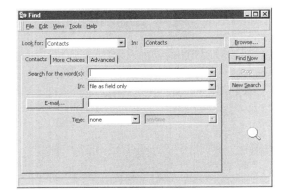

2. Click the drop-down arrow next to the Look In text box to choose the search category (contacts, messages, and so on) if necessary.

**N O T E**   Note that, depending on where you are in Outlook when you click the Find Items buttons, you may have to scroll upward in the drop-down list to find the desired category.

3. When searching for a contact, enter the word you're looking for in the Search for the Word(s) text box.

4. Choose the fields in which to search from the In box's drop-down list.

5. You may search selected categories of contacts only by choosing the More Choices tab and then choosing the category of contact you want to search.

6. If you need to conduct a search on a field other than those listed in the In box on the Contacts tab (say you remember the contact's wife's name is the same as yours and you recorded that information in the Spouse field), open the Advanced tab and click the Field button to see all your options.

7. Click Find Now when you're ready to see a list of records matching your criteria.

8. When you locate the entry you want to view or on which you want to take action, double-click the icon to the left of the its name.

 **TIP** You can use the Find Items feature for any type of Outlook item by simply selecting that item in the Look In box, as described previously in step 2.

# Editing and Deleting Address Book Entries

People are constantly moving, changing jobs, or getting new Internet service providers, which means you'll need to constantly update your address book to ensure the integrity of the information. To edit an entry, do the following:

1. If necessary, follow the previous steps to display the entry you need to edit.

2. Tab or Shift+Tab from field to field, making the necessary changes or additions as you would to text in Word.

3. Click Save and Close to save your changes.

Deleting an entry is as easy as highlighting or displaying it, choosing Edit, Delete, or clicking the Delete button on the Standard toolbar.

# Sorting Address Book Entries

Having a bunch of contact information is only useful if you have the ability to sort, group, or filter it in meaningful ways.

To sort entries in Address Card or Detailed Address Card view, follow these steps:

1. Choose View, Sort to open the dialog box shown in Figure 21.5.

2. Select the primary sort field in the Sort Items By drop-down list.

3. If you don't see the field you need, choose the appropriate category from the Select Available Fields From drop-down list, then return to the sort box you were using to see the new selection of available fields.

**FIG. 21.5**
Click the drop-down boxes to select sort criteria, then choose Ascending or Descending order. Click OK to perform the sort.

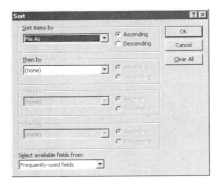

4. You may want to specify a second sort criteria in the first Then By box to eliminate ties. For instance, you may want to sort address book entries by their corporate affiliation, then by their last names.

5. Click OK to process the sort.

# Grouping Address Book Entries

You may find it useful to view your entries as a group as well. To do so, follow these steps:

1. Click the Contacts button on the Outlook Bar.

2. Enter Phone List view by choosing View, Current View, Phone List.

3. Choose View, Group By to open a Group By box identical to the Sort dialog box (refer to Figure 21.5).

4. Select the primary field by which you want to group the entries in the Group Items By drop-down list.

5. If you don't see the field you need, choose the appropriate category from the Select Available Fields From drop-down list, then return to the Group By box you were using to see the new selection of available fields.

6. You may want to specify a second group by field in the first Then By box to eliminate ties. For instance, you may want to group address book entries by their corporate affiliation, then by their last names.

7. Click OK to process the Group By request.

# Dialing a Contact Automatically

If your computer is equipped with a modem, you can have Outlook dial the phone number of a contact for you. Just follow these steps:

1. Select the desired contact.

2. Click the AutoDialer button on the Standard toolbar to see the New Call dialog box.

3. If you want to dial another number for the contact, other than the one shown, click the drop-down list arrow to choose from the other numbers you have on record for that contact.

4. If you want your Journal to create an entry when starting a new call, place a check mark in that box.

5. Click Start Call.

6. The Call Status dialog box will prompt you to pick up the receiver and click Talk or Hang Up.

# Printing Out a Phone or Address List

To print your phone or address list in an attractive format, do the following:

1. Click the Contacts button on the Outlook Bar.

2. Choose File, Print to call up the Print dialog box shown in Figure 21.6.

**FIG. 21.6**
Select either Table Style
or Phone Directory
Style for your printouts.

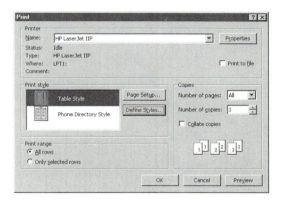

3. Select the desired print style in the Print Style box.

4. Click OK to send the output to the specified printer.

# CHAPTER 22

# Managing Your Schedule with Outlook

**Blocking out appointments**

Use Outlook to maintain your personal schedule.

**Requesting a meeting**

Learn how to request a meeting with one or many attendees and track their responses to the request.

**Printing your calendar**

Take your calendar on the road with you by printing it in the format you like best.

**Working with tasks**

Use Outlook to create a personal task list, or assign tasks to your employees.

In today's busy society, it's almost impossible to get a group of busy people together at one convenient time. You could spend hours or even days playing phone tag just to pin down someone's schedule.

Why not use Outlook to get the scheduling job done quickly and painlessly? If you work with others using Outlook on your local area network, you can check calendars of others and even have the first available meeting date checked for you. Even if you're not running Exchange Server, you can use this program to request meetings with others. ∎

# Understanding Outlook Calendar Elements

With Outlook's Calendar, you can schedule three types of activities:

- *Appointments*. Activities you allot time for in your schedule, but you do not invite others. Doctor appointments or reserved lunch hours are good examples of this type of activity.

- *Meetings*. Activities that you schedule and to which others are invited. An example might be a weekly staff meeting.

- *Events*. An activity lasting more than one day, such as a professional conference, that may have activities scheduled within it.

You may view your schedule by the day (see Figure 22.1) or by the week by clicking the Day or Week button on the toolbar in the Calendar window. You can view an entire month by choosing View, Month.

**FIG. 22.1**
View your calendar by the day to keep track of appointments and meetings for that day.

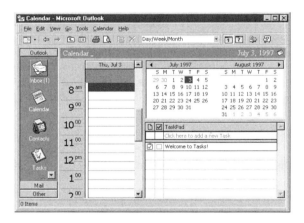

# Blocking Out Appointments and Events on Your Calendar

To block out appointments and events on your schedule, do the following:

1. Open the Untitled Appointment box, shown in Figure 22.2, by clicking the New Appointment button on the Office shortcut Bar, by choosing Calendar, New Appointment from within Outlook's Calendar window, or by clicking the New Appointment button at the far left of the Calendar window toolbar.

**FIG. 22.2**

To get an audio reminder before an appointment, check the Reminder box and click the drop-down arrow to specify how much advanced warning you want to receive, and click the sound icon to pick a favorite .WAV file as the audio reminder.

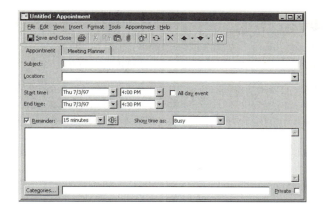

2. Fill in the Subject and Location of the appointment or event.

**N O T E**  The locations of previous appointments and events are listed in the Location drop-down list so that you don't have to retype them every time you have an appointment or event at the same location. ▨

3. Fill in the Start Time and End Time for the appointment by entering the time or by accessing the drop-down list. You can also check the All Day Event box when appropriate.

4. If you want Outlook to give you an audio reminder of the appointment, mark the Reminder box and use the drop-down list next to it to specify how much of an advanced reminder you want.

5. From the Show Time As drop-down list, select how you want the block of time to appear to others referencing your schedule. For instance, you may want to have a doctor appointment appear as "Out of the Office."

6. You can choose to enter notes about the appointment in the large text box at the bottom of the screen.

7. To Click Save and Close to complete the entry and have it appear on your calendar.

**N O T E**  You can edit an existing appointment by double-clicking it from the Calendar view shown in Figure 22.1. ▨

**T I P**  You can schedule time to work on a project, and you can even include a reference on the calendar to the files needed to do the work by clicking the Insert File button on the toolbar of the Untitled Appointment box and then by selecting the file you want to work on. When the appointment time arrives, Outlook will display an icon for the file along with the appointment reminder.

# Creating Recurring Appointments

The following steps show how to block out time for a daily lunch hour or to keep appointments from being scheduled when you need to pick up your child from school:

1. Create a new appointment, or open one to edit, as described earlier.

2. Choose Appointment, Recurrence, or click the Recurrence button on the Appointment box's toolbar to open the Appointment Recurrence dialog box (see Figure 22.3).

**FIG. 22.3**

Choose the recurrence pattern and then specify the frequency and day(s) of the week for the recurrence.

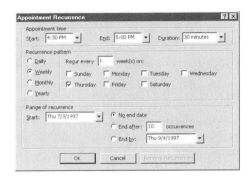

3. Click Daily, Weekly, Monthly, or Yearly, as desired.

4. Define the recurrence pattern for either:

   - *Daily*. Specify the number of days between recurrences, or select every weekday.

   - Weekly. Specify the days of the week on which the activity should recur and whether it should be scheduled every week, every other week, and so on.

   - Monthly. Specify on which days of the month the activity should recur, and whether it should be scheduled every month. Using this option, you also can specify recurrences like the third Wednesday of each month, the first weekend day of each month, and so on.

   - Yearly. Specify on which day of the year the activity should be scheduled, or specify dates such as the third Tuesday in October, and so on.

5. You may also select the start and end dates of the recurrence, or simply select the number of recurrences.

6. Click OK when you've finished defining the recurrence of the appointment to return to the appointment window; you can continue creating the appointment.

# Requesting a Meeting

Requesting a meeting with multiple attendees isn't much different from scheduling an appointment—you just need to add two short steps: check the calendars of other attendees to see when they're free, and send a note requesting their attendance.

**CAUTION**

Unless you are connected to a network running Microsoft Exchange Server, the ability to request a meeting with multiple attendees has serious limitations. To check the calendars of other attendees for a free date and time, they have to be using Outlook and have to be connected to your Exchange Server network. Although you can send meeting notices to people by using other Internet mail programs and services, you need to track and chart their attendance status manually.

Use Outlook to request a meeting with other Outlook users on your Microsoft Exchange Server network by following these steps:

1. Create an appointment as described in the prior sections, but do NOT click Save and Close.
2. From the Appointment window (refer to Figure 22.2), open the Meeting Planner tab.
3. Click the Invite Others button to see the Select Attendees and Resources dialog box, and then choose the attendees needed for the meeting. After this button is clicked, the Appointment window automatically turns into a Meeting window. Be sure to specify whether each person's attendance is required or optional; Outlook uses this information to search for a mutually free meeting time.
4. When finished selecting the attendees, click OK to return to the Meeting Planner tab.
5. For other Outlook users on your Exchange Server–driven network, you will see colorful bars highlighting when each attendee is busy, out of the office, or tentatively busy. For non-Outlook users, you see only patterned bars throughout the entire period.
6. Click AutoPick to see the first available meeting time.
7. Click the Send button to finish scheduling the meeting.
8. The meeting will appear on your calendar and as a tentative activity on the calendar of other Outlook users.

 **TIP** If you don't need to send meeting notices to the other attendees, choose File, Close; respond Yes when asked if you want to save your entry; and then respond No when asked if you want to send the message.

# Tracking Meeting Request Responses from Non-Outlook Users

Because Outlook cannot automatically process responses from non-Outlook users, you must edit the responses manually. To do so, open the window for the meeting, access the Meeting Planner tab, and select Show attendee status. Edit the desired attendee's response by clicking the drop-down list in the response column next to their name, and then by choosing the appropriate response.

# Accepting or Rejecting a Meeting Request in Outlook

If you are an Outlook user who has been invited to a meeting, this meeting will appear as a tentative item on your schedule. You will also receive, in a majority of cases, an e-mail message detailing the meeting request.

To accept or reject the request, do the following:

1. Open the e-mail note pertaining to the meeting request.
2. Click Accept or Decline in the Message box.
3. Include a message to the meeting planner if desired.
4. Click Send to route your response back to the meeting planner. The meeting planner receives the message in his or her inbox, and Outlook automatically logs your response in the meeting attendee status box for the meeting in question.

# Printing Your Outlook Calendar

To print a copy of your calendar, follow these steps:

1. Make sure that you are in Calendar view by clicking the Calendar button on the Outlook bar.
2. Choose File, Print to open the Print dialog box.
3. Select the print style you want for your calendar and specify the Start and End dates for the printout.
4. Set the other print options, such as the number of copies.
5. Click OK to send the calendar to the specified printer.

# Creating a Task List

With Outlook's task list, you now can prioritize and keep track of all the things you need to get done. To create a task for your task list, follow these steps:

1. Choose File, New, Task, or click Ctrl+N to see the Untitled Task dialog box (see Figure 22.4).
2. Type a name for the task in the Subject box.
3. If you want, you can specify a Due and Start date, give the project a priority designation of either Low, Medium, or High, and even set an audible reminder to alert you that the due date is rapidly approaching.
4. Click Save and Close to enter the task on your task list, which will be displayed in a window under your Day and Week calendar views.

**FIG. 22.4**
The Task box enables you to track everything relating to a project, from its due date to its priority level.

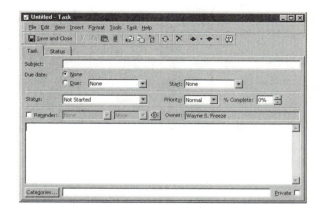

You can edit a task by double-clicking it on your task list, then editing the Task box as you would with a Word document. Remember to click Save and Close after you've made your revisions.

Deleting a task is as simple as clicking it and then clicking Delete.

# Making a Recurring Task

To assign a task to someone, do the following:

1. Create the task as previously described.
2. In the Task box's menu bar, choose Task, Assign Task to see a modified Task box such as the one shown in Figure 22.5.
3. Fill in the name of the person to whom the task will be assigned, or click the To button to select a person from your Outlook address book.
4. Set your tracking options, such as whether you want to keep a current copy of the task on your task list, or whether you want a status report when the task is complete.
5. Click Send.

If the person to whom the task is assigned is an Outlook user and on your Microsoft Exchange Server network, he or she will see the assigned task in their inbox *and* on their task list. When the person opens the message pertaining to the task, he or she can Accept or Decline it by clicking the respective button at the top of the message. If the task is accepted, the task will appear only on the task list. If it is declined, it will go to the Deleted Items folder. The person assigning the task then will receive an e-mail note regarding the disposition of the task.

# Printing Your Task List

If you're going on the road for an extended period of time, you may want to take a copy of your task list with you. To print it, put Outlook in Task view and then choose File, Print. Choose your options from the Print dialog box and then click OK to receive your output.

**FIG. 22.5**
The modified Task box, used to assign a task, enables you to select the person who will be assigned the task by clicking the To button in your Outlook address book.

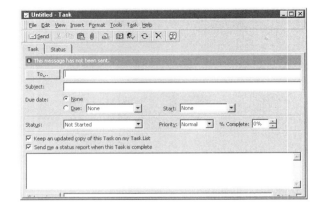

# Tracking Items with the Journal

Outlook's Journal enables you to track daily activities in a timeline format, as shown in Figure 22.6. By default, the Journal will log each file accessed in Word, PowerPoint, Access, Excel, and Binder, and place its path and file name on a timeline.

In addition, the Journal tracks when the file was opened and how long it was kept open, even if Outlook was inactive at the time. The files are grouped by application along with activities such as e-mail. This provides a powerful way to track your usage of time and enables you to find and filter Journal entries quickly, just as you can do with other Outlook items.

**FIG. 22.6**
Double-click an application type to see the files accessed in that application displayed on a timeline.

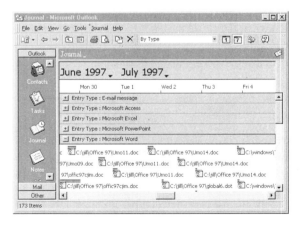

To view the Journal, launch Outlook and click the Journal icon in the Outlook bar. The Journal entries will appear as a timeline by default, but you can select alternative views by choosing View, Current View and then by choosing from the list. To open an item logged in your journal, double-click it. The appropriate application will launch along with the chosen file.

# Recording Journal Entries

In addition to the automatic entries logged by the Journal, you can add an entry in one of the following three ways:

- Drag an Outlook item to the Journal icon on the Outlook bar to record an item not automatically captured.

- If you want to record all communication with a chosen contact, create or retrieve their contact record. In the Contact dialog box, open the Journal tab and place a check mark next to Automatically record journal entries for this contact. You may also view all journal entries for that contact in the large text box at the bottom of the dialog box.

- Choose Tools, Options, and select the Journal tab, as shown in Figure 22.7. In the Options dialog box, choose for which applications you want to create entries automatically. You can even specify which items should be recorded for a selected contact in the Automatically Record These Items box.

**FIG. 22.7**

The Journal tab of the Options dialog box enables you to track specific information about a contact so that you can save the needed material without unnecessarily tracking insignificant items.

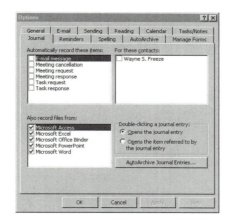

# Using Your Virtual Sticky Pad

Outlook has a feature that's the computer equivalent to sticking those little yellow pieces of paper all over the place. It's called Notes.

To make use of this virtual Post-It pad, follow these steps:

1. Click the Notes icon on the Outlook bar to enter the icon view of your "sticky pad."

2. You can create a new note in any of the following ways:

   - Double-click an empty area of the Notes window.

   - Click the New Note button on Notes' Standard toolbar.

   - Click the New Note icon on the Office Shortcut bar.

3. You will see a little yellow box into which you can enter text.

4. To close and save your note, click the X in the top-right corner of the "notepad."

The note will now appear with the rest of your notes in the Notes window.

To see a note again in its own window, double-click its name or icon from any Notes view. To toggle between the note and an open application, click Alt+Tab. If that note was some piece of wordsmith art, you can drag the mouse across the text to select it, click Ctrl+C to copy it to the Clipboard, and then paste it into the chosen application. ●

# Working Together to Achieve Even Greater Results

# CHAPTER 23

# Sharing Data Between Documents and Applications

**O**ne of the best things about Office 97 is its versatility. You can create something in one application and use it or reference it in another with minimal work. You can paste part of one document into another, or link them for a more dynamic presentation because the source data will change what the reader of the document containing the link sees. You can even place documents from Word, Excel, and PowerPoint together in a Binder where they become one file divided into sections. This simplifies printing and is a great way to bundle files for a single project—no matter what application they were created in. ∎

**Pasting Word text into another application**

Discover how to use the Clipboard to hold selected data while you prepare the second document to receive the text.

**Using alternate data sources for mail merges in Word**

Learn how to use Outlook's address book, Excel information, or an Access database as the source document for a Word mail merge.

**Including Excel data in a Word document**

Find out how to paste, embed, or link Excel data to your Word document.

**Working with hyperlinks**

Learn how to reference other Office 97 documents, Internet sites, or even sound files, in your current document.

**Using binders to achieve a uniform appearance**

Consider binding together files from a variety of Office 97 applications that pertain to the same project into a single file to create a uniform appearance when printing the results.

# Pasting Word Text and Graphics into Another Application

With Microsoft's Clipboard, it's a snap to copy text or graphics from Word and import it into another Office application (including Microsoft Publisher). Just follow these steps:

1. Select the text or graphic to be copied.

2. Choose Edit, Copy, click the Copy icon on the Standard toolbar, or press Ctrl+C to copy the selected text or graphic to the Clipboard.

3. Access the document into which you want to insert the selected text or graphic.

4. Make a spot for the item to be imported as required by the application. For instance, PowerPoint and Publisher require special boxes to be drawn for text and graphics.

5. After the Clipboard contents has a spot in which to be placed, be sure the insertion point is set in the desired location by clicking it.

6. Choose Edit, Paste, click the Paste icon on the Standard toolbar, or press Ctrl+V to place the Clipboard's contents in the desired location.

# Using Alternate Data Sources for Mail Merges in Word

In Chapter 10, "Mail Merges, Envelopes, and AutoText," you learned how to create a simple mail merge using Word for both the main document and the data source. Office 97's tight interoperability and flexibility enable you to use other application files as data sources as well.

Which data source is best for you? Consider the points in Table 23.1.

**Table 23.1   Which Data Source Meets Your Needs Best?**

| To Get This | Use This |
| --- | --- |
| A small to medium sized list of names and addresses to which you don't expect to make many changes | Word |
| Names and addresses of contacts based on your Outlook Address Book | Outlook |
| An automatically numbered list of entries from which you can select the desired records by number | Word |
| A longer list that you may want to add, delete, and change entries in, or for a numbered list of entries | Excel or Access |

| For | Use |
|---|---|
| Powerful sorting and searching capabilities | Access or Excel |
| A list with full relational database capabilities, for a large list, or for a list you can share with others | Access |

# Merging from Outlook's Contact List

If you maintain a contact list in Outlook's Address Book, you can use it as the data source by following these steps:

1. Open the Mail Merge Helper in Word as described in Chapter 10 in the section titled, "Using Mail Merge to Get Personalized Results."

2. Specify the main document, as described in Chapter 10.

3. Click Get Data in step 2, and then choose Use Address Book from the drop-down list. The Use Address Book dialog box appears (see Figure 23.1).

**FIG. 23.1**

Choose Outlook Address Book from the list to turn your contact list into a Word data source.

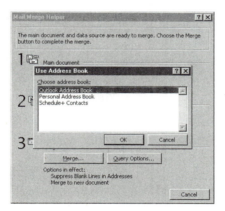

4. Select the Outlook Address Book, and then click OK.

5. Depending on how your system is set up, you may be asked to provide a profile or user name.

6. Your address book will then be converted to a Word data source file that you can edit and filter, as described in the mail merge sections of Chapter 6.

7. Edit the main document and perform the merge as usual to receive output based on your Address Book entries.

**N O T E**  Because merging from Outlook builds a new Word data source, changes to your contacts'
information after the initial data source, document was created will not be reflected in this
file. You may want to create a new data source, or at least double-check the entries the next time you
want to perform a mail merge with Outlook, to avoid embarrassing errors due to changes of address
and so on.

# Merging from Excel

If you maintain a database in Excel, you can merge from it to create personalized output as
well. Simply follow these steps:

1. Open the Mail Merge Helper in Word, as described in the section in Chapter 10, "Using
   Mail Merge to Get Personalized Results."

2. Specify the main document, as described in Chapter 10.

3. Click Get Data in step 2, and then choose Open Data Source from the drop-down list.
   The Open Data Source dialog box appears.

4. Mark the Select Method check box.

5. In the Files of Type drop-down list, Choose MS Excel Worksheets, and then click OK.

6. Double-click the file name of the Excel workbook you want to use. The Confirm Data
   Source dialog box shown in Figure 23.2 appears.

**FIG. 23.2**

Select Microsoft Excel
Worksheet via Converter
to continue with the
mail merge.

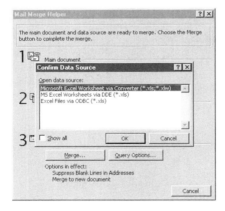

7. Choose Microsoft Excel Worksheet via Converter, and then click OK.

8. In the Open Worksheet dialog box, choose the worksheet to be used and, if necessary,
   the named range within the worksheet.

9. Click OK to return to the Mail Merge Helper where you'll continue with the merge
   process.

Your Excel database will be linked to Word where you can format the main document to accommodate the fields in your Excel database, then proceed with the merge process as described in Chapter 10.

# Merging from Access

The process for merging from Access is nearly identical to that of Excel. Follow the instructions for Excel, except choose "MS Access 7.0 Database via ODBC" in the Files of Type drop-down list.

**N O T E**  ODBC stands for Open Database Connectivity. This option is much quicker than the DDE method because you don't need to open Access. ▪

This links the chosen Access database to Word where you will edit the main document and prepare it for the merge. Complete the merge process as described in Chapter 10.

# Understanding Object Linking and Embedding

You can share data between Office 97 applications in three different ways: pasting, linking, and embedding. The main differences between them are where the data is stored and how the data is updated after it has been placed in the destination file. For a quick peek at the techniques, take a look at the following explanations:

- *Pasting*. When you paste data from one document into another, that data is stored in the destination file as well as the source file. If changes need to be made to the data, it must be edited in both the source and the destination document. Furthermore, the destination document's data must be edited using the destination document's application tools. For instance, if you paste part of an Excel spreadsheet into Word, the Excel data in Word would need to be edited in Word, not Excel, and you would have to edit both the destination and source documents to ensure consistency.

- *Linking*. With linked data, the information must be updated in the source file where it is stored. The destination document merely stores a reference to the linked data, then displays only the selected section of the data in the destination document. This method has the advantage of ensuring both files contain the same data and that the linked data must be manipulated in the source data's native application. Linking data can also save file space in the destination document because that document stores only a reference to the data, not the data itself. Unfortunately, it can make things more difficult when it comes to taking the document on the road, because you'll need two documents (as well as their corresponding applications) instead of one.

- *Embedding*. Embedding an object means that information in the destination file does not change with the source file. Embedding is a good idea for archiving monthly status reports—you can write the narrative in Word, and then embed the spreadsheet of figures for the month. But why not just paste the data? Because embedding enables your CEO to double-click the object and play what-if with the data using the native application's (in the case of this example, Excel) tools without affecting the source file (see Figure 23.3). After an object is embedded, it becomes part of the destination document permanently, so there's no chance your CEO's fantasized figures will corrupt the original document. Pasting an object, however, gives you minimal opportunity to edit the data within the object.

**FIG. 23.3**

When embedding an Excel worksheet in Word, you have access to all the Excel tools. Just double-click the object to begin editing the worksheet part of the document as you would in Excel.

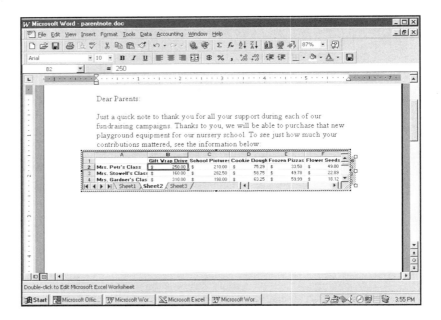

# Linking an Excel Chart or Data to a Word Document

To link an Excel worksheet to a Word document, do the following:

1. Open the Word document and the Microsoft Excel workbook that contains the data from which you want to create a linked object.

2. From Excel, select the entire worksheet, a range of cells, or the chart you want to use as the linked object.

 **TIP** Giving an up-to-the-minute status report to your board of directors at the annual meeting? Consider creating a Word document with a link to the desired Excel spreadsheet. That way the data is current the instant your accounting division updates the file. No need to go back and double-check numbers at the last minute. This is one instance where Office 97 can do the work for you, so why not let it? Refer back to Table 23.1 for more information on how to choose between pasting, embedding, and linking.

3. Choose Edit, Copy, press Ctrl+C, or click the Copy icon on the Standard toolbar.

4. Switch back to Word and then click the location you want to insert the linked object.

5. Choose Edit, Paste Special to open the Paste Special dialog box (see Figure 23.4).

**FIG. 23.4**
Click Paste Link to establish a link between the Word document and the Excel data selected.

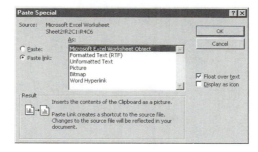

6. Click Paste link.

7. In the As box, click Microsoft Excel Worksheet Object.

8. To prevent the linked worksheet or chart from being displayed as a drawing object that you can position in front of or behind text and other objects, remove the check mark in the Float Over Text check box.

9. Click OK to complete the link.

**N O T E**  If the linked object were to remain as a drawing object, it could inadvertently become hidden behind text in your document, or it could even cover up critical text. When you're in a hurry, who wants to be faced with phantom elements? Just be sure to perform step 8 so that you can keep everything in order. ▨

# Embedding an Excel Worksheet in Word

You can embed either a new worksheet in Word, or embed an existing worksheet. Embedding a new worksheet gives you Excel functionality in Word that can be extremely useful in creating tables that need totals or other calculations run against them. Embedding existing worksheets gives people the ability to play with the worksheet numbers by making the source file's application accessible from within Word.

To create a new embedded worksheet in Word, follow these steps:

1. In the Word document, click where you want to insert a new embedded object for a worksheet or chart.

2. Choose Insert, Object. The Object dialog box appears (see Figure 23.5). Click the Create New tab.

**FIG. 23.5**

Scroll down the Object Type box to find Microsoft Excel Worksheet, or Microsoft Excel Chart— whichever you want to use.

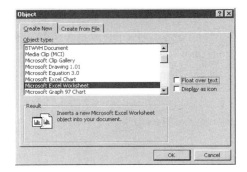

3. In the Object type box, click Microsoft Excel Worksheet or Microsoft Excel Chart as needed.

4. To prevent the embedded worksheet or chart from being displayed as a drawing object that you can position in front of or behind text and other objects, remove the check mark next to the Float over text check box.

5. Click OK.

6. Create the worksheet or chart as you would in Excel.

To embed an existing worksheet in Word, follow these steps:

1. Open both the Word document and the Microsoft Excel workbook that contains the data from which you want to create an embedded object.

2. In Excel, select the entire worksheet, a range of cells, or the chart you want to embed in Word.

3. Choose Edit, Copy; press Ctrl+C; or click the Copy icon on the Standard toolbar.

4. Switch to the Word document, then click the location where you want to insert the embedded object.

5. Choose Edit, Paste Special.

6. Click Paste.

7. In the As box, click either Microsoft Excel Worksheet Object or Microsoft Excel Chart Object, depending on your needs.

8. To prevent the embedded worksheet or chart from being displayed as a drawing object that you can position in front of or behind text and other objects, remove the check mark next to the Float over text check box.

9. Click OK to embed the selected object.

# Creating a Hyperlink

Creating a hyperlink in Word, Excel, PowerPoint, or Access follows an identical procedure:

1. Create or open the spreadsheet, document, database, or slide that will contain the hyperlinks. (This will be the document displaying the word or object you can click to be transported to another document.)

2. To use the hyperlink's address itself as the link, place the insertion point in the location you want the link to appear.

**TIP**

Do you have a stellar Web page to which you want to refer readers? Use hyperlinking when you want to include references to Web pages— these elements cannot be included in a document any other way.

You can also use hyperlinking in place of linking if the reader will have no need to manipulate the data. It can be a more secure way to provide the reader with up-to-date information that cannot be altered.

3. To use a graphic or other text for the reference, create and then select the desired graphic or text.

4. Click the Insert Hyperlink button on the Standard toolbar, or press Ctrl+K. In some cases, you will be prompted to save your work before inserting the link. Click Yes to do so before proceeding.

5. The Insert Hyperlink dialog box, shown in Figure 23.6, appears.

6. In the Link To File Or URL box, enter the desired address of the file. The file can be anything from a file created in another application to a Web site address.

**FIG. 23.6**
Enter the file name or URL in the Link to File or URL box. If you don't know the File name, click the Browse button to look for the desired file, or click the drop-down arrow to see selected URL's (addresses) from your favorite Internet sites.

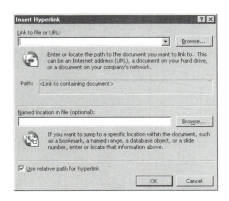

**TIP**

To reference another section in the current document, leave the Link to file or URL box blank (it defaults to the current document), and then specify a named location or bookmark in the document in the text box at the bottom of the dialog box. You will learn more about creating named locations in the following sections.

7. If you don't recall the local file name or remote URL, click the Browse button to search your hard disk for the file name or URL of choice.

8. Confirm that the Use Relative Path for Hyperlink check box is marked. This option strips the drive letters off the file name so that it can be moved to another drive without having to update your hyperlinks.

9. Click OK to complete the hyperlink.

10. Text containing a hyperlink will appear underlined in a different color for easy spotting.

# Editing or Deleting a Hyperlink

There may come a time when you need to redefine the hyperlink or delete it altogether. To do this, follow these steps:

1. Place the mouse-pointer over the hyperlink, and right-click it.

2. Select Hyperlink, Edit Hyperlink from the shortcut menu.

3. The Edit Hyperlink dialog appears. Click the Remove Link button in the lower-left corner of the box to remove the link reference but leave the pointer (text or a graphic) intact in the document.

4. To change the address, name of the file, or URL, either enter the filename or address manually or click the drop-down arrow beside the Link to File or URL text box to browse your hard disk for the new name.

# Creating a WordArt Graphic Hyperlink

This is the perfect way to create nice looking icons for your hyperlinks. The process requires two groups of steps—the first group to design the icon using WordArt, and the second group to turn the icons into hyperlinks.

To design the icon, do the following:

1. Click the Drawing button on the Standard toolbar to call up the Drawing toolbar.

2. Click the Insert WordArt button.

3. The WordArt Gallery appears (see Figure 23.7). Select a WordArt Style, and then click OK.

**FIG. 23.7**

Choose from a variety of WordArt styles in the WordArt Gallery.

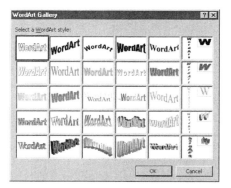

4. The Edit WordArt dialog box appears, prompting you to enter the desired text.

5. You can tweak the type size by clicking the Size drop-down arrow at the top of the dialog box.

6. Click OK.

7. The WordArt graphic appears in your text.

8. If you need to move the graphic a bit, click the object to select it. Point to the middle until the mouse-pointer becomes a four-headed arrow. Click and drag the graphic to the desired position.

9. Save the file under an easily identifiable name.

To turn the graphic into a hyperlink, follow these steps:

1. Select the WordArt graphic by clicking it.

2. Choose Insert, Hyperlink; press Ctrl+K; or click the Insert Hyperlink button on the Standard toolbar to open the Insert Hyperlink box.

3. In the Link to File or URL area, click browse to locate the resource to which you want to link.

4. Click OK to return to your document.

**NOTE** When you return to the document, click outside the graphic to deselect it. Notice that when you run your mouse pointer over the graphic, the mouse pointer now turns into a pointing hand to denote the presence of a hyperlink. You'll even see a yellow ScreenTip box appear with the address of the hyperlink file.

5. To test your hyperlink, click the graphic. The designated document/file should appear. Use the back arrow on the Web toolbar (which appeared when you clicked the graphic) to move back to the original document.

# Assigning Bookmarks in Word to Reference-Specific Sections of a Document

In addition to creating hyperlinks to other files on your computer, intranet, or the Internet, you can create hyperlinks to other sections within the current document. To do so, you must first Bookmark the section by following these steps:

1. Open the multi-sectioned file you want to reference with hyperlinks.

2. Select the text or section title of the text you want to reference in a hyperlink.

3. Choose Insert, Bookmark. The Bookmark dialog box appears (see Figure 23.8).

4. Give the bookmark a name, keeping in mind the name cannot contain spaces, and may not exceed 40 characters in length.

**FIG. 23.8**
Enter a name for the
current bookmark, then
click Add to complete
the request.

**CAUTION**

If you see the error message Error: Bookmark not defined! instead of the text you used for the link, chances are you have referred to a bookmark that does not exist, or you have misspelled the name of the bookmark. Try retyping the bookmark's name keeping in mind the parameters listed in step 4. You may also view the bookmarks in the current document by choosing Tools, Options. In the Show section of the View tab, place a check mark next to Bookmarks to see the bookmarks defined for the document in question.

5. Click the Add button at the bottom of the dialog box.

6. Repeat the prior steps as necessary to mark all necessary sections of the document.

Next, you need to specify a bookmark name in a hyperlink:

1. Create or open the document that will house the hyperlinks.

2. Select the text or graphic that will be the hyperlink object.

3. Choose Insert, Hyperlink; press Ctrl+K; or click the Insert Hyperlink button on the Standard toolbar.

4. In the Link to File or URL box, type or browse for the file name of the bookmarked document.

5. Click in the Named Location In File box to enter or browse for the name of the desired bookmark.

6. Select the bookmark, and then click OK to complete the hyperlink.

# Hyperlinks and Named Locations in Excel

The process of creating a hyperlink in Excel is identical to that of placing a hyperlink in Word, but creating Named Locations (Excel's equivalent to a Word Bookmark) is a bit different.

To specify a cell range for the hyperlink, do the following:

1. Select the range of data you want to reference in the named location.

2. Choose Insert, Name, Define.

3. When the Define Name dialog box appears (see Figure 23.9), enter a name for the Named Location. Keep in mind that name may not contain spaces and must be less than 255 characters long.

**FIG. 23.9**

In the Define Name dialog box, you can give the named location an easily identifiable name.

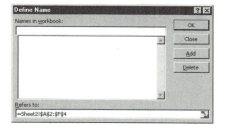

4. Click Add, and then click OK to complete the definition.

5. Repeat these steps to define multiple named locations in a worksheet or workbook.

To reference this named location in a hyperlink, do the following:

1. Create or open the document that will house the hyperlinks.

2. Select the text or graphic that will be the hyperlink object.

3. Choose Insert, Hyperlink; press Ctrl+K; or click the Insert Hyperlink button on the Standard toolbar.

4. In the Link to File or URL box, type or browse for the file name of the destination worksheet.

5. Click the Named Location In File box to enter or browse for the name of the desired named location.

6. Select it, and then click OK to complete the hyperlink.

# Hyperlinks in PowerPoint

Most frequently, you will want to hyperlink to other PowerPoint slides to maintain your presentation's design quality, even though in theory you can link to any type of file just as you can in other Office 97 applications.

To hyperlink to another PowerPoint slide, follow these steps:

1. Create or select text or a graphic to act as the hyperlink.

2. Choose Insert, Hyperlink; click the Insert Hyperlink button on the Standard toolbar; or press Ctrl+K.

3. When the Insert Hyperlink dialog box appears, enter the filename for the other PowerPoint presentation, if necessary. If the reference is contained in the same presentation, you will only have to work with the Named Location in File text box.

4. Click the Browse button to see a listing of slides in the current presentation.

5. Choose the slide you want to define as the destination of the link, and then click OK.

6. The link is inactive until you enter Slide Show mode. To do this, click the Slide Show button at the bottom left of the PowerPoint screen.

# Expanding Outlook's Capabilities by Using Hyperlinks

By using Word as your e-mail editor in Outlook, you can do some incredible things. You can include hyperlinks to Internet sites in your e-mail message, assuming the recipient's e-mail program is capable of dealing with hyperlinks in its messages. Or, even more impressive is the concept of e-mailing hyperlinks to documents on your company's intranet to others in your company for their review.

1. Launch Outlook.

2. Choose Tools, Options, and then open the E-Mail tab as shown in Figure 23.10.

**FIG. 23.10**

Place a check mark next to Use Microsoft Word as the E-Mail Editor to be able to insert hyperlinks in your e-mail.

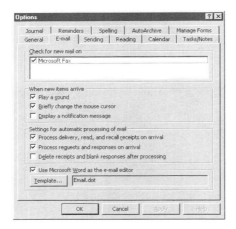

3. Place a check mark by the last item on the list: Use Microsoft Word as the e-mail editor.

4. Click OK to confirm your choice.

5. Create a new e-mail message, as you usually do.

6. To create the hyperlink(s), follow the procedures for creating hyperlinks in Word as described above.

7. Click Send to send the message containing hyperlinks to recipients capable of accessing the information you have included in your links.

**N O T E**  Keep in mind that if you reference documents on your intranet with your links, the recipient obviously must be connected to that intranet to see the documents.

# Creating a Word Outline to Use in Designing a PowerPoint Presentation

If you've written a complex report or long-range plan for your organization, you may want to present this data to your board of directors or senior management in a fancy PowerPoint presentation. To make sure you cover all the important issues, you may want to use the Word outline of the document as a guide in designing your presentation. To do so, launch PowerPoint and follow these steps:

1. For best results, use a Word document formatted with heading styles. This simplifies PowerPoint's job of creating slides by basing slide creation on header titles.

2. Choose File, Open.

3. In the Files of Type box, click All Outlines.

4. In the Name box, double-click the document you want to use.

5. The imported outline opens in PowerPoint in outline view. Each major heading is converted to an individual slide title.

# Importing Excel Information into a PowerPoint Presentation

To use Excel worksheet data in a PowerPoint presentation, do the following:

1. On the Excel worksheet, select the range you want to copy.

2. Choose Edit, Copy; press Ctrl+C; or click the Copy button on the Standard toolbar.

3. Switch to the presentation, and then click where you want to insert the cells.

4. In PowerPoint, choose Edit, Paste Special to see the Paste Special dialog box.

   Choose your options based on the following:

   - To paste the cells so that you can resize and position them as you would a picture, choose Microsoft Excel 8.0 Worksheet Object.

   - To keep only the current result of a formula, click Paste.

   - To make sure the result is updated if the original data changes in Microsoft Excel, click Paste link.

**N O T E**   The Paste link option is available only if you select the Microsoft Excel 8.0 Worksheet Object format. ▪

5. Click OK to complete the request.

# Putting It All Together in a Binder

A Microsoft Binder acts the same way a loose-leaf binder works with paper—all of the documents or papers are stored as one. With Microsoft Binders, each document or file becomes a section of the binder, which can be edited as individual documents just as they could before being added to the binder.

Binders can be a wonderful way to organize related documents created in various applications, but they have some limitations, too. Before deciding to use a binder, consider the following points:

- All related documents are stored in a single file, which will save time when you need to pull all of a project's files together.
- A single binder makes taking your project files home or posting them to a shared folder a breeze.
- You can standardize the appearance of the documents by applying headers and footers that carry through the entire binder, no matter what application was used.
- Print the entire binder at once without having to send each document to the printer separately.
- You can place only certain types of files into a binder—files created in Word, Excel, or PowerPoint. Binder will not work with Access databases or Outlook contact information.
- Documents stored in a binder cannot be viewed or manipulated in Windows Explorer or the Open dialog box.

# Creating a Binder

To create an Office 97 Binder, do the following:

1. On the Office Shortcut Bar, click the New Office Document button. The New dialog box appears.
2. Open the General tab, if necessary.
3. Click Blank Binder to select it, then click OK. The Blank Binder screen, shown in Figure 23.11, appears.
4. To increase the size of your workspace, click the Maximize button at the top of the Office Binder Window.
5. Choose File, Save Binder to open the Save Binder As dialog box.
6. Select the text in the File Name box, and then enter a name for the Binder.
7. Click Save to complete the process.

**FIG. 23.11**
When filled with documents, the white strip down the left side of the Binder workspace will hold icons representing each section of the binder.

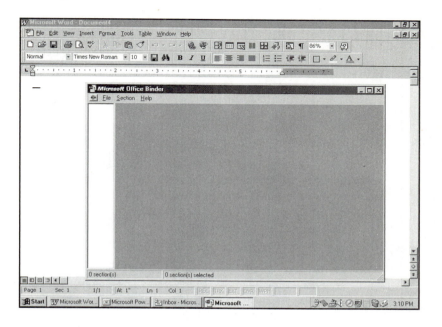

# Adding Existing Files to a Binder

Files added to a binder are known as Sections rather than files or documents. To create these binder sections from existing files, follow these steps:

1. From the Binder workspace, choose Section, Add from File. The Add from File dialog box appears.

2. Browse the files until you find one you want to add to the binder.

3. Click on that file, and then click Add to include it in the binder.

4. Repeat the steps until all the files you want to use have been added to your binder.

# Rearranging the Order of the Sections

Rearranging the order of your binder's sections is important when preparing to print the contents, especially if you plan to use page numbers and other elements that might identify the order of the contents.

Rearrange the sections of a binder by following these steps:

1. Confirm that icons for all the files you intend to include in the binder are represented in the left pane of the Binder window.

2. Choose Section, Rearrange to open the Rearrange Sections dialog box.

3. Select the section you want, then use the Move Up and Move Down buttons to rearrange the sections as needed.

**N O T E**   Perhaps one of the biggest strengths of the Binder function is the capability to share it with others using the Windows Briefcase feature. All the members of your workgroup can work on their respective sections of the Binder without the fear of separate documents getting lost on various peoples' hard drives, for example.

4. Click OK to save your placement changes.

**N O T E**   The contents of a binder are edited with the specific section's native application tools, so there's no need to learn new editing techniques.

# Printing the Binder

You can either print the entire contents of a binder by choosing File, Print, and then choosing the desired options in the Print dialog box as you do in other applications; or print a specific section of the binder by clicking the desired section's icon, choosing Section, Print, and then selecting the printing options as usual.

To print a single section of a binder, select the icon of that section, then choose Section, Print and choose your options in the Print dialog box.

# CHAPTER 24

# Collaborating on Documents

In this day of increased work demands and job specialization, working together on documents has become more of a necessity than a luxury.

Office provides a host of tools to simplify collaboration on documents, including the capability to save versions in Word, to secure data in spreadsheets while making them available on your intranet, and to schedule group meetings in Outlook.

**Routing documents for review by others**

You can combine the features of Word and Outlook to route a document for review by multiple people.

**Tracking changes in Word and Excel**

Learn how to track, then accept and reject, changes made to a document throughout multiple reviews.

**Working with people using other versions of Office applications**

We can't all afford to upgrade our software with each new release, so learn how to make Office 97 documents downward-compatible.

# Routing Documents for Review by Others

If a document is being worked on by a team, or if others need to double-check it for accuracy, you may want to consider routing it to make sure it gets to everyone it's supposed to.

If you are the originator of the document to be routed, you'll need to create a "virtual routing slip" by following these steps:

1. Open the document to be routed.
2. Choose File, Send To, and then click Routing Recipient.
3. To select recipients of the routed document, click Address.
4. In the Type Name Or Select From list box, type a recipient's name and then click Tars for a date and time that the recipients are free; the attendees *must* be using Outlook and *must* be connected to your Exchange Server network. Although you can send meeting notices to people who are using other Internet mail programs and services, you need to track and chart their attendance status manually. To request a meeting with others using Outlook on your Microsoft Exchange Server, see "Requesting a Meeting," later in this chapter.
5. To route the document to a person who is not on the list, choose File, Send To, and then click Other Routing Recipient.

# Using In-Place Comments to Synthesize Reviewer Feedback

One way to make notes to yourself regarding a document in Word or Excel is to include in-place comments. These comments also work well in synthesizing group feedback because they do not alter the text. Simply read these invisible comments and incorporate the changes needed, or make notes to yourself about new sections to be written or data to be researched.

Text containing a comment will appear highlighted in light yellow in Word, whereas Excel cells containing comments have a little red triangle in the upper-right corner of the cell. When you move the mouse pointer over a comment in either application, a yellow ScreenTip-like box also pops up showing the author of the comment and the comment text.

To create in-place comments, do the following:

1. Select the text/cell(s) or place the insertion point inside the word or cell that should be highlighted with a comment.
2. Choose Insert, Comment.
3. The chosen Word text will be highlighted in yellow, and a comment box similar to the one shown in Figure 24.1 will open. In Excel, the red triangle appears in the selected cell and a square box appears beside it, ready for you to insert your comments.

**FIG. 24.1**
Enter your comments in Word's Comments From box, in which you can view comments from a specific person or from all reviewers.

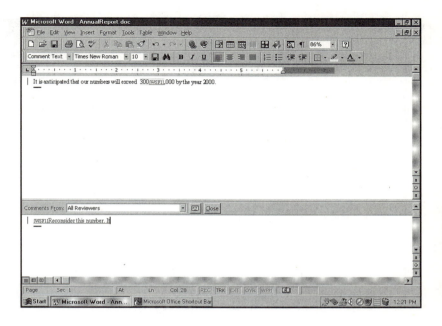

4. Your name, as defined in the User Information tab of the Options dialog box, will appear to label the comments.

5. If you want to change the name specified, choose Tools, Options, and then select the User Information tab (the General tab in Excel), where you can redefine your Name or Initials. Click OK to save your changes.

6. Enter your comments or even a sound file if you have a microphone and sound card installed on your computer.

7. When you've finished commenting in Word, click the Close button at the top of the comment box. In Excel, just click outside the comment box.

# Viewing and Editing In-Place Comments

When you see a block of text highlighted in a faint yellow color, place the mouse pointer over the top of it. The highlight will turn a darker shade of yellow. A comments icon will flash briefly, followed by the yellow comment box, which itself displays the name of the reviewer and their comments.

For more controlled comment viewing, right-click any visible toolbar, then place a check mark next to Reviewing on the drop-down menu. The Reviewing toolbar will appear (see Figure 24.2).

The Reviewing toolbar provides a number of comment viewing and editing options. The comment buttons (and their corresponding functions) on the Reviewing toolbar are shown in Table 24.1.

**FIG. 24.2**
The Reviewing toolbar enables you to locate comments in a document quickly by using the Previous Comment or Next Comment buttons.

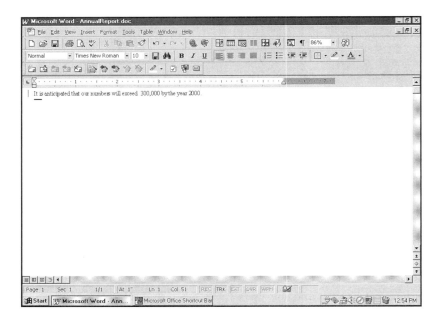

**Table 24.1   The Reviewing Toolbar Buttons and Their Functions**

| Button | Button Name | Function |
|---|---|---|
| | Insert Comment | Add a comment to the document |
| | Edit Comment | Change a comment in the document |
| | Previous Comment | View the previous comment |
| | Next Comment | View the next comment |
| | Delete a Comment | Deletes the comment after the issue has been addressed or resolved |

# Tracking Changes in a Document

Word and Excel's Track Changes feature enables you to monitor changes made to a document or worksheet. The revisions are indicated with colored text in Word, or a blue triangle in the upper-left corner of an Excel cell. Word can accommodate multiple reviewers of a document by assigning a different text color for each reviewer. Excel defines comments from different reviewers by allowing you to select the reviewer's name from a drop-down list in the Accept or Reject comments dialog box.

To turn on the Track Changes feature, follow these steps:

1. Choose Tools, Track Changes, Highlight Changes to bring up the Highlight Changes dialog box.

2. If you want changes to be tracked while editing, check the Track Changes While Editing box. By default, all added text in Word will be underlined and all deleted text will have strikethrough formatting. In Excel, the blue triangle will appear along with the suggested cell contents. If you run the mouse pointer over the changed cell, a box will pop up describing the changes made.

To accept or reject changes made by others, do the following:

1. To accept or reject changes, click Tools, Track Changes, Accept or Reject Changes to open the Accept or Reject Changes dialog box (see Figure 24.3).

Part
III

Ch
24

**FIG. 24.3**
Word's Accept or Reject Changes dialog box lets you accept or reject all changes in a document at once, or address them one at a time.

2. In Word, click Accept All or Reject All to accept or reject all changes made to the document. In Excel, choose which changes you want to review by making the appropriate selection from the drop-down lists, and then press OK to move to the first change.

3. To accept or reject changes one-by-one in Word, click the Find button with the arrow pointing to the right. You may also choose Find with the left-pointing arrow to process changes made earlier in the document. Information about the change will be displayed and highlighted, and you will have the option of accepting or rejecting only that change.

   Changes can be treated similarly in Excel. When the first change appears, you can accept it, reject it, accept all changes, or reject all changes. Excel then moves to the next change automatically.

4. Click Close to return to the document.

# Saving Versions of a Document

In earlier versions of Word, you had to rename files in order to save multiple revisions of a document. With Word 97's new Save Version option, the days of conjuring up creative file names are over. To take advantage of this new feature, follow these steps:

1. Choose File, Versions to open the Versions dialog box shown in Figure 24.4.

**FIG. 24.4**
Click the Save Now
button in the upper-left
corner to continue the
Save Version process.

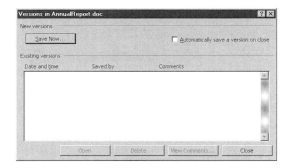

2. Click the Save Now button.
3. Enter any applicable comments for the version that you want to save in the Comments on Version text box.
4. Click OK to save this version of the document.

**N O T E**  Note that the version saving feature is only available for Word 97 files. Other file types and previous versions of the software do not support this feature. ▪

 By saving versions of a document, you are archiving them. This means a saved version of a document cannot be modified without being saved as a new version.

# Protecting Workbook Cells Before Sharing It with Others

If you have drafted a budget and need others to fill in specific information—without intentionally or inadvertently altering other data—you may want to consider protecting certain cells of your workbook.

To specify which cells can be edited by others, follow these steps:

1. Open the workbook you want to protect and then move to the appropriate worksheet.
2. Select the cells others will be allowed to edit.
3. Right-click the highlighted text, then choose Format Cells from the shortcut menu.
4. The Format Cells dialog box appears. Select the Protection tab, as shown in Figure 24.5.
5. Deselect the Locked check box to free the cells you selected for collaboration, and then click OK.
6. Repeat the prior steps as necessary to free up all needed cells.
7. Choose Tools, Protection, Protect Sheet to activate the cell locks for the remaining cells.

**FIG. 24.5**
Use this dialog box to determine which cells are locked or unlocked.

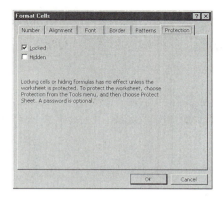

8. When the Protect Sheet dialog box appears, select the protection options you want to use, add a password if you feel it's necessary, and then click OK.

# Avoiding Word File Conversion Nightmares

If you share documents created or edited in Word 97 with users of earlier versions of Word, there are some file formats you should be aware of. While it's true that Word offers Save As options for converting Word 97 files to Word 6.0/95, these files aren't converted to true Word 95 documents. Instead, they are converted to Rich Text Format (.rtf) files.

What does this mean to the average user?

- Rich Text Format files are less efficient at handling graphics, which results in a larger file size.
- Formatting files in this manner can create inconsistencies in the formatting and layout of your documents.
- Rich Text Format files are incompatible with Microsoft FrontPage, WordPerfect, and other popular products.

Luckily, Microsoft rectified the problem after taking so much heat over it. They posted an update on their Web site that is available for free download.

But, before you link up, follow these steps to make sure you really need the update:

1. On the Windows Taskbar, click Start, and then choose Find, Files or Folders.
2. The Find: All Files dialog box appears. Open the Name & Location tab, as shown in Figure 24.6.
3. In the Named text box, enter **wrd6ex32.cnv**.
4. Click Find Now to search all the files and subfolders on your system.
5. After a few seconds, information for a file should appear in the large box at the bottom of the dialog box.
6. Use the horizontal scroll bar at the bottom of the box to view the Modified column of the located file.

Part
III

Ch
24

**FIG. 24.6**

Use this box to search for the Word 6.0/95 conversion file specified in step 3.

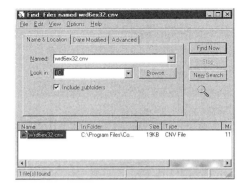

7. If the date reads 11/17/96, follow the next set of steps to download the update.

8. If the date is 6/10/97 or more recent, then your system has been updated already, either by your network administrator or by purchasing a copy of Office that was manufactured recently enough to include the update.

To download the update, make sure you have an active Internet connection and then do the following:

1. Launch Word 97.

2. Choose <u>H</u>elp, Microsoft on the <u>W</u>eb, <u>F</u>ree Stuff to access Microsoft's Web page of free stuff for Word 97 users.

3. Look for a link to the Word 6.0/95 Binary Converter for Word 97. Follow the directions for downloading and installing the update.

**N O T E**   The 600K file should take three to six minutes to download via a 28.8K or 14.4K modem.

# Preventing Loss of Work when Working with Other Versions of Excel

Excel 97 provides the option to save workbooks in a dual Excel 97/Excel 5.0/95 format so that you can continue to use all of the new Excel features while sharing the workbook with others, but there's a catch. When Excel 5.0/95 users open the file, they will be advised to use the file as read-only. If users ignore this message, make edits, save it, and then send the worksheet back to you, the file, which is now in Excel 5.0/95 format, will lose any Excel 97 features that you used to create it.

The solution? If you must get input from others, consider passing around a basic worksheet and saving all the fancy formatting for last, or simply ask for their contributions via an e-mail note.

# CHAPTER 25

# Office 97 and the Web

**P**erhaps the most significant enhancement to the Office 97 suite is its extensive Web capabilities. Whether you're posting an Excel worksheet to your company's intranet, building a basic Web page in Word, or publishing to the Web your organization's newsletter created in Publisher, Office 97 can do it all. You can even take a break from it all and launch your favorite Web browser from within any Office application to surf your favorite sites, or do some marketing analysis.

This chapter explores posting Office 97 documents to your intranet versus making them available in a public folder. It also gives you all the information you need to build your own Web page and publish it to the Internet for the world to see. Of course, first you'll need your network administrator's permission or space allocated to you by your Internet service provider. ■

### Web or public folder—which is best?

Learn how the techniques differ in publishing a document to the Web versus making it available in a public folder, and which meets your needs best.

### Publishing your Office 97 documents to the Web

See all the steps needed to successfully transfer your documents to the Web.

### Using Creative design elements

From textured backgrounds to scrolling text—learn how to make your Web page stand out.

### Viewing the source code

With a little knowledge of HTML, truly adventurous users can open the source code of their HTML documents and apply even more advanced capabilities.

### Publishing your creation to the Web

After you've designed your Web page, find out what you need to do to publish it to the Web.

# Web or Public Folder—Which Is Best?

There are essentially two ways to share your documents with others, in addition to e-mailing them or giving someone a disk with the document on it: you can place them in a public folder on your company's network, or you can post them to the Web, be it on the Internet or your company's intranet.

Although it is common for everyone to have read-and-write access to the contents stored in the public folder, documents posted to the Web generally cannot be updated by anyone other than the creator.

By posting documents to a public folder, colleagues can access them and edit or contribute to them as the need arises. However, for sensitive data such as budget spreadsheets, this can pose some security concerns if the documents haven't been secured by using passwords or other methods of protection.

▶ **See** "Protecting Workbook Cells Before Sharing It with Others," **p. 292**

By saving your documents in HTML format, you can prevent others from updating the document, while providing easy access via a Web browser. This means that you don't need the document's native software to view the document.

So which method is best? It depends on your needs. If others need to view the document without editing it and your company has its own Web server, publishing it to the Web may be a good choice, especially if everyone in the organization may be running different versions of various software packages.

If, however, you need to collaborate on a document, a public folder is the only method besides e-mail or cutting a disk that you can use to get the document to others for editing or reviewing.

# Readying Word Documents for the Internet or Intranet

Word is Office 97's HTML editor, so the process of converting an existing Word document to Web-ready HTML is fairly simple:

1. Open the Word document you want to publish on the Web (see the example in Figure 25.1).
2. Make any heading or formatting changes you want to make to the Word document to reflect the document's Web presence, such as omitting page headers and footers.
3. Choose File, Save as HTML.
4. The Save as HTML dialog box appears with the name of the current file followed by the new .html extension.
5. Click the Save button on the right side of the dialog box.
6. The document may look a little different because HTML formatting has been applied.

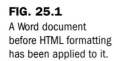

**FIG. 25.1**
A Word document before HTML formatting has been applied to it.

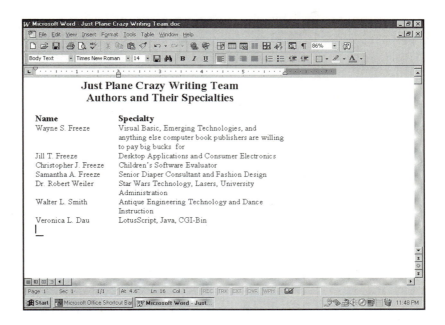

7. The true test is how the document looks through a Web browser. Make a note of where you stored your HTML file, then launch Internet Explorer. If your Internet connection starts, cancel it because you're just doing testing on a local machine.

8. Choose File, Open from Internet Explorer's toolbar.

9. Enter the file name, or browse your system for the desired file, and then click Open in the dialog box.

10. You will see your document as viewed in Internet Explorer (see Figure 25.2).

One of the most common problems encountered when converting a Word document to HTML occurs when the document's author uses multiple tabs instead of converting text to a table. This is what happened in Figure 25.2.

To fix the problem, do the following:

1. Open the original Word document file.

2. Make sure the text to be converted into a table has only one tab stop between each column.

3. Highlight the block of text to be converted into a table.

4. Choose Table, Convert Text to Table to open the Text to Table dialog box, pictured in Figure 25.3.

5. Word will open the dialog box with information it gathered from the selected text. Simply click OK to turn the text into a table (see Figure 18.4).

6. Repeat steps 3 through 10 of the previous section to test how the document looks with its new formatting.

Part
III

Ch
25

**FIG. 25.2**
Using tabs to create the look of a table can really cause trouble when converting a document to HTML.

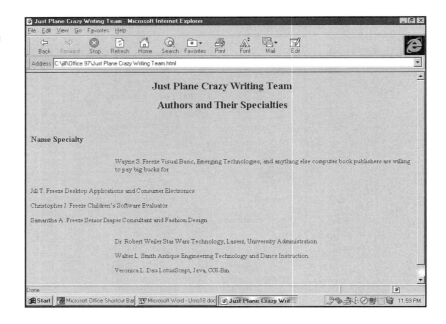

**FIG. 25.3**
The settings provided by Word should give you the desired result. Click OK to turn the selected block of text into a table.

# Getting Excel Workbooks Ready for the Web

With Microsoft's Internet Assistant Wizard, readying Excel data for the Web is a breeze. Just follow these steps:

1. Open the Excel workbook you want to convert to HTML.
2. Select the range of cells you want to include on the Web page.
3. Choose File, Save as HTML.
4. Step 1 of the Internet Assistant appears, as shown in Figure 25.5.
5. The ranges you select should appear in the Ranges and Charts To Convert box. Click Next to go to Step 2.
6. Choose Create an independent, ready-to-view HTML document, then click Next to move to Step 3.

**FIG. 25.4**
Converting the Word text to a table goes a long way toward improving the document's appearance on the Web.

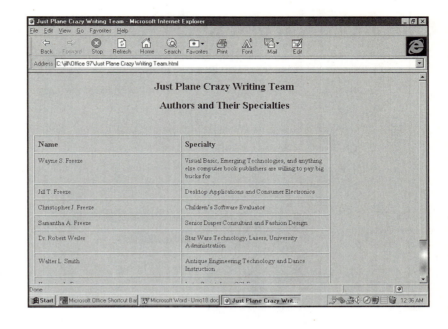

**FIG. 25.5**
Step 1 of the Internet Assistant asks you to confirm your selected range, then click Next to continue.

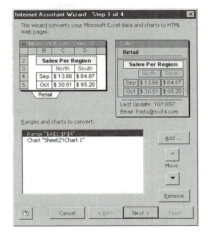

7. Enter the information that you want to appear on the Web browser's Title Bar, along with any other header information you may want to include. Click Next to proceed to the Internet Assistant's final step.

8. Choose Save The Result As An HTML file, specify where on your hard disk you want to store the file, and then click Finish.

---

**T I P**  You may test the results of the Excel conversion just as you did with Word in the preceding section.

---

Part
III

Ch
25

# Bringing PowerPoint to the Web

PowerPoint slide presentations on the Web are instant attention-grabbers with their deep colors and easy-to-create navigation tools.

To ready your presentation for the Web, just follow these steps and any tips provided by the Save As HTML wizard:

1. Open or create your PowerPoint presentation.
2. Choose File, Save as HTML.
3. The Save as HTML Wizard appears (see Figure 25.6). Click Next to begin working your way through the steps.

**FIG. 25.6**

PowerPoint's Save as HTML wizard guides you painlessly through the process of converting a presentation to HTML.

4. Because this is your first time converting a PowerPoint presentation to HTML, the New Layout option will be selected. You can save your answers to the questions that follow to instantly select the same options next time around. Click Next to continue.
5. Choose the Standard page style because not all browsers support frames. Click Next.
6. Select your preferred graphic type. The GIF files are most commonly used on the Web; however, if you're using photographs, you may want to choose JPEG to enhance image quality. Click Next.

**N O T E**   If you use animation in your presentation, be forewarned that unless the viewer has the PowerPoint Animation Player installed on their system, they won't see the special effects you've worked so hard to create.

7. When asked to choose the desired graphic resolution, simply select the default because that's the resolution used by most computers. Click Next to continue the process.
8. On the information Page step, provide your e-mail address and the URL of your home page if it is different from the slide presentation. Click Next.
9. The Colors and Buttons steps give you the opportunity to select all kinds of colors and button styles to coordinate with your slide presentation. Click Next after each step.

10. On the Layout Options page, determine where you want your navigation buttons placed, and then click Next.

11. Name the folder in which you want to store the presentation, and then click Next.

12. Click Finish to save the presentation with the specified settings.

# Creating Your Own Web Page from Scratch Using Word's Web Page Wizard

To create a Web page from the ground up, follow these steps to begin the process with Word's Web Page Wizard:

1. Launch Word.

2. Choose File, New.

3. When the New dialog box appears, click the Web Pages tab.

4. Double-click the Web Page Wizard icon to launch the Wizard.

5. Select the type of Web page you want to create (see Figure 25.7), and then click Next.

**FIG. 25.7**

The first step in the Web Page Wizard involves selecting the type of Web page you want to create.

6. Choose your visual style (click once to preview), and then click Finish.

7. You now have a basic Web page with which to begin designing your own page. Start by inserting your own text into the predefined sections. Click a text area; the text inside the brackets will be replaced by whatever you type. You will learn how to customize your page even more in the sections that follow.

# What Does and Doesn't Work with Word on the Web

Virtually anything you can paste into a Word document—Excel cells, graphics, or whatever—can be uploaded to the Web. But the irony is that some of the neatest special effects available in Word 97 are lost when saving the file as HTML. Special text effects like embossing and animation get tossed out when the Web is where they could really shine. You could make the document available on the Web in .doc format, but the person would need to have Word 97 in order to experience those effects you worked so hard to incorporate.

WordArt is another thing that doesn't convert to HTML. There are plans for Microsoft to release a fix to this problem, which you will be able to download from their Web site. So be sure to visit Microsoft on the Web from within Word by choosing Help, Microsoft on the Web, and then selecting Free Stuff or Product News.

Finally, all those newspaper columns will need to be converted to tables after you have saved the document as HTML in order to maintain their appearance.

# New Available Web Authoring Tools

Now that you've saved your own .html document, you may notice some new buttons on Word's Standard and Formatting toolbars (see Figure 25.8).

**FIG. 25.8**
New toolbar buttons give you instant access to some of the most popular Web authoring tools.

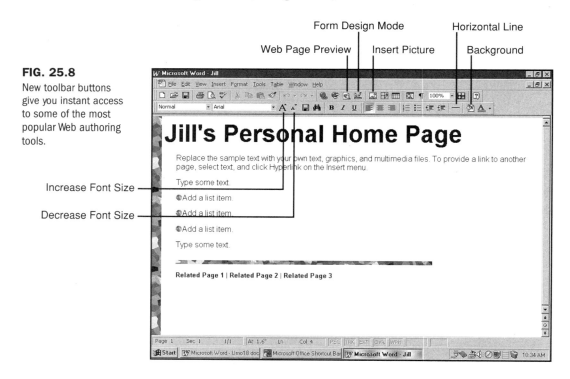

The function of these newly visible buttons is presented in Table 25.1.

**Table 25.1  New Web Authoring Buttons and Their Functions**

| Button | Button Name | Function |
|---|---|---|
| 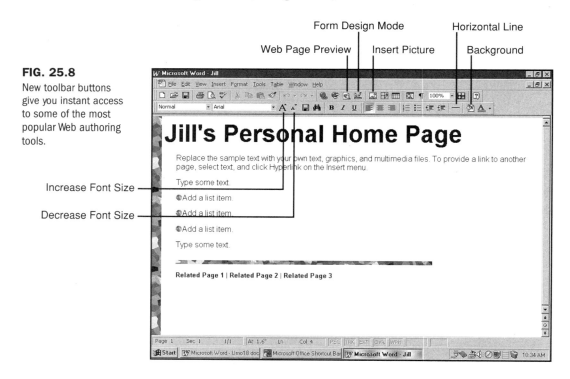 | Web Page Preview | Enables you to see what your saved HTML document will look like in the Internet Explorer browser. |

| Button | Button Name | Function |
|--------|-------------|----------|
| | Form Design Mode | Enables you to create forms to capture user feedback. |
| | Insert Picture | Presents the Clip Art Gallery from which you can select images for your Web page. |
| | Increase Font Size | Click to make the selected text larger. |
| | Decrease Font Size | Click to make the selected text smaller. |
| | Horizontal Line | Draws a horizontal line in the specified location on your Web page. |
| | Background | Select or change the background color or texture of your page. |

## Saving an HTML File

After a Web page has been created with the Web Page wizard and saved, its default Save file type is .html or .htm (the formats needed to display the document properly on the Web), so all you need to do is choose File, Save, click Ctrl+S, or click the Save button on the toolbar. You also have the new option under the File menu to save the page as a Word document.

## Selecting a Background Color or Texture for Your Web Page

Choosing a background for your Web pages will be one of the most visible enhancements you make. Word makes it easy to see the effect of your choice before you apply it.

To add or change the color or texture of your background, do the following:

1. Open the Web page for which you want to choose a new background.
2. Choose Format, Background, or click the Background button at the right end of the Formatting toolbar.
3. Choose a color to see how it looks. If you don't find what you're looking for, click More colors to see a large palette full of choices.
4. If you don't like the color you've selected, use Ctrl+Z to undo it, then pick another color.

**N O T E**  If you're working with a design effect containing artwork down the left side of the page, it may be lost if you choose a different background color.

5. If you want to add a texture or image for added impact, choose Format, Background, and then click Fill Affects. The Fill Effects box shown in Figure 25.9 will appear.

**FIG. 25.9**
Select a texture you like from the ones pictured, or click Other Texture to search your system for picture files you may want to use as a background.

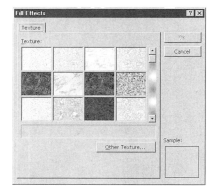

6. Choose from the textures pictured, or click Other Texture to search your system for picture files you may want to consider using for a background.

 7. To preview your selection as seen in Internet Explorer, choose File, Web Page Preview.

 **TIP** If you have any trouble undoing your selections, close the Web page WITHOUT saving the changes, and then reopen it.

# Choosing Text to Match Your Background

If you change background color, there's a fair possibility that you'll want or even need to change the color of your text to complement your selection.

Change text color by following these steps:

1. Choose Format, Text Colors to open the Text Colors dialog box, shown in Figure 25.10.

**FIG. 25.10**
Use the drop-down arrows at the right side of each text box to see more color options.

2. Make your selections for Body Text, Hyperlinks, and Followed Hyperlink colors by using the drop-down arrows, and then click OK to apply them.

# Adding Horizontal Lines

Horizontal lines are graphical elements that subdivide the page for easier viewing by the reader. They act as separators between subjects to clarify the structure of your page.

To insert a horizontal line, follow these steps:

1. Click the location where you want to place a horizontal line.

2. Choose Insert, Horizontal Line, or click the Horizontal Line button near the right end of the Formatting toolbar.
3. The Horizontal Line dialog box presents you with a number of options. Select one, and then click OK.
4. To size or reposition the line, click it and use the sizing handles to drag it into position.
5. To delete the line, select it and click Delete.
6. To move or copy the line, select it, and then use cut and paste, or copy, as appropriate.

# Using Graphical Bullets

For a Web page, you'll probably want to use something a bit more fancy than the typical bullet. To do this, follow these steps:

1. Select the previously bulleted text.

2. Choose Format, Bullets and Numbering to open the Bullets and Numbering dialog box.

3. Make your selection from those shown in the Bullets tab, or click More for a larger selection.
4. Click OK when you're finished.

# Adding Scrolling Text to Give Your Page Punch

Scrolling text, or Marquees, are one of those elements that, when used sparingly and tastefully, can set the amateurs apart from the pros of Web page design. Nearly anyone can create a static Web page and put it online with a little help, but with Office 97, you have the tools to make that Web page actually do something!

To add scrolling text to your page, follow these steps:

1. Choose Insert, Scrolling Text.
2. Enter the text that you want to scroll in the Type the Scrolling Text Here box.
3. Select the Behavior of the text from the drop-down list, and then look in the Preview box to see if it does what you expect it to.
4. Choose the Background color for the scroll box, and then preview it before selecting the next option.
5. Specify which Direction you want the text to scroll—left or right—and then preview it before moving on.

6. In the Loop box, you can define how many times you want the text to loop, from one time to infinite times. You may want to preview your settings before choosing the next option.

7. Drag the speed bar right or left to accelerate or decelerate the speed of the scroll.

8. Click OK when you're satisfied with the result.

**N O T E** The marquees created in Office 97 are supported only by the Internet Explorer Web browser (except for release 1.0, which does not support marquees). Readers using other browsers will see the text, but it will not be animated.

# Other Necessary Web Page Elements

Review Chapter 23, "Sharing Data Between Documents and Applications," to find out how to add hyperlinks and embedded objects to your Web page.

# HTML Editing: For the Brave and Adventurous

If you're already familiar with HTML coding or would like to learn how to add extra functionality and design elements to your Web pages, Word gives you the capability to view and manipulate the HTML source code. See Figures 25.11 and 25.12 for shots of a Web page and its HTML source code, respectively.

**FIG. 25.11**

This Web page was generated using Word's Web Page Wizard.

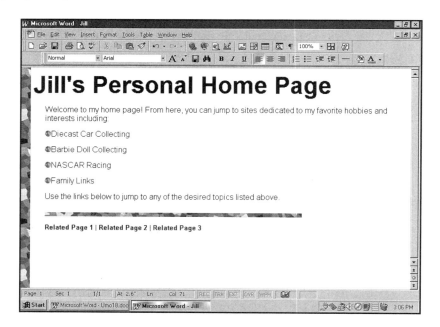

**FIG. 25.12**
The same Web page's HTML source code.

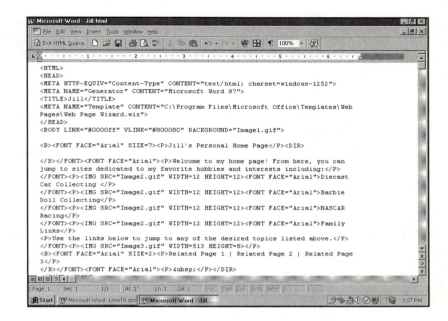

To learn more about HTML programming, you may want to take a look at the following book from Que: *Special Edition Using HTML, Third Edition*.

## Saving Your Work as a Web Template

If you've heavily customized your Web page, you may want to save it as a template so that you can create similar Web pages in the future. It's also a great way to achieve a uniform look throughout your entire Web site.

To save your design as a template for future use, open the desired Web page and choose File, Save As to open the Save As dialog box. In the Save As type box, click the drop-down arrow and use the scroll bars if necessary to locate the Document Template (.dot).

When you choose this file type, the various template folders are shown so that you can place your template in an easy-to-find location. Click Save to save your HTML document as a template in the chosen folder. Now when you go to create a new Web page, you can select your template from the Web Pages tab where you found the Web Page wizard.

## Publishing to the Web

When it comes to actually publishing to the Web, circumstances can vary greatly. If you want to publish to an intranet or public folders, check with your company's network administration for specifics on where the files should be placed. The same applies for uploading documents to your company's Web server.

If you're designing a Web page from home or as a small business, check with your Internet service provider to find out first whether you do, in fact, have space to upload Web documents in your current subscription arrangement; and second, what path and file names you should use for those files.

There are some basic steps you have to follow to publish to a Web server:

1. Copy all the HTML files created by your application to the intranet or Web server as appropriate.
2. Also copy all supporting files such as images, movies, sound files, and so on.
3. From your Web browser, test your Web page's navigational buttons and all its links to make sure it's working properly.

**TIP** If the Web page is a critical commercial venture, you may want to view it on multiple Web browsers to see how it will look to others using various browsers. That way, you can be sure you're putting your best foot forward to prospective clients or customers.

# CHAPTER 26

# Using Macros to Save Time and Automate Tasks

**D**o you perform the same set of commands in Word all the time? Do you have a complex formula in Excel that you use in many places? Do you wish you could write a short program to scan through your documents and make simple changes?

Macros can offer big benefits when used with Microsoft Office applications. They can be used to provide simple solutions to simple problems. They can also be used to develop very complex solutions for very complex problems. ■

## Recording and playing macros

Record your own macros in Word 97 and Excel 97, then play them back to make changes to your document.

## Editing macros

Use Visual Basic for Applications to edit and change your macros, even if you aren't familiar with Visual Basic.

## Using VBA to build better macros

Use the objects available with Visual Basic for Applications to include additional functions in your macro.

# Macros and Visual Basic for Applications

A macro is simply a way of recording a set of keystrokes used in an application and playing them back when you need them. In the previous versions of Microsoft Office, each application had its own macro programming language. However, with Microsoft Office 97, Microsoft has created a common macro language for all of the applications. It is called Visual Basic for Applications (VBA).

**N O T E**   Although you should be able to construct a practical, workable VBA macro after reading this chapter, the information presented here is really just a primer on the subject. For more detailed information, see *Special Edition Using Visual Basic for Applications 5.0* by Paul Sanna, also published by Que. ▪

VBA is a special version of Visual Basic that has been developed for use as a macro language within another application. So even though a macro is built by entering a series of keystrokes, the keystrokes translate into statements in a Visual Basic program. A limited Visual Basic development environment is also available to create and edit macros. This enables you to develop complex macros that are capable of very complex tasks.

# Recording a Macro in Word 97

To record a macro in Word 97, follow these steps:

1. Select Tools, Macro, Record New Macro from the main menu bar.
2. The Record Macro dialog box appears (see Figure 26.1). Select a new name for the macro and enter a description of the macro (if desired).

**FIG. 26.1**
Use the Record Macro dialog box to create a new macro.

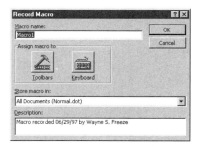

3. In the same dialog box, you can specify where the macro is saved. The default is All Documents (Normal.dot). You can also choose any other active document.

 While you can save the macro into the Normal.dot template and make it available to all documents, it is not a very good idea. Save the macro into the current document, and once you are satisfied that it works properly, copy it into Normal.dot.

4. By using the Record Macro dialog box, you can click either the Toolbars or the Keyboard buttons to continue the recording process. Clicking the Toolbars button displays the Customize dialog box for the toolbar. Clicking Keyboard displays the Customize Keyboard dialog box.

5. The Customize dialog box (see Figure 26.2) enables you to add the macro to any existing toolbar by simply dragging the icon onto the toolbar. You can also use the dialog box to create a new toolbar to hold the new macro. Click the Close button to display the Stop Recording box and to begin recording your macro.

**FIG. 26.2**

Use the Customize dialog box to add a macro to the toolbar.

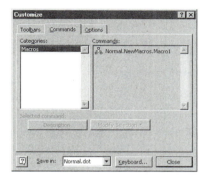

6. The Customize Keyboard dialog box (see Figure 26.3) lets you define a key sequence that will call the macro. First, you select the Press New Shortcut Key text box with your mouse and then type the keystroke you want to use. The keystroke appears in the text box. If the keystroke is already assigned, the current assignment will be listed below the text box in the Currently Assigned To area of the window. If the keystroke isn't used, this area says [unassigned]. Click the Assign button to assign the macro to the keystroke and then click the Close button to display the Stop Recording box and to begin recording the macro.

Part
III

Ch
26

**FIG. 26.3**

Use the Customize Keyboard dialog box to define the key used to activate the macro.

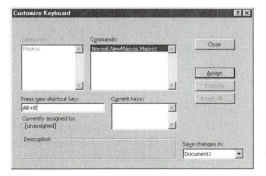

> **T I P** Don't replace any key sequence that is already assigned. Because Alt+A through Alt+Z, Alt+Shift+A through Alt+Shift+Z, and Alt+0 through Alt+9 are unused in normal Word documents, these are good candidates to use as macros.

7. When the Stop Recording box displays, you may begin using the mouse and keyboard to perform the sequence of events for the macro. You can click the Pause Recording button to temporarily suspend the recording process, and click it a second time to continue recording. Clicking the Stop Recording button will stop recording the macro and close the Stop Recording box.

# Recording a Macro in Excel 97

To record a macro in Excel 97, follow these steps:

1. Select Tools, Macro, Record New Macro from the main menu bar.

2. The Record Macro dialog box appears (see Figure 26.4). Select a new name for the macro, enter a description of the macro (if desired), and specify where the macro should be stored. You can also specify a key that will activate the macro.

**FIG. 26.4**
Use the Record Macro dialog box to create a new macro.

3. When the Stop Recording box displays, you may begin using the mouse and keyword to perform the sequence of events for the macro. Clicking the Stop Recording button stops recording of the macro and closes the Stop Recording box.

> **N O T E** You can click the Relative Reference button to record a macro with relative addresses rather than absolute addresses. Use relative addresses when you want to refer to cells based on their position relative to the current cell when the macro is invoked. Use absolute addresses when you want to refer to the same cell no matter where you invoke the macro.

# Running a Macro

To run a macro in Word 97 and Excel 97, press the key sequence associated with the macro, click the macro name in the toolbar, or select Tools, Macro, Macros from the main menu bar. The Macros dialog box appears (see Figure 26.5), from which you can select the name of the macro and click the Run button.

**FIG. 26.5**
Select the macro you
want to run.

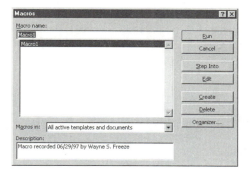

# Running a Macro from Inside Another Macro

When creating very large macros, it is best to break down the large macro into several smaller
macros and one larger macro that calls the smaller ones. After all, it is much easier to enter,
test, and debug ten five-step macros than it is to do the same on one fifty-step macro.

To call a macro from another macro, follow this procedure:

1. Begin recording a macro, as previously explained.
2. Enter the keystroke to the macro or select Tools, Macros, Macros from the main menu
   bar. Then run the desired macro.

# Deleting a Macro

To delete a macro in Word 97 or Excel 97, follow these steps:

1. Select Tools, Macro, Macros from the main menu bar. The Macros dialog box appears
   with a list of available macros.
2. Select the name of the macro you want to delete and then click the Delete button. The
   macro will be deleted.

# Understanding and Using the Visual Basic Editor

A macro is stored internally as a Visual Basic for Applications program. In many cases, there is
a one-to-one correspondence between a keystroke and a line of VBA code. Even if you are not
an experienced VBA programmer, you often can determine which line of code corresponds to
the keystroke you entered.

The Visual Basic for Applications Editor gives you the ability to edit existing macros or create
new macros from scratch. The main window in the VBA Editor is the Edit Window and contains the Visual Basic code for the macro (see Figure 26.6).

The Project window shows the objects available in the workbook. Selecting one of these
objects will display its properties in the Property window.

Part
III

Ch
26

The menu bar at the top of the window contains all the functions available. It works just like the menu bars in each Office application. A toolbar is also available that contains many of the most commonly used functions.

**FIG. 26.6**

The Visual Basic for Applications Editor gives you the ability to edit existing macros or create new macros from scratch.

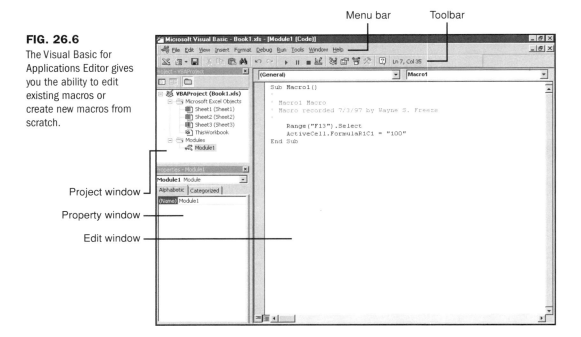

Menu bar          Toolbar

Project window

Property window

Edit window

# Editing a Macro Using Visual Basic for Applications

To edit a macro in Word 97 and Excel 97, proceed as follows:

1. Select Tools, Macro, Macros from the main menu bar.

2. The Macros dialog box appears (refer to Figure 26.5). Select the name of the macro and click the Edit button.

3. Visual Basic for Applications will start and you will see the code for the macro (refer to Figure 26.6).

   In the figure, the Range object is used to select cell F13 and make it the active cell. A value of 100 is assigned to the active cell (F13) by using the ActiveCell object and the FormulaR1C1 property.

4. After you have finished editing your macro, choose File, Close to return to the Office application you were using.

# Ideas and Tips for Your VBA Macro

After trying a few different macros, you may want to try some of the following simple ideas and tips to improve your macros:

- If you make a mistake while recording your macro, simply repeat the sequence. Then use the VBA Editor to delete the incorrect statement.

- Some macro names are reserved to perform automatic functions. These are known as Auto Macros. A macro named AutoExec will run each time an Office 97 application is started or you load a global template. AutoNew is run each time that you create a new document or worksheet. AutoOpen is run each time that you open a new document or worksheet. AutoClose is run each time that you close a document or worksheet. AutoExit is run each time that you exit an Office 97 application.

- While in the VBA editor, you will see parts that may be familiar to you. These will be blocks of text inside quotes. This may be the string you specified in the Find dialog box in a Word document or a formula you were assigning to a cell in Excel. Simply change the contents of the text to alter the effect of the macro.

- To make the macro a more general-purpose macro, try replacing the text string including the quotes with a call to `InputBox`. The following line is typical of a line in a macro; it assigns a value of 100 to the currently selected cell in Excel:

```
ActiveCell.FormulaR1C1 = "100"
```

By using the `InputBox` function, you can display an input box to the user that states, `Enter Value`. This box will be a blank area in which the user can enter a value and an OK button that the user clicks when finished entering the text (see Figure 26.7). Use the following line to create this input box:

```
ActiveCell.FormulaR1C1 = InputBox ("Enter value")
```

**FIG. 26.7**

Using an InputBox to get a value from a user.

- The `MsgBox` statement displays a message box with a message on-screen that you supply and an OK button. This statement is useful for displaying where you are in a macro. When the `MsgBox` is executed, everything in the application is suspended until the user clicks the OK button. To use this statement, place it on a line by itself, like this example:

```
MsgBox "After step 2"
```

- Comments are a useful tool that you can use to make notes to yourself in a macro. Every macro you create contains comments about the name of the macro and the name of the person that created it. To use this statement, place a single quote at the start of the line and then include your comments, like the following example:

```
' Sort columns A, B and C in descending order
```

Part **III**

Ch **26**

# Using Variables and Objects with Your Macro

One of the strengths of using VBA for macros is that you can create and use variables in your macro. Using variables, you can save and compute values that are independent of the objects in the macro.

Visual Basic for Applications offers a rich assortment of variable types. However, for most macros, all you really need are four: String, Long, Boolean, and Single. Although VBA doesn't require that you declare variables to use them, it is a good idea to declare a variable before using it. This ensures that you create the variable with the type you want rather than letting Visual Basic guess what type you want.

Objects are a collection of properties, methods, and events that represent a single element of an application. Objects are heavily used within Visual Basic for Applications and Microsoft Office. An object can correspond to a Word document, an Excel worksheet, or even a single spreadsheet cell. Here is a list of some common variable types and how objects are used:

- The most commonly used variable type in VBA is String. This type is used to declare a variable containing a string of characters.

  ```
  Dim MyString As String
  ```

- The next most important variable type is Long. Long contains a whole number, which is very useful when counting objects, or computing a row or column location.

  ```
  Dim MyLong As Long
  ```

- One variable type you will encounter from time to time is Boolean. Boolean can take on only two values: True and False. It is most often used when you want to know if something has or has not occurred.

  ```
  Dim MyBoolean As Boolean
  ```

- The last important variable type is Single. Single can hold any numeric value. It is useful for doing mathematical calculations.

  ```
  Dim MySingle As Single
  ```

- A property is very similar to a variable in concept. You can assign values to a property and copy a value from the property. A sample property definition would be as follows:

  ```
  Object.Property = value
  ```

- An object can also contain another object, which can contain another object, and so forth. This is done by using a property that contains another object. So if `Object.Property` refers to another object, a more complex property might look like:

  ```
  Object.Property.NewObjectsProperty
  ```

- A method is a way for a VBA macro to request the object to perform a service. Often, methods have one or more parameters that provide information about the requested service. A sample method definition is as follows:

  ```
  Object.Method parameter1, parameter2
  ```

■ An event is a way for the object to notify your macro that a situation has occurred. Using events in your macro is outside the scope of this book and I recommend looking at Que's *Special Edition Using Visual Basic for Applications* for more information.

# Some Simple VBA Statements

VBA is a powerful language for writing programs. While developing complex programs is beyond the scope of this book, here are a few VBA statements that you may find useful while writing simple macros:

■ The assignment statement is probably the most used statement in Visual Basic. It enables you to assign an expression to an object or a variable. The expression may be another object or variable. It may also be a constant like the string "Christopher" or the number 22. An expression can also be a formula, where multiple objects, variables, and constants are combined with operators such as + (addition), – (subtraction), * (multiplication), / (division), and & (string concatenation):

```
<object or variable> = <expression>
```

■ The If statement is also important because it allows you to test for a condition. If the condition is True, a list of statements may be executed. Optionally, if the condition is False, then another list may be executed:

```
If <condition> Then
<list of statements executed when condition is True>
End If
--- OR ----
If <condition> Then
<list of statements executed when condition is True>
Else
<list of statements executed when condition is False>
End If
```

■ The For statement is useful for repeating a list of statements multiple times. The variable will have a different value each time the list of statements is executed. The variable used should be a Long.

```
For <variable> = <starting value> To <stopping value>
<list of statements executed multiple times>
Next <variable>
```

■ The With statement simplifies using complex objects. It is frequently used in macros recorded in Word where multiple properties are set inside a single object. You can use an object's properties and methods beginning with a period (.):

```
With <object>
<list of statements>
End With
```

Part
**III**

Ch
**26**

# Some Common Objects in Word 97

Word provides a large number of objects that contain various pieces of information about the currently opened document(s). Here is just a sample of some of these objects:

- Many objects (such as the `Selection` object) use the `Font` object to describe how text is presented. Some common properties are the following:

| | |
|---|---|
| Font.Bold | `True` if all of the text is in bold, `False` if all the text is not in bold; `wdUndefined` means some text is bold and the rest is not. |
| Font.Italic | `True` if all of the text is in italic, `False` if all the text is not in italic; `wdUndefined` means some text is italic and the rest is not. |
| Font.Name | A string containing the font name. |
| Font.Size | A Single containing the size of the font in points. |

- The `Selection` object contains methods that are used to select and change portions of the document. Some common properties are the following:

| | |
|---|---|
| Selection.Font | An object reference to a `Font` object. |
| Selection.Text | Holds the currently selected text. You can replace the existing text by assigning a new value to this property. |

# Some Common Objects in Excel 97

Like Word, there are many objects in Excel. Unlike Word, Excel's objects are more hierarchical. There is a strong top organization from the highest level object to the lowest. While the following objects represent only a tiny fraction of those available in Excel, they contain sufficient information for you to write meaningful Excel macros:

- The basic object in Excel is the `Workbook` object. Each `Workbook` object corresponds to the Excel file containing the collection of worksheets and charts.
- In each workbook, there is a set of objects called `Worksheets` and another called `Charts`. These correspond to the worksheets and charts that can be found in a workbook. Some common methods are:

| | |
|---|---|
| Worksheets(<key>).Activate | Makes the worksheet identified by <key> the active worksheet. Note that only one worksheet may be active at any time. <key> can be either a number corresponding to the worksheet's order in the workbook or a string containing the title of the worksheet. |

```
Worksheets(<key>).Cell(<row>,<col>)
```
An object reference to a cell object as specified by <row> and <col>.

▨ The `Cell` object describes the contents of a single cell on a particular worksheet. If the cells are on the active worksheet, you do not need to reference the `Worksheet` object. The following properties assume that the `Cell` object is on the currently active worksheet:

```
Cells(<row>,<col>).Font
```
Reference to a `Font` object containing information about the font used within the cell.

```
Cells(<row>,<col>).Formula
```
A String containing an Excel formula.

```
Cells(<row>,<col>).FormulaR1C1
```
A String containing an Excel formula. however, Instead of using the normal A1 notation (letters for columns, numbers for rows), this property describes the cell in R1C1 notation. R1C1 is equivalent to A1. You specify cells in terms of `R<row>C<col>` where `<row>` and `<col>` represent row and column numbers. This is done primarily for macro programmers who find it easier to compute a cell address based on a column number rather than an alphabetic string. Note that the formula is stored only once and this property merely translates the formula to this notation.

```
Cells(<row>,<col>).NumberFormat
```
A string containing the format used to display a number. This is the same string from the Format Cells dialog box.

# Index

## Symbols

# Check out Que® Books on the World Wide Web
## http://www.quecorp.com

As the biggest software release in computer history, Windows 95 continues to redefine the computer industry. Click here for the latest info on our Windows 95 books

Make computing quick and easy with these products designed exclusively for new and casual users

Examine the latest releases in word processing, spreadsheets, operating systems, and suites

Find out about new additions to our site, new bestsellers, and hot topics

The Internet, The World Wide Web, CompuServe®, America Online®, Prodigy®—it's a world of ever-changing information. Don't get left behind!

In-depth information on high-end topics: find the best reference books for databases, programming, networking, and client/server technologies

A recent addition to Que, Ziff-Davis Press publishes the highly-successful *How It Works* and *How to Use* series of books, as well as *PC Learning Labs Teaches* and *PC Magazine* series of book/disc packages

Stay on the cutting edge of Macintosh® technologies and visual communications

Find out which titles are making headlines

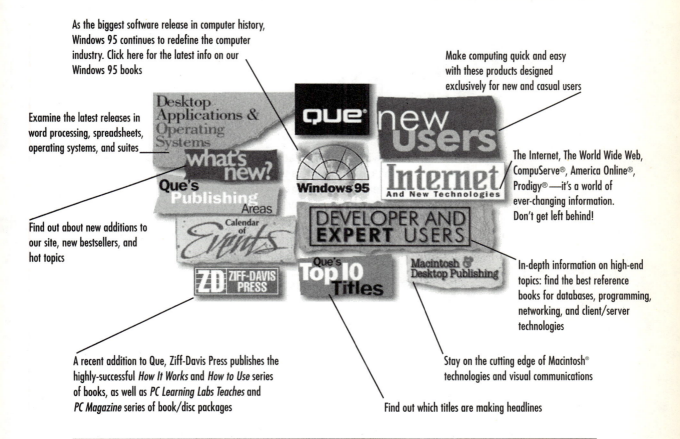

With 6 separate publishing groups, Que develops products for many specific market segments and areas of computer technology. Explore our Web site and you'll find information on best-selling titles, newly published titles, upcoming products, authors, and much more.

- Stay informed on the latest industry trends and products available
- Visit our online bookstore for the latest information and editions
- Download software from Que's library of the best shareware and freeware

que®
Copyright © 1997, Macmillan Computer Publishing-USA, A Viacom Company

MACMILLAN COMPUTER PUBLISHING USA

A VIACOM COMPANY

# Technical ---- Support:

If you need assistance with the information in this book or with a CD/Disk accompanying the book, please access the Knowledge Base on our Web site at **http://www.superlibrary.com/general/support**. Our most Frequently Asked Questions are answered there. If you do not find the answer to your questions on our Web site, you may contact Macmillan Technical Support **(317) 581-3833** or e-mail us at **support@mcp.com**.